THE PRIMEVAL FOREST

THE ALBERT SCHWEITZER LIBRARY

The Albert Schweitzer Library, published in association with the Albert Schweitzer Institute for the Humanities, presents new editions of the writings of Albert Schweitzer in English translation. The library will reflect the extraordinary scope of Schweitzer's knowledge and achievements in theology, music, history, and humanitarian philosophy. It will also restore to print his autobiographical writings and include new translations and collections of works never published in book form.

ALBERT SCHWEITZER, 1930
*Courtesy of the Albert Schweitzer Institute
for the Humanities*

The Primeval Forest

ALBERT SCHWEITZER

Including
ON THE EDGE OF THE PRIMEVAL FOREST
and
MORE FROM THE PRIMEVAL FOREST

With a new foreword by
WILLIAM H. FOEGE, M.D.

THE JOHNS HOPKINS UNIVERSITY PRESS
Baltimore and London
in association with
THE ALBERT SCHWEITZER INSTITUTE
FOR THE HUMANITIES

Johns Hopkins Paperbacks edition, 1998
9 8 7 6 5 4 3 2 1

This edition authorized by Rhena Schweitzer Miller and the Albert
Schweitzer Institute for the Humanities, Dr. Harold Robles, President.

The Johns Hopkins University Press
2715 North Charles Street
Baltimore, Maryland 21218-4363
The Johns Hopkins Press Ltd., London
www.press.jhu.edu

Library of Congress Cataloging-in-Publication Data

Schweitzer, Albert, 1875–1965.
    [Zwischen Wasser und Urwald. English]
    The primeval forest : including On the edge of the primeval forest ; and,
More from the primeval forest / Albert Schweitzer ; with a new foreword by
William H. Foege. — Johns Hopkins paperbacks ed.
        p.   c.m — (The Albert Schweitzer Library)
    Originally published: New York : Macmillan, 1931.
    ISBN 0-8018-5958-1 (pbk.)
    1. Schweitzer, Albert, 1875–1965. 2. Missionaries, Medical—Gabon—
Biography. 3. Physicians—Gabon—Biography. 4. Missions, Medical—
Gabon. 5. Missions—Gabon. 6. Lambaréné (Moyen-Ogooué, Gabon)
I. Schweitzer, Albert 1875–1965. Mitteilungen aus Lambarene. English.
II. Albert Schweitzer Institute for the Humanities. III. Title. IV. Series.
R722.32.S35A3   1998
610.69´5´092—dc21
[B]   98-6946
                                                                                    CIP

A catalog record for this book is available from the British Library.

CONTENTS

PART II

MORE FROM THE PRIMEVAL FOREST

FOREWORD, 1998

More than forty-five years ago, a body cast constricted my teen-age world. A copy of *On the Edge of the Primeval Forest*, Schweitzer's account of building a medical service in Africa, per-mitted a vicarious escape to a far different place. His demonstra-tion that Western medical science has much to offer the develop-ing areas of the world molded my own vocational choices in inter-national health.

To read again, after almost half a century, his very readable account of Africa at the beginning of this century is to bounce repeatedly between new insights and a feeling of déjà vu. The Africa of Schweitzer's first visit was almost beyond the under-standing of his European supporters. The Africa of today has changed so dramatically that it includes skyscrapers, CNN, com-puters, toxic wastes, and traffic jams. Yet Africa is as unfamiliar to many Europeans and Americans today as it was eighty years ago.

Schweitzer's account of relating to a new culture is as fresh as if it had been written today. But be forewarned—you will be jarred by some of Schweitzer's descriptions as he combines his insights, compassion, and tolerance for new ideas and cultural beliefs with a background that reflects the colonial stance of the West as it then interacted with the rest of the world.

One of the most compelling revelations is to see again through the clear window Schweitzer had on the relatedness of things. He was far ahead of his time in understanding that everything affects everything, both across geography and over time. Two hundred years after his death, Johann Sebastian Bach contributed to health in Africa: Schweitzer funded his first trip there with royal-ties from the biography he wrote of Bach.

Schweitzer's "Reverence for Life" is actually the philosophical basis for what the world now understands as the need to preserve biodiversity. He cautions against living today at the expense of tomorrow. He was an ecologist before the word was known and he provides a theological, philosophical, and scientific foundation for global security and sustainability.

The Primeval Forest is more than a story of a person. It is the story of a thinker who chose to place himself—in that wonderful phrase of Saul Bellow—"knee deep in the garbage of life." Living is hard, suffering is real, illness is overwhelming, amenities are few, and death stalks the land. Schweitzer quotes an old chief: "Our country devours its own children."

The Primeval Forest is also the story of geography, the story of intersecting cultures, of the dependence, even then, of Europeans on remote forests of Central Africa, and the increasing dependence of African villagers on European money.

It is an exciting story of medicine at the dawn of the pharmaceutical age, which would in a few short years give new hope to persons suffering from sleeping sickness, leprosy, and tropical ulcers. It is a reminder that "pain is a more terrible lord of mankind than even death itself," but also a reminder of the interdependence of "those who bear the mark of pain." It is the story of a calling and a purpose in life, of a gifted scholar who had golden opportunities to enrich himself, but who concluded that his gifts led to obligations. "We are not free to confer benefits . . . as we please; it is our duty."

The Primeval Forest reflects on what constitutes successful living. Schweitzer recounts his request to a person to give a hand in moving some wood. The man responded that he was an intellectual who did not drag wood about. Schweitzer replied, "You're lucky. I too wanted to be an intellectual, but I didn't succeed."

William H. Foege, M.D.

PART I

ON THE EDGE OF
THE PRIMEVAL FOREST

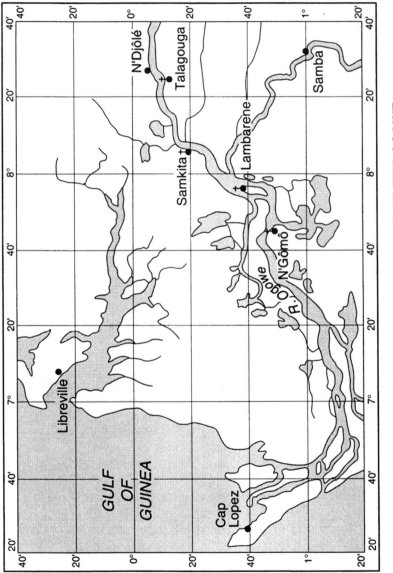

SKETCH MAP OF THE LOWER COURSE OF THE OGOWE

(Based on a map by the Rev. Mr. Haug.)

1 *HOW I CAME TO BE A DOCTOR IN THE FOREST*
THE LAND AND THE PEOPLE OF THE OGOWE

I GAVE up my position of professor in the University of Strasbourg, my literary work, and my organ-playing, in order to go as a doctor to Equatorial Africa. How did that come about?

I had read about the physical miseries of the natives in the virgin forests; I had heard about them from missionaries, and the more I thought about it the stranger it seemed to me that we Europeans trouble ourselves so little about the great humanitarian task which offers itself to us in far-off lands. The parable of Dives and Lazarus seemed to me to have been spoken directly of us! We are Dives, for, through the advances of medical science, we now know a great deal about disease and pain, and have innumerable means of fighting them: yet we take as a matter of course the incalculable advantages which this new wealth gives us! Out there in the colonies, however, sits wretched Lazarus, the coloured folk, who suffers from illness and pain just as much as we do, nay, much more, and has absolutely no means of fighting them. And just as Dives sinned against the poor man at his gate because for want of thought he never put himself in his place and let his heart and conscience tell him what he ought to do, so do we sin against the poor man at our gate.

The two or three hundred doctors whom the European States maintain as medical officers in the colonial world could undertake only a very small part (so I argued to myself) of the huge task, even if the majority of them were not there for the benefit, first of all, of the white colonists and the troops. Society in general must recognise this work of humanity to be its task, and there must come a time when doctors go

11

out into the world of their own free will, but sent and supported by society and in numbers corresponding to the need, to
work for the benefit of the natives. Then only shall we be
recognising and beginning to act upon the responsibility in
respect of the coloured races which lies upon us as inheritors
of the world's civilisation.

Moved by these thoughts I resolved, when already thirty
years old, to study medicine and to put my ideas to the test
out there. At the beginning of 1913 I graduated as M.D. That
same spring I started with my wife, who had qualified as a
nurse, for the River Ogowe in Equatorial Africa, there to
begin my active work.

I chose this locality because some Alsatian missionaries in
the service of the Paris Evangelical Mission had told me
that a doctor was badly needed there on account of the
constantly spreading sleeping sickness. The mission was prepared also to place at my disposal one of the houses at their
station at Lambaréné, and to allow me to build a hospital
in their grounds, promising further to give me help with the
work.

The actual expenses of the undertaking, however, I had to
provide myself, and to that I devoted what I had earned by
giving organ concerts, together with the profits from my
book on Bach, which had appeared in German, French, and
English. In this way the old Thomas Cantor of Leipsig,
Johann Sebastian himself, helped me in the provision of a
hospital for negroes in the virgin forest, and kind friends
in Germany, France, and Switzerland contributed money.
When we left Europe, the undertaking was securely financed
for two years, the expenses—apart from the journey out and
back—being, as I reckoned, about 15,000 francs[1] a year,
and this calculation proved to be very nearly correct.

The keeping of the accounts and the ordering of all the
things needed had been undertaken by self-sacrificing friends
in Strasbourg, and the cases, when packed, were sent to Africa
by the mission with their own.

My work then lived—to use a scientific term—in symbiosis
with the Paris Evangelical Mission, but it was, in itself,
undenominational and international. It was, and is still, my
conviction that the humanitarian work to be done in the world

---

[1] *i.e.,* about three thousand dollars.

should, for its accomplishment, call upon us as men, not as members of any particular nation or religious body.

Now for a word about the country which was the scene of our labours. The Ogowe district belongs to the Colony of Gaboon, and the Ogowe itself is a river, 700 to 800 miles long, north of, and roughly parallel to, the Congo. Although smaller than the latter, it is yet a magnificent river, and in the lower part of its course its width is from 1,200 to 2,200 yards. For the last 120 miles it divides into a number of arms which enter the Atlantic near Cape Lopez, but it is navigable for fairly large river steamers as far as N'Djôle, about 250 miles up stream. At that point begins the region of hills and mountains which leads up to the great plateau of Central Africa. Here also begins a series of rapids which alternate with stretches of ordinary open river, and these rapids can only be surmounted by small screw steamers, built for the purpose, and by native canoes.

While along the middle and upper course of the Ogowe the country is a mixture of prairie and wood, there is along the lower part of the river, from N'Djôle downwards, nothing but water and virgin forest. This damp, low-lying ground is admirably suited for the cultivation of coffee, pepper, cinnamon, vanilla, and cocoa; the oil palm also grows well in it. But the chief business of Europeans is neither the cultivation of these things, nor the collection of rubber in the forest, but the timber trade. Now on the west coast of Africa, which is very poor in harbours, especially in such as have rivers discharging into them, conditions are very seldom favourable for the loading of timber cargoes. But the Ogowe has the great advantage of discharging into an excellent roadstead without any bar; the huge rafts can lie alongside the steamers which are to take them away without danger of being broken up and scattered on a bar or by a heavy swell. The timber trade, therefore, is likely to be for an indefinite period the chief industry of the Ogowe district.

Cereals and potatoes it is, unfortunately, impossible to cultivate, since the warm, damp atmosphere makes them grow too fast. Cereals never produce the usual ear, and potato haulms shoot up without any tubers below. Rice, too, is for various reasons not cultivable. Cows cannot be kept along the lower Ogowe because they cannot eat the grass that grows there, though further inland, on the central plateau, they flourish splendidly. It is necessary, therefore, to import from Europe flour, rice, potatoes, and milk, a fact which makes living a complicated business and very expensive.

Lambaréné lies a little south of the Equator, so that its seasons are those of the Southern hemisphere: winter when it is summer in Europe, and vice-versa. Its winter is characterised by its including the dry season, which lasts from the end of May to the beginning of October, and summer is the rainy season, the rain falling from early in October to the middle of December, and from the middle of January to the end of May. About Christmas one gets three to four weeks of continuous summer weather, and it is then that the thermometer record is highest.

The average shade temperature in the rainy season is 82-86 degrees Fahrenheit, in the dry season about 77-82 degrees Fahrenheit, the nights being always nearly as hot as the days. This circumstance, and the excessive moisture of the atmosphere, are the chief things which make the climate of the Ogowe lowlands such a trial for a European. After a year's residence fatigue and anaemia begin to make themselves disagreeably perceptible. At the end of two or three years he becomes incapable of real work, and does best to return to Europe for at least eight months in order to recruit.

The mortality among the whites at Libreville, the capital of Gaboon, was, in 1903, 14 per cent.

*   *   *

Before the war there lived in the Ogowe lowlands about two hundred whites: planters, timber merchants, storekeepers, officials, and missionaries. The number of the natives is hard to estimate, but, at any rate, the country is not thickly inhabited. We have at present merely the remains of eight once powerful tribes, so terribly has the population been thinned by three hundred years of alcohol and the slave trade. Of the Orungu tribe, which lived in the Ogowe delta, there are scarcely any left; of the Galoas, who belonged to the Lambaréné district, there remain still 80,000 at most. Into the void thus created there swarmed from inland the cannibal Fans, called by the French Pahouins, who have never yet come into contact with civilisation, and but for the opportune arrival of the Europeans this warrior folk would by this time have eaten up the old tribes of the Ogowe lowlands. Lambaréné forms in the river valley the boundary between the Pahouins and the old tribes.

Gaboon was discovered by the Portuguese at the end of the fifteenth century, and by 1521 there was a Catholic mission settlement on the coast between the mouths of the Congo and the Ogowe. Cape Lopez is named after one of them, Odoardo Lopez, who came out there in 1578. In the eighteenth century the Jesuits had extensive plantations on the coast, with thousands of slaves, but they were as far from penetrating to the hinterland as were the white traders.

When, in the middle of the nineteenth century, the French and the English combined to fight the slave trade on the west coast, they chose, in 1849, the bay which lies north of that of Cape Lopez for the headquarters of their fleet, establishing there also a settlement to which they could send the rescued slaves: hence the name Libreville. That the narrow channels which empty themselves here and there into Cape Lopez bay belonged to a great river, the whites did not yet know, for the natives inhabiting the coast had withheld the information in order to keep the inland trade in their own hands. It was not till 1862 that Lieutenant Serval, while on an excursion to the south-east of Libreville, discovered the Ogowe in the neighbourhood of Lambaréné. Then began the exploration, from Cape Lopez, of the lower course of the river, and the chiefs were gradually brought to acknowledge the French protectorate.

When in the eighties the need was felt of finding the most convenient route for trade from the coast up to the navigable parts of the Congo, de Brazza believed that it was to be found in the Ogowe, since this river rises only some 125 miles northwest of Stanley Pool, and is separated from the Alima, a navigable tributary of the Congo, only by a narrow watershed. He even succeeded in getting to the Congo by this route a steamer which could be taken to pieces and transported by land, but the route proved to be impracticable for trade on account of the difficulties caused by the rapids in the upper part of the Ogowe. The construction of the Belgian-Congo railway between Matadi and Brazzaville was finished in 1898, and this put a final end to any idea of making the Ogowe a way to the Congo. To-day the Ogowe is used only by the traffic which goes up to its own still comparatively unexplored hinterland.

The first Protestant missionaries on the Ogowe were Americans, who came there about 1860, but as they could not comply with the requirement of the French Government that they should give their school instruction in French, they resigned their work later on to the Paris Missionary Society.

To-day this society owns four stations: N'Gômô, Lambaréné, Samkita, and Talagouga. N'Gômô is about 140 miles from the coast, and the others follow one another in that order at intervals of about 35 miles. Talagouga is situated on a picturesque island just in front of N'Djôle, which is the farthest point to which the river steamer goes.

At each Protestant mission station there are generally one unmarried and two married missionaries, and, as a rule, a woman teacher also, making five or six persons, without reckoning the children.

The Catholic mission has three stations in the same district: one in Lambaréné, one in N'Djôle, and one near Samba, on the N'Gounje, the largest tributary of the Ogowe, and on each station there live about ten whites: usually three priests, two lay brothers, and five sisters.

The administrative officials of the district are stationed at Cape Lopez, at Lambaréné, at Samba, and at N'Djôle, with about five hundred coloured soldiers distributed over it to act as a police force.

Such was the country, and such the people among whom for four and a half years I worked as the forest doctor. What I experienced during that time and the observations I made previous to the outbreak of the war, I shall now describe with the help of the reports which I wrote every six months in Lambaréné and sent as printed letters to my friends and supporters. During the war such correspondence was, of course, impossible, and for that later period and for what is said about the religious and social problems treated of, I rely on memoranda which I made for my own use.

2 THE JOURNEY

THE church bells in my native Alsatian village of Güns-bach, in the Vosges, had just ceased ringing for the afternoon service on Good Friday, 1913, when the train appeared round the corner of the wood, and the journey to Africa began. We waved our farewells from the platform of the last coach, and for the last time saw the *flêche* on the church tower peeping up among the trees. When should we see them again? When next day Strasbourg Cathedral sank out of sight we seemed to be already in a foreign land.

On Easter Sunday we heard once more the dear old organ of S. Sulpice's Church in Paris and the wonderful playing of our friend Widor. At two o'clock the Bordeaux train glided out of the underground station at the Quai d'Orsay, and we began a delightful journey. Everywhere we saw people in their holiday dress; the sunshine was brilliant, and the warm spring breeze brought out of the distance the sound of the village church bells, which seemed to be greetings to the train that was hurrying past. It was an Easter Day which seemed a glorious dream.

The Congo steamers do not start from Bordeaux but from Pauillac, which is an hour and a half by train nearer the sea. But I had to get my big packing case, which had been sent in advance by goods train, out of the custom house at Bordeaux, and this was closed on Easter Monday. There would have been no time on Tuesday to manage it, but fortunately an official observed and was touched by our anxiety, and enabled me to get possession of my goods without all the prescribed formalities. But it was only at the last minute that two motor-cars got us and our belongings to the harbour station, where the train was already waiting which was to convey

17

the passengers for the Congo to their ship. The feeling of relief
can hardly be described with which, after all the excitement
and the payment of all those who had helped us off, we sank
into our seats in the railway carriage. The guard blew his
whistle; the soldiers who were also going took their places; we
moved out into the open, and for a time had the enjoyment of
blue sky and pleasant breeze, with the sight here and there of
water and yellow broom in flower, and cows quietly grazing.
In an hour and a half we are at the quay among packing
cases, bales, and barrels, ten yards from the ship, called the
Europe, which is gently tossing on the somewhat restless waters
of the Gironde. Then came a time of crushing, shouting,
signalling to porters; we push and are pushed till, over the
narrow gangway, we get on board and, on giving our names,
learn the number of the cabin which is to be our home for
three whole weeks. It is a roomy one, well forward and away
from the engines, which is a great advantage. Then we had
just time to wash before the bell rang for lunch.

We had at our table several officers, the ship's doctor, an
army doctor, and two wives of colonial officials who were returning to their husbands after a voyage home to recruit. All
of them, as we soon discovered, had already been in Africa
or in other colonies, so that we felt ourselves to be poor un-
travelled home birds. I could not help thinking of the fowls
my mother used to buy every summer from Italian poultry
dealers to add to her stock, and which for several days used
to walk about among the old ones very shyly and humbly!
One thing that struck me as noticeable in the faces of our
fellow travellers was a certain expression of energy and de-
termination.

As there was still a great deal of cargo to come aboard we
did not start till the following afternoon, when under a
gloomy sky we drew slowly down the Gironde. As darkness
gradually set in the long roll of the waves told us that we had
reached the open sea, and about nine o'clock the last shimmering lights had disappeared.

Of the Bay of Biscay the passengers told each other horrid
tales. "How I wish it were behind us!" we heard at every
meal-time; but we were to make full proof of its malice. On
the second day after starting, a regular storm set in, and the
ship pitched and tossed like a great rocking-horse, and rolled
from starboard to port, and back from port to starboard, with

impartial delight. The Congo boats do this more than others in a heavy sea because, in order to be able to ascend the river as far as Matadi, whatever the state of the water, they are of a comparatively shallow build.

Being without experience of ocean travel, I had forgotten to make the two cabin trunks fast with cords, and in the night they began to chase each other about. The two hat cases also, which contained our sun helmets, took part in the game without reflecting how badly off they might come in it, and when I tried to catch the trunks, I nearly got one leg crushed between them and the wall of the cabin. So I left them to their fate and contented myself with lying quietly in my berth and counting how many seconds elapsed between each plunge made by the ship and the corresponding rush of our boxes. Soon there could be heard similar noises from other cabins and, added to them, the sound of crockery, etc., moving wildly about in the galley and the dining saloon. With morning came a steward, who showed me the scientific way of making the baggage fast.

For three days the storm lasted with undiminished force. Standing or even sitting in the cabins or the saloons was not to be thought of; one was thrown about from one corner to the other, and several passengers received more or less serious injuries. On Sunday we had cold food only, because the cooks were unable to use the galley fire, and it was not till we were near Teneriffe that the storm abated.

I had been looking forward to the first sight of this island, which is always said to be so magnificent, but, alas! I overslept myself and woke only as we were entering the harbour. Then, scarcely had the anchor been dropped, when we were hemmed in on both sides by coaling-hulks from which were hoisted sacks of food for the engines, to be emptied through the hatch into the ship's hold.

*   *   *

Teneriffe lies on high ground which slopes rather steeply into the sea, and has all the appearance of a Spanish town. The island is carefully cultivated, and produces potatoes enough to supply the whole coast of West Africa, besides bananas, early potatoes, and other vegetables for Europe.

We weighed anchor about three o'clock, and I stood in the

bows and watched how the anchor slowly left the bottom and came up through the transparent water. I watched also, with admiration, what I took for a blue bird flying gracefully above the surface of the sea, till a sailor told me it was a flying fish.

Then, as we moved from the coast southwards, there rose slowly up behind the island the snow-capped summit of its highest mountain, till it lost itself in the clouds, while we steamed away over a gently heaving sea and admired the entrancing blue of the water.

It was during this portion of the voyage that we found it possible to become acquainted with one another. The other passengers were mostly army officers and doctors and civil service officials; it surprised me to find so few traders on board. The officials, as a rule, are told only where they are to land, and not until on shore do they get to know their ultimate destination.

Among those whom we got to know best were a lieutenant and a Government official. The latter was going to the Middle Congo region and had to leave his wife and children for two years. The lieutenant was in much the same position, and was expecting to go up to Abescher. He had already been in Tonquin, and in Madagascar, on the Senegal, the Niger, and the Congo, and he was interested in every department of colonial affairs. He held crushing views about Mahommedanism as it prevails among the natives, seeing in it the greatest danger there is for the future of Africa. "The Mahommedan negro," he said, "is no longer any good for anything. You may build him railways, dig him canals, spend hundreds of thousands of pounds to provide irrigation for the land he is to cultivate, but it all makes no impression on him; he is absolutely and on principle opposed to everything European, however advantageous and profitable it may be. But let a marabout—a travelling preacher of Islam—come into the village on his ambling horse with his yellow cloak over his shoulders, then things begin to wake up! Everybody crowds round him, and brings his savings in order to buy with hard cash charms against sickness, wounds, and snake bite, against bad spirits and bad neighbours. Wherever the negro population has turned Mahommedan there is no progress, either socially or economically. When we built the first railway in Madagascar, the natives stood for days together round the locomotive and wondered at it; they shouted for joy when it let off steam, and kept trying to explain to each other how the thing could move. In an African town inhabited by Mahommedan negroes, the local water power was used once for an installation of electric light, and it was expected that the people would be surprised at the novel brightness. But the evening that the lamps were first used the whole population remained inside their houses and huts and discussed the matter there, so as to show their indifference to the novelty."

Very valuable I found my acquaintance with a military doctor who had already had twelve years experience of Equatorial Africa, and was going to Grand Bassam as director of the Bacteriological Institute there. At my request he spared me two hours every morning, during which he gave me an account of the general system of tropical medicine, illustrated by his own experiments and experiences. It was very necessary, he thought, that as many independent doctors as possible should devote themselves to the care of the native population; only so could we hope to get the mastery of the sleeping sickness.

The day after we left Teneriffe the troops were ordered to wear their sun-helmets whenever they were outside the saloons and cabins. This precaution struck me as noticeable, because the weather was still cool and fresh, hardly warmer than it is with us in June, but on the same day I got a warning from an "old African," as I was enjoying the sight of the sunset with nothing on my head. "From to-day onwards," he said, "you must, even though the weather is not yet hot, regard the sun as your worst enemy, and that whether it is rising, or high in heaven, or setting, and whether the sky is cloudy or not. Why this is so, and on what the sun's power depends, I cannot tell you, but you may take it from me that people get dangerous sunstrokes before they get close to the Equator, and that the apparently mild heat of the rising or setting sun is even more treacherous than the full glow of that fiery body at midday."

At Dakar, the great harbour of the Colony of Senegambia, my wife and I set foot for the first time on the soil of Africa to which we were to devote our lives, and we felt it as a somewhat solemn moment. Of Dakar itself I have no kindly remembrance, for I cannot forget the cruelty to animals which is universal there. The town lies on a steep slope, the streets are mostly in very bad condition, and the lot of the poor beasts of burden which are at the mercy of the negroes is terrible: I have never seen such overworked horses and mules as here. On one occasion when I came on two negroes who were perched on a cart heavily laden with wood which had stuck in the newly-mended street, and with loud shouts were belabouring their poor beast, I simply could not pass by, but compelled them to dismount and to push behind till the three of us got the cart on the move. They were much disconcerted, but obeyed without replying. "If you cannot endure to see animals ill-treated, don't go to Africa!" said the lieutenant to me when I got back. "You will see plenty of that kind of horror here."

At this port we took on board a number of Senegalese tirailleurs with their wives and children. They lay about the foredeck, and at night crept, head and all, into big sacks, as they had to sleep in the open. The wives and children were heavily loaded with charms, enclosed in little leather bags, even the babies at the breast not being exempt.

The shores of Africa I had pictured to myself as desert, and when, on the way to Konakri, the next place of call to Dakar, we put in towards the coast, I was surprised to see nothing but magnificently green woods coming down right to the water's edge. With my telescope I could see the pointed huts of the negro villages, and rising between us and them, like a cloud, the spray of the waves on the bar; the sea, however, was fairly calm, and the coast, so far as I could see, was flat.

"A shark! A shark!" I rushed from the writing saloon, and was shown a black triangular object projecting from the water and moving in the direction of the ship. It was a fin of that dreaded sea-monster, and whoever has once seen it never forgets it or confuses it with anything else. The West African harbours all swarm with sharks. In Kotonou I saw one, enticed by the kitchen refuse, come to about twelve yards from the ship. The light being good and the water very transparent, I could see for several minutes the whole length of its glistening grey and yellow body, and observe how the creature turned over nearly on to its back to get what it considered worth devouring into its mouth, which, as we all know, is placed on the underside of its head.

In spite of the sharks the negroes in all these harbours are ready to dive for coins, and accidents seldom happen to them, because the noise they make during the proceedings gets on the nerves of even these wolves of the sea. At Tabou I was astonished to see one of the divers quite silent while the rest were crying out for more coins, but I noticed later that he was the most skilful of the lot and had to keep silent because his mouth served as his purse, and he could hardly shut it for the number of nickel and silver coins that were in it.

From Konakri onwards we were almost always within sight of the coast. The Pepper Coast, the Ivory Coast, the Gold Coast, the Slave Coast! If only that line of forest on the horizon could tell us about all the cruelty it has had to witness! Here the slave dealers used to land and ship their living cargoes for transport to America. "It is not all as it should be, even to-day," said to me an employee of a big trading firm, who was returning for a third period of work to his post in Africa. "We bring the negroes strong drink and diseases which were previously unknown among them. Do the blessings we bring the natives really outweigh the evils that go with them?"

Several times during meals I found myself watching the guests at the different tables. All had already worked in Africa, but with what objects? What ideals had they? So pleasant and friendly here, what sort of people were they away in their places of work? What responsibility did they feel? In a few days the three hundred of us who left Bordeaux together will have landed in Africa, and in a few weeks we shall be separated, taking up our duties on the Senegal, on the Niger, on the Ogowe, on the Congo and its tributaries, some even as far away as Lake Chad, to work in these different regions for three years or so. What shall we accomplish? If everything could be written down that is done during these years by all of us who are now here on this ship, what a book it would be! Would there be no pages that we should be glad to turn over as quickly as possible? . . .

But the ship is carrying us on and on. Grand Bassam . . . Kotonou . . . Each time there are hearty farewells exchanged between many who have hardly spoken to each other. "Good health to you!" The words are spoken with a smile, but again and again, and in this climate they have a serious sound. How will those to whom they are spoken look when they come on board next? And will they all come back? . . . The windlasses and cranes begin to creak; the boats are dancing on the waves; the red roofs of the seaside town throw us a bright greeting from out of the mass of greenery; the waves breaking on the sandy bar send up their clouds of spray . . . and behind them all lies the immeasurable stretch of land, at some place in which every one who leaves us here is to be a lord and master, all his doings having a significance of some sort for the great land's future. "Good health to you! Good health to you!" It seems to be scarcely a solemn enough farewell for all that lies in the future!

At Tabou and at Grand Bassam, on the Ivory Coast, and at Kotonou, the swell is so heavy even in good weather that passengers cannot get into the boats by the rope-ladder, but must be lowered into them four at a time in wooden boxes, such as one sees on merry-go-rounds at village fairs. It is the duty of the engineer who manages the crane to seize the right moment for letting the cradle with its four occupants safely down into the bottom of the boat which is dancing up and down on the waves; the negro in the boat has to see that his craft is exactly below the cradle as it descends, and accidents are not infrequent. The unloading of cargo is also a very difficult operation and only possible in calm weather. I now understand the assertions that West Africa is very poor in good harbours.

At Tabou we took on board, as is done on every voyage, some fifty negroes for handling the cargo. They are taken as far as the Congo, to be landed again on the return voyage, and they helped with the unloading at Libreville, Cape Lopez, and Matadi, the places to which most of the freight is consigned. They do their work perfectly, almost better than the dock labourers at Pauillac, but their behaviour towards the other coloured folk on board is brutal. Whenever the latter get the least bit in their way they come to blows.

Every evening the glimmer of the sea, as the ship ploughs her way through it, is wonderful: the foam is phosphorescent, and little jelly-fishes spring up through it like glowing balls of metal. After leaving Konakri we saw almost every night the reflection of storms that swept across the country, and we passed through several deluges of rain accompanied by tornadoes that did nothing, however, to cool the air. On cloudy days the heat was worse than on others, and the sun, although not shining directly on us, was said to be much more dangerous in such weather than at other times.

Early on April 13th, a Sunday, we reached Libreville, and were welcomed by Mr. Ford, the American missionary, who brought us a preliminary gift from Africa of flowers and fruit from the mission-house garden. We thankfully accepted his invitation to visit the mission station, which is called Baraka, and is situated on a hill about two and a half miles along the coast from Libreville. As we mounted the hill through the rows of neat bamboo huts belonging to the negroes, the chapel doors opened after service. We were introduced to some of the congregation and had a dozen black hands to shake. What a contrast between these clean and decently clothed people and the blacks that we had seen in the seaports, the only kind of native we had met up to now! Even the faces are not the same. These had a free and yet modest look in them that cleared from my mind the haunting vision of sullen and unwilling subjection, mixed with insolence, which had hitherto looked at me out of the eyes of so many negroes.

From Libreville to Cape Lopez it is only an eight hours run. When, early on Monday, April 14th, we came in sight of the harbour, an anxiety seized me which I had felt before occasionally during the last week or so. The custom house and the duties! During the latter part of the voyage all sorts of tales had been told at meal times about the colonial duties. "Ten per cent on the value of all you bring you'll have to fork out!" said an old African. "And whether the things are new or old doesn't matter in the least!" added another. However, the customs officer was fairly gracious to us. Perhaps the anxious faces we showed, as we laid before him the list of the things in our seventy cases, toned him down to a gentler mood, and we returned to the ship with a delightful feeling of relief, to sleep in it for the last time. But it was an uncomfortable night: cargo was being unloaded and coal taken in, till the negroes at the cranes could no longer stand for weariness.

*   *   *

Early on Tuesday we transferred to the *Alembe*, which, being a river boat, was built broad and shallow, and its two paddle-wheels were side by side at the stern, where they are safe from wandering tree-trunks. It took up only the passengers and their personal luggage, being already full of cargo. Our cases were to follow in the next boat a fortnight later. We started at 9 a.m., so as to pass safely at high tide over the sandbanks which block the mouth of the Ogowe, and a few passengers who had stayed on shore too long were left behind. They overtook us, however, later on in a motor-boat.

River and forest . . . ! Who can really describe the first impression they make? We seemed to be dreaming! Pictures of antediluvian scenery which elsewhere had seemed to be merely the creation of fancy, are now seen in real life. It is impossible to say where the river ends and the land begins, for a mighty network of roots, clothed with bright-flowering creepers, projects right into the water. Clumps of palms and palm trees, ordinary trees spreading out widely with green boughs and huge leaves, single trees of the pine family shooting up to a towering height in between them, wide fields of papyrus clumps as tall as a man, with big fan-like leaves, and amid all this luxuriant greenery the rotting stems of dead giants shooting up to heaven. . . . In every gap in the forest a water mirror meets the eye; at every bend in the river a new tributary shows itself. A heron flies heavily up and then settles on a dead tree-trunk; white birds and blue birds skim over the water, and high in the air a pair of ospreys circle. Then—yes, there can be no mistake about it!—from the branch of a palm there hang and swing—two monkey tails! Now the owners of the tails are visible. We are really in Africa!

So it goes on hour by hour. Each new corner, each new bend, is like the last. Always the same forest and the same yellow water. The impression which nature makes on us is immeasurably deepened by the constant and monotonous repetition. You shut your eyes for an hour, and when you open them you see exactly what you saw before. The Ogowe is not a river but a river system, three or four branches, each as big as the Rhine, twisting themselves together, and in between are lakes big and little. How the black pilot finds his way correctly through this maze of watercourses is a riddle to me. With the spokes of the great wheel in his hand he guides the ship, without any map before him, from the main stream into a narrow side channel, from this into the lake, and from the lake back into the main stream; and so again and again. But he has worked up and down this stretch of water for sixteen years, and can find his way along even by moonlight!

The current in the lower part of the river is sluggish, but it is very different higher up, though it nowhere becomes as strong as that of the Rhine. Invisible sandbanks and tree-trunks floating just below the surface demand very cautious navigation, and the boat's average speed is not more than eight miles an hour.

After a long run we stop at a small negro village, where, stacked on the river bank, are several hundred logs of wood, such as bakers often use, and we lie to in order to ship them, as wood is the fuel used for the engines. A plank is put out to the bank; the negroes form a line and carry the logs on board. On the deck stands another negro with a paper, and as soon as ten logs have passed, another on the plank calls to him in musical tones, "Put a one." When the hundredth log comes, the call, in the same pleasant tone, is, "Put a cross." The price is from four to five francs a hundred, which is rather high when one considers that the logs are all windfalls and only have to be collected.

The captain abuses the village elder for not having had logs enough ready. The latter excuses himself with pathetic words and gestures. At last they come to an agreement that he shall be paid in spirits instead of cash, because he thinks that the whites get their liquor cheaper than the blacks do, so that he will make a better bargain. . . . Every litre of alcohol pays two francs duty on coming into the colony, and I pay for the absolute alcohol which I use for medical purposes the same duty as is paid on the ordinary liquor for drinking.

Now the voyage continues. On the banks are the ruins of abandoned huts. "When I came out here fifteen years ago," said a trader who stood near me, "these places were all flourishing villages." "And why are they so no longer?" I asked. He shrugged his shoulders and said in a low voice, "L'alcohol. . . ."

A little after sunset we lay to opposite a store, and two hours were spent in shipping 3,000 logs. "If we had stopped here in daylight," said the merchant to me, "all the negro passengers" (there were about sixty of them) "would have gone ashore and bought spirits. Most of the money that the timber trade brings into the country is converted into rum. I have travelled about in the colonies a great deal, and can say that rum is the great enemy of every form of civilisation."

Thus with the ennobling impressions that nature makes are mingled pain and fear; with the darkness of the first evening on the Ogowe there lowers over one the shadow of the misery of Africa. Through the gloaming chimes the monotonous call,

"Make a one," "Make a cross"; and I feel more convinced than ever that this land needs to help it men who will never let themselves be discouraged.

With the help of the moon we are able to go further. Now we see the forest like a gigantic border on the river bank; now we seem to graze its dark wall, from which there streams out a heat that is almost unendurable. The starlight lies gently on the water; in the distance there is summer lightning. Soon after midnight the vessel is anchored in a quiet bay, and the passengers creep into their mosquito nets. Many sleep in the cabins; others on the couches along the walls of the dining saloon, under which are stored the mail sacks.

About 5 a.m. the engines are set in motion again. We have now covered nearly 130 miles (200 kilometres), and the forest is more imposing than further downstream. In the distance appears a hill with red roofs upon it: the mission station of N'Gômô; and the two hours spent in shipping logs gives us time to see the station and its sawmill.

Five hours later the slopes of Lambaréné come in sight, and the steamer sounds its syren, though it will take another half-hour to reach the village. But the inhabitants of the widely scattered stores must be warned in good time, so that they can bring their canoes to the landing stage and take possession of the goods that we have brought for them.

The Lambaréné mission station is an hour further on by canoe, so that no one could be at the landing stage to greet us, but while the cargo was being unloaded I suddenly saw a long, narrow canoe, rowed by merrily singing boys, shoot round the ship, and so fast, indeed, that the white man in the stern had only just time to throw himself backwards and save his head from contact with the ship's cable. It is Mr. Christol, with the lower class of the boys' school, and behind them comes another boat with Mr. Ellenberger, rowed by the upper class. The boys had made it a race, and the younger ones had won; perhaps, however, because they were given the lighter boat. They were, therefore, allowed to convey the doctor and his wife; the others took the luggage aboard. What charming young faces! One little man walked solemnly about, carrying my heavy rifle.

The canoe journey we found at first anything but comfortable. These vessels are only tree-trunks hollowed out and are therefore both flat and narrow, so that their equilibrium is very easily disturbed. Moreover, the rowers do not sit, but stand, which, again, does not contribute to their stability. With a long, narrow paddle, which is held freely in the hands, the crew strike the water singing also so as to keep in time with each other, and a single awkward movement of one of the rowers may upset the canoe. However, in half an hour's time we had overcome our anxiety, and enjoyed the trip thoroughly. The steamer was by now again on its way upstream, and the boys raced it, with such eagerness, too, that they nearly ran into another canoe with three old negresses in it.

In half an hour's time we leave the main stream for a branch one, the singing still going on as merrily as ever, and we can see some white spots on a hill that is flooded with light from the setting sun: the houses of the mission station! The nearer we get, the louder is the singing, and, after crossing a stream which gusts of wind make rather rough, the canoe glides into a quiet little bay.

First there are a dozen black hands to shake, but that seems now quite natural. Then, Mrs. Christol, Miss Humbert, the schoolmistress, and Mr. Kast, the manual worker, conduct us to our little house, which the children have hastily decorated with palms and flowers. Built of wood, the house stands on some forty iron piles, which raise it about twenty inches from the ground, and a verandah runs all round its four small rooms. The view is entrancing: below us is the stream, which here and there widens into a lake; all round is forest, but in the distance can be seen a stretch of the main stream, and the background is a range of blue hills.

We have scarcely time to unpack the things we need at once when night comes on, as it does here always just after six. Then the bell summons the children to prayers in the school-room, and a host of crickets begin to chirp, making a sort of accompaniment to the hymn, the sound of which floats over to us, while I sit on a box and listen, deeply moved. But there comes an ugly shadow creeping down the wall; I look up, startled, and see a huge spider, much bigger than the finest I had ever seen in Europe. An exciting hunt, and the creature is done for.

After supper with the Christols the school children appear in front of the verandah, which has been decorated with paper lanterns, and sing in two parts to the tune of a Swiss *Volkslied* some verses composed by Mr. Ellenberger in honour of the doctor's arrival. Then we are escorted by a squad of lantern-bearers up the path to our house, but before we can think of retiring to rest we have to undertake a battle with spiders and flying cockroaches, who seem to regard as their own domain the house which has been so long uninhabited.

At six o'clock the next morning the bell rings; the hymn sung by the children in the schoolroom is soon heard, and we prepare to begin our new work in our new home.

3 FIRST IMPRESSIONS AND EXPERIENCES

LAMBARÉNÉ, *July*, 1913.

STRICT orders had been widely published that only the most serious cases were to be brought to the doctor for the first three weeks, so that he might have time to settle in; but, naturally, not much attention was paid to them. Sick people turned up at every hour of the day, but practical work was very difficult, as, first of all, I had to rely on any interpreter who might be picked up on the road, and, secondly, I had no drugs, instruments, or bandages except what I had brought in my trunk.

A year before my arrival a black teacher in the mission school at Samkita, N'Zeng by name, had offered his services as interpreter and doctor's assistant, and I had sent word to him to come to Lambaréné immediately on my arrival, but he did not come because in his native village, sixty miles away, he had to carry through a legal dispute over a will. At last I had to send a canoe with a message that he must come at once, and he promised to do so, but week after week went by and still he did not arrive. Then Mr. Ellenberger said to me with a smile: "Doctor, your education has begun. You are finding out for the first time, what every day will prove to you more conclusively, how impossible it is to rely upon the blacks."

During the night of April 26th we heard the whistle of the

steamer and soon learnt that our cases had been unloaded at
the Catholic mission station, which is on the river bank, the
captain having refused to venture on the, to him, unknown
water of our branch stream. Fortunately, however, Mr. Cham-
pel and Mr. Pelot, the industrial missionaries from N'Gômô,
had come to Lambaréné, with ten of their native labourers,
to help us. I was extremely anxious about the conveyance
of my piano with pedal attachment, built for the tropics,
which the Bach Society of Paris had given me, in recognition of many years' service as their organist, so that I
might keep myself in practice even in Africa. It seemed to
me impossible that such a piano, in its heavy zinc-lined case,
could be carried in a hollowed-out tree-trunk, and yet there
are no other boats here! One store, however, possessed a
canoe, hewn out of a gigantic tree, which would carry up to
three tons weight, and this they lent me. It would have carried five pianos!

Soon, by dint of hard work, we got our seventy cases across,
and to get them up the hill from the river bank every
sound set of limbs in the station came to help, the school
children working as zealously as any one. It was amusing to
see how a case suddenly got a crowd of black legs underneath
it and two rows of woolly heads apparently growing out of its
sides, and how, amid shouting and shrieking, it thus crept up
the hill! In three days everything had been carried up, and
the N'Gômô helpers were able to go home. We hardly knew
how to thank them enough, for without their help we could
not possibly have managed the job.

Unpacking was a trial, for it was difficult to dispose of the
various articles. I had been promised a corrugated-iron building as a hospital, but it was impossible to get its framework
erected, as there were no labourers to be had. For several
months the timber trade had been very good, and the traders
paid the labourers wages with which the Mission could not
compete. In order, however, that I might have ready at
hand, at any rate the most necessary drugs, Mr. Kast, the
industrial missionary, fixed some shelves in my sitting-room,
the wood for which he had himself cut and planed. One must
be in Africa to understand what a boon some shelves on the
wall are!

That I had no place in which to examine and treat the sick
worried me much. Into my own room I could not take them

for fear of infection. One arranges at once in Africa (so the missionaries impressed on me from the beginning) that the blacks shall be in the white people's quarters as little as possible. This is a necessary part of one's care for oneself. So I treated and bandaged the sick in the open air before the house, and when the usual evening storm came on, everything had to be hastily carried into the verandah. Treating patients in the sun was, moreover, very fatiguing.

* * *

Under the pressure of this discomfort I decided to promote to the rank of hospital the building which my predecessor in the house, Mr. Morel, the missionary, had used as a fowl-house. I got some shelves fixed on the walls, installed an old camp-bed, and covered the worst of the dirt with whitewash, feeling myself more than fortunate. It was, indeed, horribly close in the little windowless room, and the bad state of the roof made it necessary to wear my sun-helmet all day, but when the storm came on I did not have to move everything under cover. I felt proud the first time I heard the rain rattling on the roof, and it seemed incredible that I could go quietly on with my bandaging.

At the same time I discovered an interpreter and assistant. Amongst my patients there turned up a very intelligent-looking native, who spoke French remarkably well, and said he was a cook by trade but had had to give up that kind of work as it disagreed with his health. I asked him to come to us temporarily, as we could not find a cook, and at the same time to help me as interpreter and surgical assistant. His name was Joseph, and he proved extremely handy. It was hardly surprising that, as he had acquired his knowledge of anatomy in the kitchen, he should, as a matter of habit, use kitchen terms in the surgery: "This man's right leg of mutton (*gigot*) hurts him." "This woman has a pain in her upper left cutlet, and in her loin!" At the end of May N'Zeng arrived, the man whom I had written to engage beforehand, but as he did not seem to be very reliable, I kept Joseph on. Joseph is a Galoa, N'Zeng a Pahouin.

Work was now fairly well started. My wife had charge of instruments and made the necessary preparations for the surgical operations, at which she served as assistant, and she also looked after the bandages and the washing of the linen. Consultations begin about 8:30, the patients waiting in the shade of my house in front of the fowlhouse, which is my surgery, and every morning one of the assistants reads out—

THE DOCTOR'S STANDING ORDERS

1. Spitting near the doctor's house is strictly forbidden.
2. Those who are waiting must not talk to each other loudly.
3. Patients and their friends must bring with them food enough for one day, as they cannot all be treated early in the day.
4. Any one who spends the night on the station without the doctor's permission will be sent away without any medicine. (It happened not infrequently that patients from a distance crowded into the schoolboys' dormitory, turned them out, and took their places.)
5. All bottles and tin boxes in which medicines are given must be returned.
6. In the middle of the month, when the steamer has gone up the river, none but urgent cases can be seen till the steamer has gone down again, as the doctor is then writing to Europe to get more of his valuable medicines. (The steamer brings the mail from Europe about the middle of the month, and on its return takes our letters down to the coast.)

These six commandments are read out every day very carefully in the dialects of both the Galoas and the Pahouins, so that no long discussion can arise afterwards. Those present accompany each sentence with a nod, which indicates that they understand, and at the finish comes a request that the doctor's words shall be made known in all the villages, both on the river and on the lakes.

At 12.30 the assistant announces: "The doctor is going to have his lunch." More nods to show that they understand, and the patients scatter to eat their own bananas in the shade. At 2 p.m. we return, but at 6 p.m. there are often some who have not yet been seen, and they have to be put off till the next day. To treat them by lamplight cannot be thought of because of the mosquitoes and the risk of fever infection.

Each patient is given, on leaving, a round piece of cardboard on a string of fibre, on which is the number under which his name, his complaint, and the medicines given him are recorded in my register, so that if he comes back I have only to turn to the page to learn all about the case, and be spared a time-wasting second diagnosis. The register records also all the bottles, boxes, bandages, etc., which were given; only with this means of control is it possible to demand the return of these things, which in about half the cases we do get back. How valuable bottles and boxes are away from the civilised world only he can rightly estimate who has had to get medicines ready in the primeval forest for patients to take home with them!

The atmosphere is so damp here that medicines, which in Europe can be wrapped in paper or distributed in cardboard boxes, can only be kept in good condition in a corked bottle or in a tin box which closes perfectly. I had not taken sufficient account of this, and I found myself in such difficulty about it that I had to fall out with patients who said they had forgotten or lost a tin box. My friends in Europe were entreated by every post to collect from their acquaintances bottles big and little, glass tubes with corks, and tin boxes of all sorts and sizes. How I look forward to the day when I shall have a sufficient supply of such things!

The round cardboard ticket with the number on it most of the patients wear round their neck, together with the metal one which shows that they have paid their five-franc poll tax for the current year. It is seldom lost or forgotten, and many of them, especially among the Pahouins, regard it as a kind of fetish.

My name among the natives in Galoa is "Oganga," *i.e.,* fetishman. They have no other name for a doctor, as those of their own tribesmen who practise the healing art are all fetishmen. My patients take it to be only logical that the man who can heal disease should also have the power of producing it, and that even at a distance. To me it is striking that I should have the reputation of being such a good creature and yet, at the same time, such a dangerous one! That the diseases have some natural cause never occurs to my patients: they attribute them to evil spirits, to malicious human magic, or to "the worm," which is their imaginary embodiment of pain of every sort. When they are asked to describe their symptoms, they talk about the worm, telling how he was first in their legs, then got into their head, and from there made his way to their heart; how he then visited their lungs, and finally settled in their stomach. All medicines have to be directed to expelling him. If I quiet a colic with tincture of opium, the patient comes next day beaming with joy and tells me the worm has been driven out of his body but is now settled in his head and is devouring his brain: will I please give him something to banish the worm from his head too?

A great deal of time is lost trying to make them understand how the medicines are to be taken. Over and over again the interpreter tells them, and they repeat it after him; it is written, also, on the bottle or box, so that they can hear the directions again from any one in their village who can read, but in the end I am never sure that they do not empty the bottle at one go, and eat the ointment, and rub the powders into their skins. I get, on the average, from thirty to forty people a day to treat, and the chief complaints are skin diseases of various sorts, malaria, the sleeping sickness, leprosy, elephantiasis, heart complaints, suppurating injuries to the bones (osteomyelitis), and tropical dysentery. To stop the discharge from the sores the natives cover the place with powder made from the bark of a certain tree. This hardens gradually into a paste which hinders the escape of the pus and, of course, makes the case much worse.

From the list of the complaints which come oftenest to be treated, the itch (scabies) must not be omitted. It causes the black very great distress, and I have had patients who had not slept for weeks because they had been so tortured by the itching; many had scratched their whole body till the blood came, so that there were festering sores to treat as well as scabies. The treatment is very simple. The patient first washes in the river, and is then rubbed all over, however tall he is, with an ointment compounded of flower of sulphur (*sulphur depuratum*), crude palm oil, remains of oil from sardine tins, and soft soap. In a tin which once contained sterilised milk he receives a quantity of this ointment with which to give himself at home two more rubbings. The success of this is wonderful, the itching ceasing to worry on the second day, and this ointment has in a very few weeks made me famous far and wide.

The natives have great confidence in the white man's medicine, a result which is partly, at any rate, due to the self-sacrificing spirit and the wise understanding with which they have been treated for a generation here on the Ogowe. In this connection I may specially mention Mrs. Lantz, of Talagouga, a native of Alsace, who died in 1906, and Mr. Robert, of N'Gômô, a Swiss, who is now lying seriously ill in Europe.

My work is rendered much harder by the fact that I can keep so few medicines in the fowlhouse. For almost every patient I have to cross the court to my dispensary, there to weigh out or to prepare the medicine needed, which is very fatiguing and wastes much time. When will the iron building for the hospital be seriously taken in hand? Will it be ready before the autumn rainy season begins? What shall I do if it is not ready? In the hot season I shall not be able to work in the fowlhouse.

I am worried, too, by the fact that I have hardly any medicines left, for my *clientèle* is much more numerous than I had expected. By the June mail I sent off an extensive order, but the things will not be here for three or four months, and my quinine, antipyrin, bromide of potassium, salol, and dermatol are almost exhausted.

Yet what do all these disagreeables count for compared with the joy of being here, working and helping? However limited one's means are, how much one can do with them! Just to see the joy of those who are plagued with sores, when these have been cleanly bandaged up and they no longer have to drag their poor, bleeding feet through the mud, makes it worth while to work here. How I should like all my helpers to be able to see on Mondays and Thursdays—the days set apart for the bandaging of sores—the freshly bandaged patients walking or being carried down the hill, or that they could have watched the eloquent gestures with which an old woman with heart complaint described how, thanks to digitalis, she could once more breathe and sleep, because the medicine had made "the worm" crawl right away down to her feet!

As I look back over the work of two months and a half, I can only say that a doctor is needed, terribly needed, here; that for a huge distance round the natives avail themselves of his help, and that with comparatively small means he can accomplish a quite disproportionate amount of good. The need is terrible. "Here, among us, everybody is ill," said a young man to me a few days ago. "Our country devours its own children," was the remark of an old chief.

4 *JULY, 1913-JANUARY, 1914*

LAMBARÉNÉ, *February*, 1914.

THE Lambaréné mission station is built on hills, the one which lies farthest upstream having on its summit the buildings of the boys' school, and on the side which slopes down to the river the storehouse and the largest of the mission houses. On the middle hill is the doctor's little house, and on the remaining one the girls' school and the other mission house. Some twenty yards beyond the houses is the edge of the forest. We live, then, between the river and the virgin forest, on three hills, which every year have to be secured afresh against the invasion of wild Nature, who is ever trying to get her own back again. All round the houses there are coffee bushes, cocoa trees, lemon trees, orange trees, mandarin trees, mango trees, oil palms, and pawpaw trees. To the negroes its name has always been "Andende." Deeply indebted are we to the first missionaries that they took so much trouble to grow these big trees.

The station is about 650 yards long and 110 to 120 yards across. We measure it again and again in every direction in our evening and Sunday constitutionals, which one seldom or never takes on the paths that lead to the nearest villages. On these paths the heat is intolerable, for on either side of these narrow passages rises the forest in an impenetrable wall nearly 100 feet high, and between these walls not a breath of air stirs. There is the same absence of air and movement in Lambaréné. One seems to be living in a prison. If we could only cut down a corner of the forest which shuts in the lower end of the station we should get a little of the breeze in the river valley; but we have neither the money nor the men for such an attack on the trees. The only relief we have is that in the dry season the river sand-

37

banks are exposed, and we can take our exercise upon them and enjoy the breeze which blows upstream.

It had been originally intended to put the hospital buildings on the ridge of high ground on which the boys' school stands, but as the site was both too far away and too small, I had arranged with the staff of the station that I should be given a place for it at the foot of the hill on which I myself lived, on the side next the river. This decision had, however, to be confirmed by the Conference of Missionaries which had been called to meet at Samkita at the end of July. So I went there with Mr. Ellenberger and Mr. Christol, to put my case, and that was my first long journey in a canoe.

*　　*　　*

We started one misty morning two hours before daybreak, the two missionaries and myself sitting one behind the other in long folding chairs in the bow. The middle of the canoe was filled with our tin boxes, our folded camp-bedsteads, the mattresses, and with the bananas which formed the rations of the natives. Behind these things were the twelve rowers in six pairs one behind the other; these sang about the destination to which we were bound and about who was on board, weaving in plaintive remarks about having to begin work so early and the hard day's work they had in front of them! Ten to twelve hours was the time usually allowed for the thirty to thirty-five miles upstream to Samkita, but our boat was so heavily laden that it was necessary to allow somewhat longer.

As we swung out from the side channel into the river, day broke and enabled us to see along the huge sandbank, some 350 yards, some dark lines moving about in the water. The rowers' song stopped instantly, as if at a word of command. The dark lines were the backs of hippopotami, which were enjoying their morning bath after their regular grazing time on land. The natives are much afraid of them and always give them a wide berth, for their temper is very uncertain, and they have destroyed many a canoe.

There was once a missionary stationed in Lambaréné who used to make merry over the timidity of his rowers, and challenge them to go nearer to the great animals. One day, just as he was on the point of bursting into laughter, the canoe was suddenly shot up into the air by a hippopotamus which rose from its dive immediately beneath it, and he and the crew only saved themselves with difficulty. All his baggage was lost. He afterwards had a square patch, with the hole that the creature had made, sawn out of the bottom of the canoe, that he might keep it as a souvenir. This happened some years ago, but the story is told to any white man who asks his crew to row nearer to a hippopotamus.

In the main stream the natives always keep close to the bank where the current is not so strong: there are even stretches of river where one finds a counter-current flowing upstream. And so we creep along, as far as possible in the shade of the overhanging trees. This canoe has no rudder, but the rower nearest the stern guides it in obedience to signals from the one in front, who keeps a sharp lookout for shallows, rocks, and floating tree-trunks. The most unpleasant thing on these trips is the way in which the light and heat are reflected from the water. One feels as if from the shimmering mirror one were being pierced with arrows of fire. To quench our thirst we had some magnificent pineapples, three for each of us.

Sunrise brought the tsetse fly, which is active only by day, and compared with which the worst mosquito is a comparatively harmless creature[1]. It is about half as large again as our ordinary house fly, which it resembles in appearance, only its wings, when closed, do not lie parallel to each other but overlap like the blades of a pair of scissors. To get blood it can pierce the thickest cloth, but it is extremely cautious and artful, and evades cleverly all blows of the hands. The moment it feels that the body on which it has settled makes the slightest movement, it flies off and hides itself on the side of the boat. Its flight is inaudible and a small fly-whisk is the only means of protecting oneself to some extent from it. Its habit of caution makes it avoid settling on any light-coloured object, on which it would be easily detected: hence white clothes are the best protection against it. This statement I found fully confirmed during this trip, for two of us wore white, and one yellow clothes. The two of us hardly ever had a fly upon us: our companion had to endure continual annoyance, but the blacks were the worst sufferers.

At midday we stopped at a native village, and while we ate the provisions we had brought with us, our crew roasted their bananas. I wished that after such hard work they could

---

[1] The *Glossina palpalis*, which conveys the germs of the sleeping sickness, belongs, as is well known, to the Tsetse family.

have had some more substantial food. It was very late in the evening before we reached our destination.

With the conference, which sat for a whole week, I was strongly impressed. I felt it inspiring to be working with men who for years had practised such renunciation in order to devote themselves to the service of the natives, and I enjoyed thoroughly the refreshing atmosphere of love and goodwill. My proposal had a most friendly reception: it was decided that the iron shed and the other hospital buildings should be erected on the place I had in view, and the mission gave me £80 (4,000 fr.) towards the cost of building.

On our return journey we crossed the river twice in order to avoid groups of hippopotami, one of which came up only fifty yards away. Darkness had already come on when we reached our side channel, and for a whole hour we had to pick our way between sandbanks, the crew having now and again to jump out and pull or push the canoe forward. At last we got into deep water: the song of the crew deepened into a roar, and soon we saw lights moving, which advanced in zigzag lines down to a lower level and there came to a halt together. It was the ladies of Lambaréné and the negro women who had come to meet the returning travellers at the landing-place. The canoe cuts through the water with a whish, and with a last spurt is carried high up the beach. The rowers give a yell of triumph, while black hands without number reach out for the boxes, the beds, the bags, and the vegetables we have brought from Samkita. "This is Mr. Christol's." "This is Mr. Ellenberger's." "This is the Doctor's." "Two of you to that; it's too heavy for one!" "Don't drop it!" "Be careful with the guns!" "Wait: not here; put it over there!" and so on. At last the whole cargo has been distributed to the right places, and we go joyfully up the hill.

Our immediate task now was to level the site for the hospital by the removal of several cubic metres of soil. After a world of trouble the Mission managed to secure four or five labourers whose laziness was perfectly magnificent, till my patience at last gave way. A timber merchant whom we knew, Mr. Rapp, had just arrived with a working party in order to examine the neighbouring forest, in which he wanted to secure a concession, and he was staying at the Catholic mission in order to clear off his correspondence. At my request he put eight of his sturdy carriers at my disposal. I promised them handsome pay and took a spade in hand myself, while the black foreman lay in the shade of a tree and occasionally threw us an encouraging word. With two days of steady work we had got the soil cleared away and the spot levelled. The labourers went off with their pay, but on the way back, I regret to say, they stopped at a store and, in spite of my warnings, turned it all into spirits. They reached home in the middle of the night, blind drunk, and the next day were fit for nothing. But we were now in a position to begin building the hospital.

* * *

Joseph and I were now doing all the work without help. N'Zeng went off to his village on leave in August, and as he did not return at the time agreed on, he was discharged. Joseph gets 70 francs (£2 16s.) a month, though as a Cook at Cape Lopez he used to get 120 (£4 16s.). He finds it hard that work demanding some education should be worse paid than the common kinds.

The number of people with heart complaints astonishes me more and more. They, on the other hand, are astonished that I know all about their trouble as soon as I have examined them with the stethoscope. "Now I believe we've got a real doctor!" said an old woman to Joseph not long ago. "He knows that I can often hardly breathe at night, and that I often have swollen feet, yet I've never told him a word about it and he has never even looked at my feet." I cannot help saying to myself that there is something really glorious in the means which modern medicine has for treating the heart. I give digitalis according to the new French method (daily doses of a tenth of a milligram of digitalin continued for weeks and months) and am more than pleased with the results obtained. It must be said that it is easier to treat heart disease here than it is in Europe, for when patients are told that they must rest and keep quiet for weeks, they are never obliged to object that they will lose their wages and perhaps their work. They simply live at home and "recruit," and their family, in the widest sense of that word, supports them.

Mental complaints are relatively rarer here than in Europe, though I have already seen some half-dozen such. They are a great worry as I do not know how to dispose of them. If they are allowed to remain on the station they disturb us with their cries all the night through, and I have to get up again and again to quieten them with a subcutaneous injection. I can look back on several terrible nights which resulted in my feeling tired for many a day afterwards. The difficulty can be surmounted in the dry season, for then I can make the mental patients and their friends camp out on a sandbank about 600 yards away, although getting across to see them twice a day consumes a great deal both of time and of energy.

The condition of these poor creatures out here is dreadful. The natives do not know how to protect themselves from them. Confinement is impossible, as they can at any time break out of a bamboo hut. They are therefore bound with cords of bast, but that only makes their condition worse, and the final result almost always is that they are somehow or other got rid of. One of the Samkita missionaries told me once that a couple of years before, while sitting one Sunday in his house, he had heard loud cries in a neighbouring village. He got up and started off to see what was the matter, but met a native who told him it was only that some children were having the sand flies cut out from their feet; he need not worry, but might go home again. He did so, but learnt the next day that one of the villagers, who had become insane, had been bound hand and foot and thrown into the water.

My first contact with a mentally-diseased native happened at night. I was knocked up and taken to a palm tree to which an elderly woman was bound. Around a fire in front of her sat the whole of her family, and behind them was the black forest wall. It was a glorious African night and the shimmering glow of the starry sky lighted up the scene. I ordered them to set her free, which they did, but with timidity and hesitation. The woman was no sooner free than she sprang at me in order to seize my lamp and throw it away. The natives fled with shrieks in every direction and would not come any nearer, even when the woman, whose hand I had seized, sank quietly to the ground as I told her, and offered me her arm for an injection of morphia and scopolamin. A few moments later she followed me to a hut, where, in a short time, she went to sleep. The case was one of an attack of recurrent maniacal disturbance, and in a fortnight she was well again, at least for a time. In consequence of this the report spread that the doctor was a great magician and could cure all mental diseases.

Unfortunately, I was soon to learn that there are forms of maniacal disturbance here with which our drugs can do little or nothing. The second case was an old man, and he, too, was brought with hands and feet bound. The ropes had cut deeply into his flesh, and hands and feet alike were covered with blood and sores. I was amazed at the small effect produced by the strongest doses of morphia, scopolamin, chloral hydrate, and bromide of potassium. On the second day Joseph said to me: "Doctor, believe me, the man is out of his mind because he has been poisoned. You will make nothing of him; he will get weaker and wilder, and at last he will die." And Joseph was right; in a fortnight the man was dead. From one of the Catholic fathers I learnt that he had robbed some women, and, therefore, had been followed up and poisoned by their relatives.

A similar case I was able to study from the beginning. One Sunday evening there arrived in a canoe a woman who was writhing with cramp. I thought at first that it was simple hysteria, but the next day maniacal disturbance supervened, and during the night she began to rave and shriek. On her, too, the narcotics had hardly any effect, and her strength rapidly diminished. The natives surmised that she had been poisoned, and whether they were right or not I am not in a position to decide.

From all I hear it must be true that poison is much used in these parts, and further south that is still oftener the case: the tribes between the Ogowe and the Congo are notorious in this respect. At the same time there are, among the natives, many inexplicable cases of sudden death which are quite unjustifiably regarded as the result of poison.

Anyhow, there must be many plants the juices of which have a peculiarly stimulating effect on the system. I have been assured by trustworthy persons that there are certain leaves and roots which enable men to row for a whole day without experiencing either hunger, thirst, or fatigue, and to display at the same time an increasingly boisterous merriment. I hope in time to learn something more definite about these "medicines," but it is always difficult to do so, because the knowledge about them is kept a strict secret. Any one who is suspected of betraying anything about them, and, above all, if it is to a white man, may count with certainty on being poisoned.

That the medicine men employ poison to maintain their authority I learnt in a peculiar way through Joseph. About the middle of the dry season his village went off to a sandbank about three hours upstream from here, on a fishing expedition. These fishing days are not unlike the Old Testament harvest festivals, when the people "rejoiced before Yahweh." Old and young live together for a fortnight in "booths" made with branches of trees and eat at every meal fresh fish, boiled, baked, or stewed. Whatever is not consumed is dried and smoked, and if all goes well, a village may take home with it as many as ten thousand fish. As Joseph's eyes nearly start from their sockets whenever the conversation turns on fish, I proposed to allow him to go out with his village for the first afternoon, and asked him to take a small tub in which to bring back a few fishes for the doctor. He showed, however, no enthusiasm at the prospect, and a few questions put me in possession of the reason. On the first day there is no fishing done, but the place is blessed. The "elders" pour rum and throw tobacco leaves into the water to put the evil spirits into a good humour, so that they may let the fish be caught in the nets and may injure no one. These ceremonies were once omitted several years ago, but the following year an old woman wrapped herself up in a net and let herself be drowned. "But—why? Most of you are Christians!" I exclaimed; "you don't believe in these things!" "Certainly not," he replied, "but any one who spoke against them or even allowed himself to smile while the rum and tobacco were being offered, would assuredly be poisoned sooner or later. The medicine men never forgive, and they live among us without any one knowing who they are." So he stayed at home the first day, but I allowed him to go some days later.

*　　*　　*

Besides the fear of poison there is also their dread of the supernatural power for evil which one man can exert over another, for the natives here believe that there are means of acquiring such powers. Whoever has the right fetish can do anything; he will always be successful when hunting, and he can bring bad luck, sickness, and death on any one whom he wishes to injure. Europeans will never be able to understand how terrible is the life of the poor creatures who pass their days in continual fear of the fetishes which can be used against them. Only those who have seen this misery at close quarters will understand that it is a simple human duty to bring to these primitive peoples a new view of the world which can free them from these torturing superstitions. In this matter the greatest sceptic, did he find himself out here, would prove a real helper of mission work.

What is fetishism? It is something born of the fears of primitive man. Primitive man wants to possess some charm to protect him from the evil spirits in nature and from those of the dead, as well as from the power for evil of his fellow men, and this protecting power he attributes to certain objects which he carries about with him. He does not worship his fetish, but regards it as a little bit of property which cannot but be of service to him through its supernatural powers.

What makes a fetish? That which is unknown is supposed to have magical power. A fetish is composed of a number of little objects which fill a small bag, a buffalo horn, or a box; the things most commonly used are red feathers, small parcels of red earth, leopard's claws and teeth, and . . . bells from Europe! Bells of an old-fashioned shape which date from the barter transactions of the eighteenth century! Opposite the mission station a negro has laid out a small cocoa plantation, and the fetish which is expected to protect it hangs on a tree in a corked bottle. Nowadays valuable fetishes are enclosed in tin boxes, so that they may not be damaged by termites, from whose ravages a wooden box gives no permanent protection.

There are big fetishes and little ones. A big one usually includes a piece of human skull, but it must be from the skull of someone who was killed expressly to provide the fetish. Last summer at a short distance below the station an elderly man was killed in a canoe. The murderer was discovered, and it is considered to have been proved that he committed the crime in order to secure a fetish by means of which he hoped to ensure the fulfilment of their contracts by people who owed him goods and money!

A few weeks later my wife and I took a walk one Sunday through the forest to Lake Degele, which is about two hours distant. In the village in which we took a midday rest the people had nothing to eat because for several days the women had been afraid to go out to the banana field. It had become known that several men were prowling about the neighbourhood who wanted to kill someone in order to obtain a fetish. The women of Lambaréné asserted that these men had also been seen near one of our wells, and the whole district was in a state of excitement for several weeks.

I am myself the possessor of a fetish. The most important objects in it are two fragments of a human skull, of a longish oval shape and dyed with some sort of red colouring matter; they seem to me to be from the parietal bones. The owner was ill for many months, and his wife also, both suffering tortures from sleeplessness. Several times, however, the man heard in a dream a voice which revealed to him that they could only get well if they took the family fetish he had inherited to Mr. Haug, the missionary in N'Gômô, and followed Mr. Haug's orders. Mr. Haug referred him to me, and made me a present of the fetish. The man and his wife stayed with me several weeks for treatment, and were discharged with their health very much improved.

The belief that magical power dwells in human skulls which have been obtained expressly for this purpose, must be a quite primitive one. I saw not long ago in a medical periodical the assertion that the supposed cases of trephining which have often been recognised during the excavation and examination of prehistoric graves were by no means attempts at treatment of tumours on the brain or similar growths, as had been assumed, but were simply operations for the securing of fetish objects. The author of the article is probably right[1].

* * *

In the first nine months of my work here I have had close on two thousand patients to examine, and I can affirm that most European diseases are represented here; I even had a child with whooping-cough. Cancer, however, and appendicitis I have never seen. Apparently they have not yet reached the negroes of Equatorial Africa. On the other hand, chills play a great part here. At the beginning of the dry season there is as much sneezing and coughing in the church at Lambaréné as there is in England at a midnight service on New Year's Eve. Many children die of unrecognised pleurisy.

In the dry season the nights are fresher and colder than at other times, and as the negroes have no bedclothes they get so cold in their huts that they cannot sleep, even though according to European standards the temperature is still fairly high. On cold nights the thermometer shows at least 68 de-

---

[1] In Keith's *Antiquity of Man* (William & Norgate, 1915), p. 21, is a picture of a prehistoric skull in which there is a hole made by trephining, as is shown by the fact that the edges are bevelled off. The condition of the bone shows further that the wound had healed prior to death.

grees F., but the damp of the atmosphere, which makes people sweat continually by day, makes them thereby so sensitive that they shiver and freeze by night. White people, too, suffer continually from chills and colds in the head, and there is much truth in a sentence I came across in a book on tropical medicine, though it seemed at the time rather paradoxical: "Where the sun is hot, one must be more careful than elsewhere to avoid chills." Especially fatal to the natives is the camp life on the sandbanks when they are out on their summer fishing expeditions. Most of the old folk die of pneumonia which they have caught on these occasions.

Rheumatism is commoner here than in Europe, and I not infrequently come across cases of gout, though the sufferers cannot be said to bring it on by an epicurean diet. That they eat too much flesh food cannot possibly be alleged, as except for the fish-days in summer they live almost exclusively on bananas and manioc.

That I should have to treat chronic nicotine poisoning out here I should never have believed. At first I could not tell what to think of acute constipation which was accompanied by nervous disturbances and only made worse by aperients, but while treating a black Government official who was suffering severely I came to see clearly, through observation and questioning, that the misuse of tobacco lay at the root of it. The man soon got well and the case was much talked of, as he had been a sufferer for years and had become almost incapable of work. From that time, whenever a case of severe constipation came to me, I asked at once: "How many pipes a day do you smoke?" and I recognised in a few weeks what mischief nicotine produces here. It is among the women that cases of nicotine poisoning are most frequent. Joseph explained to me that the natives suffer much from insomnia, and then smoke all through the night in order to stupefy themselves.

Tobacco comes here from America in the form of leaves, seven of which form a head (*tête de tobac*). It is a plant which is frightfully common and also frightfully strong (much stronger than that which is smoked by white people), and it largely takes the place of small coins: e.g., one leaf, worth about a halfpenny, will buy two pineapples, and almost all temporary services are paid for by means of it. If you have to travel, you take for the purchase of food for the crew, not money, for that has no value in the forest, but a box of tobacco-leaves, and to prevent the men from helping themselves to its valuable contents you make it your seat. A pipe goes from mouth to mouth during the journey; and anybody who wants to travel fast and will promise his crew an extra two leaves each, is sure to arrive an hour or two sooner than he otherwise would.

* * *

The teeth also give the natives much trouble. Many of my patients suffer from shrinking of the gums together with purulent discharges (*pyorrhœa*) caused by accumulations of tartar. Then, in course of time, all the teeth get loose and fall out. Strange to say, these cases get well more quickly here than in Europe, where the complicated treatment often fails to attain its object. I have obtained successful results from regular painting with an alcoholic solution of thymol, only the patient has to be careful not to swallow any of the liquid, which is, of course, very poisonous.

It seems to the natives almost incredible that I can extract teeth which are not yet loose, but they do not all trust the polished forceps! A chief who was plagued with toothache would not submit to their use till he had gone home again to consult his wives. Presumably the family decision was unfavourable, as he did not present himself again. On the other hand, some request me to take all their teeth out and to get them new ones from Europe. A few old folk have, through the missionaries, actually got some double sets, "made by the white people," and they are now an object of much envy.

Abdominal tumours are very common here with the women.

My hope that I should not need to perform any major operation before the medical ward was ready for use was disappointed. On August 15th I had to operate on a case of strangulated hernia which had been brought in the evening before. The man, whose name was Aïnda, begged me to operate, for, like all the natives, he knew well enough the dangers of his condition. There was, in fact, no time to lose, and the instruments were brought together as quickly as possible. Mr. Christol allowed me to use his boys' bedroom as an operating theatre; my wife undertook to give the anaesthetic, and a missionary acted as assistant. Everything went off better than we could have expected, but I was almost staggered by the quiet confidence with which the man placed himself in position on the operating table.

A military doctor from the interior, who is going to Europe on leave, tells me that he envies me the excellent assistance I had for my first operation on hernia! He himself, he said, had performed his with one native prisoner handing him the instruments and another administering the chloroform by guesswork, while each time they moved the fetters on their legs rattled; but his regular assistant was ill and there was no one who could take his place.

The aseptic precautions were, naturally, far from perfect, but the patient recovered.

January 10th, 1914. I had scarcely finished writing the above paragraphs this afternoon when I had to hurry off to the landing place. Mrs. Faure, the wife of the missionary at N'Gômô, arrived in a motor-boat, suffering from a severe attack of malaria, and I had scarcely given her a first intramuscular injection of quinine when a canoe brought in a young man who had had his right thigh broken and badly mutilated by a hippopotamus in Lake Sonange. In other respects, too, the poor fellow was in a bad condition. He and a friend had gone out together to fish, but not far from the landing place of their village a hippopotamus had come up unexpectedly and hurled their boat into the air. The friend escaped, but my patient was chased about in the water by the enraged beast for half an hour, though he was able at last to get to shore in spite of his broken thigh. I was afraid there would be serious blood poisoning, for they had brought him the twelve hours' canoe journey with his mutilated thigh wrapped in dirty rags.

I have myself had a meeting with a hippo, but it, fortunately, ended well. One autumn evening I was called up to visit a planter, and to get to him we had to pass a narrow canal about fifty yards long with a very strong current. On the journey out we saw two hippos in the distance. For the journey home, which would be in the dark, for night had fallen, the store people advised me to make a détour of a couple of hours so as to avoid the canal and the animals, but the rowers were so tired that I would not ask them for so much extra exertion. We had just got to the entrance of the canal when the two hippos came up from a dive thirty yards ahead of us, their roar sounding much as if children were blowing a trumpet into a watering can, only louder. The crew at once drew in close to the bank, where the current was least strong, but we advanced very slowly, foot by foot, the hippos accompanying us, swimming along the other bank. It was a wonderful, exciting experience. Some palm-tree stems, which had got fixed in midstream, rose out of the water and swayed about like reeds; on the bank the forest rose straight up like a black wall, and an enchanting moonlight illuminated the whole scene. The rowers gasped with fear and encouraged each other with low calls while the hippos pushed their ugly heads out of the water and glared angrily across at us. In a quarter of an hour we had got out of the canal and were descending the narrow arm of the river, followed by a parting roar from the hippos. I vowed that never in future would I be so scrupulous about adding even two hours to a journey in order to get out of the way of these interesting animals, yet I should be sorry not to be able to look back on those wonderful minutes, uncomfortable though the experience seemed at the time.

*   *   *

Towards evening on November 1st I was again called upon to go to N'Gômô. Mrs. Faure had, without thinking, walked a few yards in the open without anything on her head, and was now prostrate with severe fever and other threatening symptoms. Truly my fellow-traveller on the *Europe* was right when he said that the sun was our great enemy. Here are some further examples:

A white man, working in a store, was resting after dinner with a ray of sunshine falling on his head through a hole in the roof about the size of a half-crown: the result was high fever with delirium.

Another lost his pith helmet when his boat was upset. As soon as he got on to the boat, which was floating away keel uppermost, he threw himself on his back and, anticipating danger, at once took off his coat and his shirt to protect his head with them. It was too late, however, and he got a bad sunstroke.

The skipper of a small merchant vessel had to make some small repairs to the keel of his craft, which had been drawn up dry on land. While working at them he bent his head so far that the sun shone upon his neck below his helmet. He, too, was for a time at death's door.

Children, however, are less affected than adults. Mrs. Christol's little daughter not long ago ran unobserved out of the house and walked about in the sun for nearly ten minutes with-

out taking any harm. I am now so used to this state of things
that I shudder every time I see people represented in illustrated
papers as walking about bareheaded in the open air, and I
have to reassure myself that even white people can do this
with impunity in Europe.

The skipper of the little steamer, who had himself been
down with sunstroke, had been kind enough to offer to fetch
me to N'Gômô, and my wife went with me to help to nurse
the patient. Following the advice of an experienced colonial
doctor, I treated the sunstroke as if it were complicated with
malaria, and gave intra-muscular injections of a strong solution of quinine. It has been proved that sunstroke is especially
dangerous to people who are already infected with malaria,
and many doctors even assert that quite half the symptoms
are to be put down to the malarial attack which is brought on
by the sunstroke. A further necessity in such cases, when the
patient can take nothing or brings everything up again, is to
introduce sufficient fluid into the system to avert such injury
to the kidneys as might endanger life. This is effected best
with a pint of distilled and sterilised water containing 65
grains (4½ grams) of the purest kitchen salt, which is introduced under the skin or into a vein in the arm with a
cannula.

On our return from N'Gômô we were agreeably surprised
to hear that the corrugated iron hospital ward was ready. A
fortnight later the internal fitting up was practically finished,
and Joseph and I left the fowlhouse and settled in, my wife
helping us vigorously. I owe hearty thanks for this building
to Mr. Kast and Mr. Ottmann, the two practical workers of
the Mission; the former a Swiss, the latter a native of the
Argentine. It was a great advantage that we could discuss all
details together, and that these two were willing to listen to
the considerations, suggested by my medical knowledge. Hence
the building, although it is so plain and so small, is extraordinarily convenient: every nook and corner is made use of.

The building has two rooms, each thirteen feet square, the
outer of which serves as consulting room, the inner as operating theatre. There are also two small side rooms under
the very wide projections of the roof: one is the dispensary,
the other the sterilising room. The floor is of cement. The
windows are very large and go right up to the roof. That
prevents any accumulation of hot air at the top of the room,

and everyone is astonished to find how cool it is, although corrugated-iron buildings are always condemned in the tropics as being intolerably hot. There is no glass in the windows, only fine wire-netting to keep out mosquitoes, but there are wooden shutters outside, which are necessary on account of the storms. Along the walls run wide shelves, many of them of the rarest woods. We had no common boards left, and it would have cost much more to have had new ones sawn than to use even the most expensive that we had ready, besides throwing the work weeks backward. Under the roof white calico is stretched tightly as a protection against mosquitoes, which otherwise would find their way in through holes.

During December the waiting-room was got ready and a shed for housing the patients. Both buildings are constructed like large native huts out of unhewn logs and raffia leaves, and I myself, under Mr. Christol's direction, took part in the work. The patients' dormitory measures 42 feet by 19 feet 6 inches. Joseph has a large hut to himself. These buildings lie along both sides of a path about 30 yards long which leads from the iron building to a bay in the river, in which the canoes of the patients are moored. The bay is overshadowed by a magnificent mango-tree.

When the roof of the dormitory was ready, I marked on the floor of beaten earth with a pointed stick sixteen large rectangles, each indicating a bed, with passages left between them. Then the patients and their attendants, who hitherto had been lodged, so far as possible, in a boathouse, were called in. Each patient was put into a rectangle, which was to be his sleeping place, and their attendants were given axes with which to build the bedsteads; a piece of bast on a peg showed the height they were to have. A quarter of an hour later canoes were going up and down stream to fetch the wood needed, and the beds were ready before nightfall. They consist of four short posts ending in forks, on which tie two strong side-poles, with shorter pieces lying across, the whole bound firmly together with creeper stalks. Dried grass serves as a mattress.

The beds are about twenty inches from the ground, so that boxes, cooking utensils, and bananas can be stored below, and they are broad enough for two or three persons to occupy them at once; if they do not provide room enough, the attendants sleep on the floor. They bring their own mosquito nets with them.

There is no separation of the sexes in the big shed; they arrange themselves in their usual way. The only thing I insist on is that the healthy shall not take possession of a bed while a patient has to sleep on the ground. I must soon build some more huts for their accommodation, as the one dormitory is not enough. I must also have some rooms in which to isolate infectious cases, especially the dysentery ones. The patients with sleeping sickness, again, I cannot keep for any length of time in hospital, as they endanger the health of the whole station, and later on I shall build a hut for them in a quiet spot on the other side of the river. There is plenty of work to do beside the mere medical treatment.

*　　*　　*

With the hospital building finished, the doctor's wife can develop her activity to the full. In the fowlhouse there was only room for Joseph and myself. She shares with me the work of teaching Joseph how to clean and handle the instruments and to prepare for operations. She also superintends the washing, and it takes a great deal of trouble to ensure that the dirty and infected bandages are properly cleaned and sufficiently boiled. She appears punctually at ten o'clock, and stays till twelve, insisting on everything being kept in good order.

To understand what it means when my wife leaves her household work to give most of the morning to the medical work as well as not a few afternoons to the operations, for which she administers the anæsthetics, one must know how complicated the simplest style of housekeeping is in Africa. This is the result of two causes: first, the strict division of duties among the native servants, and, second, their unreliability. We have to keep, as is customary, three servants: a boy, a cook and a washerman. To assign the work of the last-named to either the boy or the cook, as is often done in small households, is impossible in our case, on account of the extra washing which comes to the house from the hospital. Apart from this, a moderately good European maid could do the whole of the work quite well by herself. The cook does nothing but the cooking, the washerman the washing and ironing, and the boy looks after the rooms and the fowls. Each of them, as soon as he has finished his own work, goes off to rest! So we have to ourselves do whatever work there is which does not belong to either of their strictly defined departments. Women servants are not to be had out here. Mrs. Christol has as nursemaid for her eighteen months old baby girl a native boy of fourteen, M'Buru by name.

Then, again, all one's servants, even the best of them, are so unreliable that they must not be exposed to the slightest temptation. This means that they must never be left alone in the house. All the time they are at work there my wife must be there too, and anything that might be attractive to their dishonesty must be kept locked up. Each morning the cook is given exactly what is to be prepared for our meàls, so much rice, fat, and potato; in the kitchen he keeps just a small supply of salt, flour, and spice, and if he forgets anything, my wife will have to go up the hill again to the house from the hospital in order to give it out to him.

That one can never leave them alone in a room, that one keeps everything locked up and does not trust them with more than the exact amount of foodstuffs, is not taken by the black servants as an insult. They themselves expect us to observe these precautionary measures strictly, in order that they may not be held responsible for any occasional theft. Joseph insists on my locking the dispensary if I go into the dormitory from the iron building for even two minutes, and leave him alone in the consulting-room, from which one goes into the dispensary. If a European does not observe these precautions then his blacks steal his things with a good conscience. What is not locked up "goes for a walk," to use Joseph's language; you may steal anything from a person who is so careless!

Worse still, however, than this, the negro steals not merely what will be of value to him, but anything that attracts him for the moment. Mr. Rambaud, of Samkita, lost in this way part of a valuable work in several volumes, and there disappeared one day from my bookshelf the piano edition of Wagner's "Meistersinger" and the copy of Bach's Passion Music (S. Matthew), into which I had written the organ accompaniment, which I had worked out very carefully! This feeling of never being safe from the stupidest piece of theft brings one sometimes almost to despair, and to have to keep everything locked up and turn oneself into a walking bunch of keys adds a terrible burden to life.

*   *   *

If I went simply by what the blacks ask for, I should now have to operate on some one every day; the people with hernia quarrel as to who shall submit to the knife first! However, at present we manage to get off with two or three operations a week. For more than this my wife would be unable to manage the necessary preparations and the cleaning and putting away of the instruments afterwards; nor should I be equal to the work. I have often to operate in the afternoon when I have been busy till one o'clock or even later with bandaging and examination; and in this land one cannot take so much upon one as in a more temperate climate.

That Joseph can allow himself to collect the vessels with blood in them after an operation and to wash the instruments, is a sign of very high enlightenment. An ordinary negro will touch nothing that is defiled with blood or pus, because it would make him unclean in the religious sense. In many districts of Equatorial Africa it is difficult, or even impossible, to persuade the natives to let themselves be operated on, and why those on the Ogowe even crowd to us for the purpose I do not know. Their readiness is probably connected with the fact that some years ago an army doctor, Jorryguibert by name, stayed some time with the District Commandant at Lambaréné, and performed a series of successful operations. He sowed, and I am reaping.

Not long ago I got a rare case of injury to operate on, for which many a famous surgeon might envy me. It was a case of strangulated hernia which protruded under the ribs, the so-called lumbar hernia. There was every imaginable complication present, and when darkness fell I had not finished; for the final sutures Joseph had to hold the lamp for me. But the patient recovered.

Much notice was attracted by an operation on a boy who for a year and a half had had a piece of necrosed bone, as long as his hand, projecting from his leg below the knee. It was a case of osteomyelitis, and the pus secreted stank so horribly that no one could stay near him for long. The boy himself was reduced to a skeleton, but now he is fat and healthy and is beginning to walk again.

Hitherto all my operations have been successful, and that raises the confidence of the natives to a pitch that almost terrifies me. What impresses them most of all is the anæsthetics, and they talk a great deal about them. The girls in our school exchange letters with those in a Sunday school at home, and in one of them there was the following piece of news: "Since the Doctor came here we have seen the most wonderful things happen. First of all he kills the sick people; then he cures them, and after that he wakes them up again." For anæsthesia seems to the native the same thing as being dead, and similarly if one of them wants to make me understand that he has had an apoplectic fit, he says: "I was dead."

There are sometimes patients who try to show their gratitude. The man who in August was freed from a strangulated hernia collected twenty francs among his relations, "in order to pay the Doctor for the expensive thread with which he sewed up my belly."

An uncle of the boy with the sores on his feet, a joiner by trade, put in fourteen days' work for me making cupboards out of old boxes.

A black trader offered me his labourers in order that the roof of my house might be put in order in good time before the rains.

Another came to see me and thank me for having come out to help the natives, and when he left me he presented me with twenty francs for the medicine chest.

Another patient presented my wife with a kiboko (or sjambok) of hippopotamus hide. It is made in this way: When a hippopotamus is killed, its hide, which is from ½ inch to 1 inch thick, is cut into strips about 1½ inches wide and nearly 5 feet long. One end is nailed to a board, the strip is twisted into a spiral, and the other end is nailed down. When it is dry that supple, sharp-cornered, and justly dreaded instrument of torture is ready.

* * *

The last few weeks I have been busy stowing away the supply of drugs, etc., which arrived in October and November. The reserve stock we place in the small iron room on the hill, of which I have had the use since Mr. Ellenberger went away, and which the grateful uncle mentioned above has fitted with the necessary cupboards and shelves. It is true that they do not look handsome, being put together from cases and bearing still the addresses that were painted on them, but we have a place for everything: that is the essential thing. In Africa we learn not to be too exacting.

While I was worrying over the cost of these valuable supplies of medicines, bandages, and lint, the December mail brought me news of fresh gifts which made my heart lighter again. How can we thank sufficiently all our friends and acquaintances? By the time anything comes to Lambaréné it costs about three times its European price, and this increase is accounted for by the cost of packing, which must be very carefully done, of the railway journey, of shipping and unloading, of the voyage, of the colonial import duty, of conveyance up the river, and allowance for the general losses which result from heat or water in the hold or from rough handling at the ports.

Our health continues excellent; not a trace of fever, though we need a few days' rest.

Just as I close this chapter there arrives at the station an old man with leprosy. He and his wife have come from the Fernando Vaz lagoon, which lies south of Cape Lopez and is connected with Ogowe by one of its smaller mouths. The poor creatures have rowed themselves 250 miles upstream to visit the doctor, and can hardly stand for exhaustion.

5 *JANUARY TO JUNE, 1914*

LAMBARÉNÉ, *End of June,* 1914.

AT the end of January and the beginning of February my wife and I were in Talagouga busy looking after Mr. Hermann, a missionary, who was suffering from a bad attack of boils with high fever, and at the same time I treated the sick of the neighbourhood. Among the latter was a small boy who, with every sign of extreme terror, refused to enter the room, and had to be carried in by force. It transpired later that he quite thought the doctor meant to kill and eat him! The poor little fellow had got his knowledge of cannibalism, not from nursery tales, but from the terrible reality, for even to-day it has not been quite extirpated among the Pahouins. About the area over which it still prevails it is hard to say anything definite, as fear of the heavy penalties attached to it make the natives keep every case as secret as possible. A short time ago, however, a man went from the neighbourhood of Lambaréné into some outlying villages to collect arrears of debt, and did not come back. A labourer disappeared in the same way from near Samkita. People who know the country say that "missing" is often to be interpreted as "eaten."

Even the keeping of slaves by natives, though it is no longer acknowledged as such, is not yet a thing of the past, in spite of the war that both Government and missions carry on against it. I often notice among the attendants of a sick man some whose features are not those of any tribe that is settled here or in the neighbourhood. But if I ask whether they are slaves, I am assured with a rather peculiar smile that they are only "servants." The lot of these unacknowledged slaves is by no means a hard one. They never have to fear ill-treatment, and they never think of escaping and putting themselves under the protection of the Government. If an inquiry is held, they usually deny obstinately that they are slaves, and it often happens that after a number of years of slavery they are admitted as members of the tribe, thereby becoming free and obtaining a right of domicile in a definite place. The latter is what they regard as most valuable.

The reason for the continued secret existence of domestic slavery in the district of the lower Ogowe, is to be looked for in the food conditions of the interior. It is the disastrous lot of Equatorial Africa never to have had at any time either fruit-bearing plants or fruit-bearing trees. The banana stocks, the manioc, the yam, the potato, and the oil palm were introduced from their West Indian islands by the Portuguese, who were the great benefactors of Equatorial Africa. In the districts where these useful products have not been introduced, or where they are not well established, permanent famine prevails. Then parents sell their children to districts lower down stream, in order that these, at any rate, may have something to eat. In the upper course of the N'Gounje, a tributary of the Ogowe, there must be such a famine district; it is from there that the majority of the domestic slaves on the Ogowe come, and I have patients from there who belong to the "earth eaters." These are driven by hunger to accustom themselves to this practice, and they keep it up even when they have a sufficiency of food.

That the oil palm was imported one can notice evidence to-day, for on the river and round the lakes where there are, or once were, villages, there are whole woods of oil palms, but when one goes about on the main roads into the virgin forest, where there has never been a human settlement, there is not one to be seen.

On our return journey from Talagouga we stayed two days in Samkita with Mr. and Mrs. Morel, the missionaries from Alsace. Samkita is the leopard station, and one of these robbers broke, one night last autumn, into Mrs. Morel's fowl-house. On hearing the cries of their feathered treasures, her husband hurried off to get some one to help, while she kept a look-out in the darkness, for they supposed a native had forced his way in to steal something for his dinner. Then, hearing a noise on the roof, Mrs. Morel went nearer in hopes of identifying the intruder. The latter, however, had already vanished into the darkness with a mighty spring, and when they opened the door twenty-two fowls lay dead on the floor with their breasts torn open. It is only the leopard that kills in this fashion, his chief object being to get blood to drink. His victims were removed, but one of them, stuffed with strychnine, was left lying before the door. Two hours later the leopard returned and devoured it, and while it was writhing in cramp it was shot by Mr. Morel. Shortly before our arrival another leopard had made his appearance in Samkita, and had devoured several goats.

At the house of Mr. Cadier, a missionary, we ate monkey flesh for the first time, for Mr. Cadier is a great sportsman. With me, on the contrary, the blacks are far from pleased, because I use my rifle so little. On one of my journeys we passed a cayman, asleep on a tree which was growing out of the water, and when I merely watched it instead of shooting it the cup of their indignation ran over. "Nothing ever happens with you," the crew exclaimed through their spokesman. "If we were with Mr. Cadier, he would long ago have shot us a couple of monkeys and some birds so that we could have some meat. But you pass close by a cayman and never even touch your shooter!" I willingly put up with the reproach. Birds which circle above the water I never like shooting; monkeys are perfectly safe from my weapon. One can often bring down or wound three or four in succession and yet never secure their bodies. They get caught among the thick branches or fall into the undergrowth which covers an impenetrable swamp; and if one finds the body, one often finds also a poor little baby monkey, which clings, with lamentations, to its dying mother. My chief reason for keeping a gun is to be able to shoot snakes, which swarm on the grass around my house, and the birds of prey which plunder the nests of the weaver bird in the palm trees in front of it.

On our return journey we met a herd of fifteen hippos, who soon plunged into the water on our approach, but a quite young one remained amusing itself on the sandbank, and would not obey its mother when she called to it.

*   *   *

During our absence Joseph had carried out his duties very well, and had treated the surgical cases with intelligence. On his own initiative he had dressed the festering stump of a man's arm with a solution of hydrogen peroxide, which he had to make from biborate of sodium!

The young man who had been mauled by the hippo I found in a very bad state. My three weeks' absence had prevented me from operating at the right time, and he died during the amputation of his leg, which I now hastily undertook. As he drew his last breaths his brother began to look angrily at the companion who had gone with him on the fatal expedition, and had come to the station to help to look after him. He spoke to him also in a low voice, and as the body became cold there began an excited duel of words between them. Joseph drew me aside and explained what it meant. N'Kendju, the companion, had been with the dead man on the expedition, and they had, in fact, gone on his invitation. He was, therefore, according to native law, responsible for him, and could be called to account. That was why he had had to leave his village to stay all these weeks by his friend's bedside, and now that they were taking the dead man back to his village he was expected to go with them, that the case against him might be settled at once. He did not want to go, however, as he knew that it would mean death. I told the brother that I regarded K'Kendju as being now in my service, and that I would not let him go, which led to an angry altercation between him and myself while the body was being placed in the canoe, -where the mother and the aunts began the funeral lamentations. He asserted that N'Kendju would not be put to death, but would only have to pay a fine. Joseph, however, assured me that no reliance could be placed on such statements, and I felt obliged to remain at the riverside till they started, as they would otherwise, no doubt, have dragged N'Kendju into the canoe by force.

My wife was troubled that while the patient was breathing his last his brother showed no sign of grief, and was thinking only of the putting into force of the legal rights, and she expressed herself angrily about his want of feeling. But in that she was no doubt wronging him. He was only fulfilling a sacred duty in beginning at once to take care that the person who, from his point of view, was responsible for his brother's death, did not escape the penalty due to him. For to a negro it is unthinkable that any such act should remain unatoned for, a point of view which is thoroughly Hegelian! For him the legal side of an event is always the important one, and a large part of his time is spent in discussing legal cases[1]. The most hardened litigant in Europe is but a child compared to the negro, and yet it is not the mere love of litigation that is the latter's motive; it is an unspoilt sense of justice, such as is, on the whole, no longer felt by Europeans. I was getting ready one day to tap an old Pahouin who was suffering badly from abdominal dropsy, when he said to me: "Doctor, see that all the water runs off as soon as possible, so that I can breathe and get about again. My wife has deserted me because my body has got so big, and I must go and press for the return of the money I paid for her at the wedding." On another occasion a child was brought to me in a most miserable condition; its right leg had an open sore along it right up to the hip. "Why didn't you come before?" "Doctor, we couldn't; there was a palaver to finish." A palaver means any sort of quarrel which is brought up for a legal settlement, and the little ones are discussed in the same detail and with the same

---

[1] "No other race on a similar level of culture has developed as strict methods of legal procedure as has the negro. Many of his legal forms remind us strongly of those of medieval Europe." (Professor Boas in *The Ethnical Record*, March 1904, p. 107.)

"Everywhere in Africa where the life of the people has not been disturbed by outside influences, the people are governed by law. There is law relating to property, to morality, to the protection of life, in fact, in many portions of Africa law is more strictly regarded than in many civilised countries." (Booker Washington: *The Story of the Negro*, Vol. I, p. 70.)

earnestness as the big ones. A dispute involving a single fowl will keep the village elders employed for a whole afternoon. Every negro is a law expert.

The legal side of life is extremely complicated with them, because the limits of responsibility are, according to our notions, very wide indeed. For a negro's debts the whole of his family, down to the remotest degree of relationship, is responsible. Similarly the penalties are extraordinarily severe. If a man has used another's canoe illegally for a single day, he must pay the third of its value as a fine.

Together with this unspoilt sense of justice goes the fact that the native accepts the punishment as something obvious and needing no defence, even when it is, according to our notions, much too severe. If he did not get punished for an offence, his only conclusion would be that his victims were remarkably foolish. Yet the lightest sentence, if unjust, rouses him to great indignation; he never forgives it, and he recognises the penalty as just only if he is really convicted and obliged to confess. So long as he can lie with the slightest plausibility, he inveighs against his condemnation with most honourable-seeming indignation, even if he is actually guilty. This is a feature in primitive man which every one who has to do with him must take into account.

That N'Kendju ought to pay some compensation to the family of his companion on the unfortunate fishing expedition is obvious, even though he was only so very indirectly responsible for the other's death. But they must get the case against him settled in orderly fashion in the District Court at Lambaréné.

*　　*　　*

I am always able to rely on Joseph. True, he can neither read nor write, but in spite of that he never makes a mistake when he has to get a medicine down from the shelf. He remembers the look of the words on the label, and reads this, without knowing the individual letters. His memory is magnificent, and his capacity for languages remarkable. He knows well eight negro dialects, and speaks fairly well both French and English. He is at present a single man, as his wife left him, when he was a cook down on the coast, to go and live with a white man. The purchase price of a new life companion would be about 600 francs (£24), but the money can be paid in instalments. Joseph, however, has no mind to take another wife under these conditions, for he thinks they are an abomination. "If one of us," he said to me, "has not completely paid for his wife, his life is most uncomfortable. His wife does not obey him, and whenever an opportunity offers she taunts him with having no right to say anything to her, because she has not yet been paid for."

As Joseph does not understand how to save any better than the other natives, I have bestowed on him a money-box in which to save up for the purchase of a wife. Into this goes all his extra pay for sitting up at night or other special services, and all the tips he gets from white patients. How extravagant the "first assistant of the doctor in Lambaréné" (as he calls himself) can be, I experienced about this time. He was with me at a store, and while I was buying some nails and screws his eye was caught by a pair of patent leather shoes which, from standing a long time in a Paris shop window, had got sun-dried and rotten, and had then, like many other odds and ends, found their way to Africa. Although they cost nearly as much as the amount of his monthly wages, he meant to buy them, and warning looks from me were useless, as were also a couple of digs in the ribs which I gave him quietly while we were standing at the counter among a crowd of staring negroes. I could not venture openly to dissuade him, as it would have offended the dealer, who was thankful to get rid of the shoes. So at last I pinched him unperceived as hard as I could just above the back of his thigh till he could stand the pain no longer, and the transaction was broken off. In the canoe I gave him a long lecture on his childish taste for extravagance, with the result that the very next day he went to the store again on the quiet and bought the shoes! Quite half of what he earns from me he spends in clothes, shoes, ties, and sugar. He dresses much more elegantly than I do.

All through the last few months the work has been steadily growing. Our hospital is splendidly situated. Upstream, and downstream, from places hundreds of kilometres away on the Ogowe and its tributaries, sick people are brought here, and the fact that those who bring them can be lodged here is a further encouragement to come in great numbers. And there is yet another attraction: the fact that I am always at home, unless—and this has happened only two or three times so far—I have to go to some other mission station to treat a missionary who is ill, or some member of his family. Thus the native who has undertaken the trouble and the expense of the journey here from a distance, is sure of seeing me. That is the great advantage which the independent doctor has over one appointed by the Government. The latter is ordered now here, now there, by the authorities, or has to spend a long time with a military column on the march. "And that you have not got to waste so much time on correspondence, reports, and statistics, as we have to, is also an advantage, the reality of which you have not yet grasped," said an army doctor not long ago, during a short chat with me on his way past.

*   *   *

The hut for the sleeping sickness victims is now in course of erection on the opposite bank, and costs me much money and time. When I am not myself superintending the labourers whom we have secured for grubbing up the vegetation and building the hut, nothing is done. For whole afternoons I have to neglect the sick to play the part of foreman there.

Sleeping sickness prevails more widely here than I suspected at first. The chief focus of infection is in the N'Gounje district, the N'Gounje being a tributary of the Ogowe about ninety miles from here, but there are isolated centres round Laméné and on the lakes behind N'Gômô.

What is the sleeping sickness? How is it spread? It seems to have existed in Equatorial Africa from time immemorial, but it was confined to particular centres, since there was little or no travelling. The native method of trade with the sea coast was for each tribe to convey the goods to the boundary of its territory, and there to hand them over to the traders of the adjoining one. From my window I can see the place where the N'Gounje enters the Ogowe, and so far only might the Galoas living round Lambaréné travel. Any one who went beyond this point, further into the interior, was eaten.

When the Europeans came, the natives who served them as boats' crews, or as carriers in their caravans, moved with them from one district to another, and if any of them had the sleeping sickness they took it to fresh places. In the early days it was unknown on the Ogowe, and it was introduced about thirty years ago by carriers from Loango. Whenever it gets into a new district it is terribly destructive, and may carry off a third of the population. In Uganda, for example, it reduced the number of inhabitants in six years from 300,000 to 100,000. An officer told me that he once visited a village on the Upper Ogowe which had two thousand inhabitants. On passing it again two years later he could only count five hundred; the rest had died meanwhile of sleeping sickness. After some time the disease loses its virulence, for reasons that we cannot as yet explain, though it continues to carry off a regular, if small, number of victims, and then it may begin to rage again as destructively as before.

The first symptom consists of irregular attacks of fever, sometimes light, sometimes severe, and these may come and go for months without the sufferer feeling himself really ill. There are victims who enter the sleep stage straight from this condition of apparent health, but usually severe headaches come during the fever stage. Many a patient have I had come to me crying out: "Oh, doctor! my head, my head! I can't stand it any longer; let me die!" Again, the sleep stage is sometimes preceded by torturing sleeplessness, and there are patients who at this stage get mentally deranged; some become melancholy, others delirious. One of my first patients was a young man who was brought because he wanted to commit suicide.

As a rule, rheumatism sets in with the fever. A white man came to me once from the N'Gômô lake district suffering from sciatica. On careful examination, I saw it was the beginning of the sleeping sickness, and I sent him at once to the Pasteur Institute at Paris, where French sufferers are treated. Often, again, an annoying loss of memory is experienced, and this is not infrequently the first symptom which is noticed by those around them. Sooner or later, however, though it may be two or three years after the first attacks of fever, the sleep sets in. At first it is only an urgent need of sleep; the sufferer falls asleep whenever he sits down and is quiet, or just after meals.

A short time ago a white non-commissioned officer from Mouila, which is six days' journey from here, visited me because, while cleaning his revolver, he had put a bullet through his hand. He stayed at the Catholic mission station, and his black boy accompanied him whenever he came to have his hand dressed, and waited outside. When the N.C.O was ready to go, there was almost always much shouting and searching for his attendant, till at last, with sleepy looks, the latter emerged from some corner. His master complained that he had already lost him several times because, wherever he happened to be, he was always taking a long nap. I examined his blood and discovered that he had the sleeping sickness.

Towards the finish the sleep becomes sounder and passes at last into coma. Then the sick man lies without either feeling or perception; his natural motions take place without his being conscious of them, and he gets continually thinner. Meanwhile his back and sides get covered with bed-sores; his knees are gradually drawn up to his neck, and he is altogether a horrible sight. Release by death has, however, often to be awaited for a long time, and sometimes there is even a lengthy spell of improved health. Last December I was treating a case which had reached this final stage, and at the end of four weeks the relatives hurried home with him that, at least, he might die in his own village. I myself expected the end to come almost at once, but a few days ago I got the news that he had recovered so far as to eat and speak and sit up, and had only died in April. The immediate cause of death is usually pneumonia.

Knowledge of the real nature of sleeping sickness is one of the latest victories of medicine, and is connected with the names of Ford, Castellani, Bruce, Dutton, Koch, Martin, and Leboeuf. The first description of it was given in 1803 from cases observed among the natives of Sierra Leone, and it was afterwards studied also in negroes who had been taken from Africa to the Antilles and to Martinique. It was only in the 'sixties that extensive observations were begun in Africa itself, and these first led to a closer description of the last phase of the disease, no one even suspecting a preceding stage or that there was any connection between the disease and the long period of feverishness. This was only made possible by the discovery that both these forms of sickness had the same producing cause.

Then in 1901 the English doctors, Ford and Dutton, found, on examining with the microscope the blood of fever patients in Gambia, not the malaria parasites they expected, but small, active creatures which on account of their form they compared to gimlets, and named Trypanosomata, *i.e.*, boring-bodies. Two years later the leaders of the English expedition for the investigation of sleeping sickness in the Uganda district found in the blood of a whole series of patients similar little active creatures. Being acquainted with what Ford and Dutton had published on the subject, they asked whether these were not identical with those found in the fever patients from the Gambia region, and at the same time, on examination of their own fever patients, they found the fever to be due to the same cause as produced the sleeping sickness. Thus it was proved that the "Gambia fever" was only an early stage of sleeping sickness.

The sleeping sickness is most commonly conveyed by the *Glossina palpalis*, a species of tsetse fly which flies only by day. If this fly has once bitten any one with sleeping sickness, it can carry the disease to others for a long time, perhaps for the rest of its life, for the trypanosomes which entered it in the blood it sucked live and increase and pass in its saliva into the blood of any one it bites.

Still closer study of sleeping sickness revealed the fact that it can be also conveyed by mosquitoes, if these insects take their fill of blood from a healthy person immediately after they have bitten anyone with sleeping sickness, as they will then have trypanosomes in their saliva. Thus the mosquito army continues by night the work which the *glossina* is carrying on all day. Poor Africa[1]!

In its essential nature sleeping sickness is a chronic inflammation of the meninges and the brain, one, however, which always ends in death, and this ensues because the trypanosomes pass from the blood into the cerebro-spinal fluid. To fight the disease successfully it is necessary to kill them before they have passed from the blood, since it is only in the blood that atoxyl[2], one weapon that we at present possess, produces effects which can to any extent be relied on; in the cerebro-spinal marrow the trypanosomes are comparatively safe from it. A doctor must, therefore, learn to recognise the disease in the early state, when it first produces fever. If he can do that, there is a prospect of recovery.

In a district, therefore, where sleeping sickness has to be treated, its diagnosis is a terribly complicated business because the significance of every attack of fever, of every persistent

---

[1] I must, however, in justice add that the mosquito does not harbour the trypanosomes permanently, and that its saliva is poisonous only for a short time after it has been polluted by the blood of a sleeping sickness victim.

[2] Atoxyl (meta-arsenic anilid) is a compound of arsenic with an aniline product.

headache, of every prolonged attack of sleeplessness, and of all rheumatic pains must be gauged with the help of the microscope. Moreover, this examination of the blood is, unfortunately, by no means simple, but takes a great deal of time, for it is only very seldom that these pale, thin parasites, about one eighteen-thousandth ($\frac{1}{18000}$) of a millimetre long, are to be found in any considerable number in the blood. So far I have only examined one case in which three or four were to be seen together. Even when the disease is certainly present one can, as a rule, examine several drops of blood, one after another, before discovering a single trypanosome, and to scrutinise each drop properly needs at least ten minutes. I may, therefore, spend an hour over the blood of a suspected victim, examining four or five drops without finding anything, and even then have no right to say there is no disease; there is still a long and tedious testing process which must be applied. This consists in taking ten cubic centimetres of blood from a vein in one of the sufferer's arms, and keeping it revolving centrifugally for an hour according to certain prescribed rules, at the same time pouring off at intervals the outer rings of blood. The trypanosomes are expected to have collected into the last few drops, and these are put under the microscope; but even if there is again a negative result, it is not safe to say that the disease is not present. If there are no trypanosomes to-day, I may find them ten days hence, and if I have discovered some to-day, there may be none in three days' time and for a considerable period after that. A white official, whose blood I had proved to contain trypanosomes, was subsequently kept under observation for weeks, in Libreville, without any being discovered, and it was only in the Sleeping Sickness Institute at Brazzaville that they were a second time proved to be there.

If, then, I wish to treat such patients conscientiously, a couple of them together can tie me for a whole morning to the microscope while outside there are sitting a score of sick people who want to be seen before dinner-time! There are also surgical patients whose dressings must be renewed; water must be distilled, and medicines prepared; sores must be cleansed, and there are teeth to be drawn! With this continual drive, and the impatience of the waiting sick, I often get so worried and nervous that I hardly know where I am or what I am doing.

Atoxyl is a frightfully dangerous drug. If the solution is left for some time in the light it decomposes, just like salvarsan, and works as a poison, but even if it is prepared faultlessly and is in perfect condition, it may cause blindness by injuring the nerves of sight. Nor does this depend on the size of the dose; small ones are often more dangerous than large ones, and they are never of any use. If one begins with too small a dose, in order to see whether the patient can take the drug, the trypanosomes get inured to it; they become "atoxylproof," as it is called, and then can defy the strongest doses. Every five days my sleeping sick come to me for an injection, and before I begin I always ask in trepidation whether any of them have noticed that their sight is not as good as usual. Happily, I have so far only one case of blinding to record, and that was a man in whom the disease had already reached a very advanced stage. Sleeping sickness now prevails from the east coast of Africa right to the west, and from the Niger in the north-west to the Zambesi in the south-east. Shall we now conquer it? A systematic campaign against it over this wide district would need many doctors and the cost would be enormous. . . . Yet, where death already stalks about as conqueror, the European States provide in most niggardly fashion the means of stopping it, and merely undertake stupid defensive measures which only give it a chance of reaping a fresh harvest in Europe itself.

* * *

After the sleeping sickness it is the treatment of sores and ulcers which takes up most time. They are far more common here than in Europe—one in four of the children in our school has a permanent sore. What is the cause?

Many sores are caused by sandfleas (*Rynchoprion penetrans*), a species much smaller than the common flea. The female bores into the tenderest part of the toe, preferably under the nail, and grows under the skin to the size of a small lentil. The removal of the insect causes a small wound, and if this gets infected through dirt, there sets in a kind of gangrene, which causes the loss of a joint, or even of a whole toe. Negroes with ten complete toes are almost rarer than those who have one or more mutilated.

It is an interesting fact that the sandflea, which is now a regular plague to Central Africa, is not indigenous there, but was brought over from South America as late as 1872. In ten years from that time it had spread all over the Dark Continent from the Atlantic to the Pacific. In East Africa it is known as the "Jigger." One of the worst species of ants which we have here, the sangunagenta, is also an importation, having come over in cases of goods brought from South America.

Besides the sores caused by the sandflea we have the so-called crawcraw. These generally occur several together, most commonly on the foot and leg, and are frightfully painful, but the cause of them we do not yet know. The treatment consists in cleaning out the sore with a plug of cotton-wool till it bleeds naturally, when it is washed out with mercuric chloride and filled with boracic powder. It is then bandaged and left to itself for ten days.

Another kind of sore is that of the so-called raspberry disease (*frambœsia*), which may attack any part of the body. The name was given because it shows itself first in largish pustules, covered with a yellow crust, the removal of which reveals a slightly bleeding surface which looks exactly like a raspberry stuck on the skin. There was brought to me once an infant which had got infected through contact with its mother's breast, and looked exactly as if it had been first painted over with some viscous substance and then stuck all over with raspberries. These pustules may disappear, but for years afterwards surface sores occur in the most varied parts of the body.

This disease, which is common in all tropical countries, is very infectious, and almost all the negroes here have it at some time or other. The old treatment consisted in dabbing the sore with a solution of sulphate of copper (*cupri sulphas*) and giving the patient every day two grams of iodide of potassium (*potassii iodidum*) in water. It has recently been proved that arseno-benzol injected into the veins of the arm effects a speedy and permanent cure; the sores disappear as if by magic.

The worst sores of all are the tropical eating sores (*ulcus phagedenicum tropicum*), which spread in all directions. Not infrequently a whole leg surface is one single sore, in which the sinews and bones show like white islands. The pain is frightful, and the smell is such that no one can stay near the patient for any length of time. The sufferers are placed in a hut by themselves, and have their food brought to them;

there they gradually waste away and die after terrible sufferings. This most horrible of all the different sores is very common on the Ogowe, and merely to disinfect and bandage does no good. The sufferer must be put under an anæsthetic and the sore carefully scraped right down to the sound tissue, during which operation blood flows in streams. The sore is then bathed with a solution of permanganate of potash, but a careful inspection must be made every day so as to detect any new purulent centre that may show itself, as this must at once be scraped out like the others. It is weeks, perhaps months, before the sore is healed, and it will use up half a case of bandages. What a sum it costs us, too, to feed the patient for so long! But what joy when—limping, indeed, for the healed wounds leave the foot permanently deformed, but rejoicing at his freedom from the old pain and stench—he steps into the canoe for the journey home!

*   *   *

The lepers are another class of sick people who give one much trouble. This disease is caused by a bacillus which is closely allied to that of tuberculosis, and this was discovered in 1871 by a Norwegian doctor, Hansen by name. Isolation, which is always insisted on where possible, is not to be thought of here, and I often have four or five lepers among the other sick folk in the hospital. The most remarkable fact about it is that we have to assume that the infection passes from one individual to another, although no one has yet discovered how it does so, or succeeded in producing infection experimentally. The only drug we have at our disposal for fighting this disease is the so-called Chaulmoogra oil (*oleum gynocardiæ*), which is obtained from the seed of a tree in Further India. It is expensive, and usually comes into the market adulterated. I obtain what I want through a retired missionary, Mr. Delord, a native of French Switzerland, who had a great deal to do with leprosy when he worked in New Caledonia, and can get supplies direct from a reliable source. Following a hint from him I administer the nauseous drug in a mixture of sesame and earth-nut oils (*huile d'arachaides*), which makes it more tolerable for taking. Recently the administration of Chaulmoogra oil by subcutaneous injection has also been recommended.

A real cure of leprosy is beyond our powers, but a great

improvement in a patient's health can be effected, and the disease can be reduced to a state of quiescence which lasts so long that it is practically equivalent to a cure. The attempts which have been made in recent years to cure the disease by means of a serum prepared from the bacillus that causes it, and known under the name of Nastin, allow us to hope that some day we shall be able to fight it effectively in this way.

With swamp fever, or tropical malaria, I have, unfortunately, like every other doctor in the tropics, plenty to do. To the natives it is merely natural that every one of them should from time to time have fever with shivering fits, but children are the worst sufferers. As a result of this fever the spleen, as is well known, swells and becomes hard and painful, but with them it sometimes projects into the body like a hard stone from under the left ribs, not seldom reaching as far as the navel. If I place one of these children on the table to examine him, he instinctively covers the region of the spleen with his arms and hands for fear I should inadvertently touch the painful stone. The negro who has malaria is a poor, broken-down creature who is always tired and constantly plagued with headache, and finds even light work a heavy task. Chronic malaria is known to be always accompanied by anæmia. The drugs available for its treatment are arsenic and quinine, and our cook, our washerman, and our boy each take 7 to 8 grains (half a gram) of the latter twice a week. There is a preparation of arsenic called "Arrhenal," which enormously enhances the effect of the quinine, and I give it freely to white and black alike in subcutaneous injections.

Among the plagues of Africa tropical dysentery must not be forgotten. This disease, also, is caused by a special kind of amœba, which settles in the large intestine and injures the membrane. The pain is dreadful, and days and night alike, without intermission, the sufferer is constantly wanting to empty the bowels, and yet passes nothing but blood. Formerly the treatment of this dysentery, which is very common here, was a tedious process and not really very successful. The drug used was powdered ipecacuanha root, but it could seldom be administered in sufficient quantities to act effectively, because when taken through the mouth it caused vomiting. For some years, however, use has been made of a preparation of the essential principle contained in this root, under the title of emetin (*emetinum hydrochloricum*). Six to eight cubic

centimetres of a 1 per cent solution of this is injected sub-
cutaneously for several days in succession, and this is followed
at once by a great improvement and usually by a permanent
cure; in fact, the results attained border on the miraculous.
There is no need for care about diet; the patient can eat what
he likes—hippopotamus steak, if he is black; potato salad,
if he is white. If a doctor could effect no cures in the tropics
beyond what these newly-discovered means of healing, arseno-
benzol and emetin, make possible, it would still be worth
his while to come out here. At the fact that a great part of the
labour entailed upon a doctor in the tropics consists in combating various diseases, each one more loathsome than the
last, which have been brought to these children of nature by
Europeans, I can here only hint. But what an amount of misery
is hidden behind the hint!

* * *

As to operations, one undertakes, naturally, in the forest
only such as are urgent and which promise a successful result.
The one I have had to perform oftenest is that for hernia, a
thing which afflicts the negroes of Central Africa much more
than it does white people, though why this should be so we
do not know. They also suffer much oftener than white people from strangulated hernia, in which the intestine becomes
constricted and blocked, so that it can no longer empty itself.
It then becomes enormously inflated by the gases which form,
and this causes terrible pain. Then after several days of torture death takes place, unless the intestine can be got back
through the rupture into the abdomen. Our ancestors were
well acquainted with this terrible method of dying, but we
no longer see it in Europe because every case is operated upon
as soon as ever it is recognised. "Let not the sun go down
upon your—strangulated hernia," is the maxim continually
impressed upon medical students. But in Africa this terrible
death is quite common. There are few negroes who have not
as boys seen some man rolling in the sand of his hut and
howling with agony till death came to release him. So now,
the moment a man feels that his rupture is a strangulated
one—rupture is far rarer among women—he begs his friends to
put him in a canoe and bring him to me.

How can I describe my feelings when a poor fellow is
brought me in this condition? I am the only person within

hundreds of miles who can help him. Because I am here and am supplied by my friends with the necessary means, he can be saved, like those who came before him in the same condition and those who will come after him, while otherwise he would have fallen a victim to the torture. This does not mean merely that I can save his life. We must all die. But that I can save him from days of torture, that is what I feel as my great and ever new privilege. Pain is a more terrible lord of mankind than even death himself.

So, when the poor, moaning creature comes, I lay my hand on his forehead and say to him: "Don't be afraid! In an hour's time you shall be put to sleep, and when you wake you won't feel any more pain." Very soon he is given an injection of omnipon; the doctor's wife is called to the hospital, and, with Joseph's help, makes everything ready for the operation. When that is to begin she administers the anæsthetic, and Joseph, in a long pair of rubber gloves, acts as assistant.

The operation is finished, and in the hardly-lighted dormitory I watch for the sick man's awaking. Scarcely has he recovered consciousness when he stares about him and ejaculates again and again: "I've no more pain! I've no more pain!" . . . His hand feels for mine and will not let it go. Then I begin to tell him and the others who are in the room that it is the Lord Jesus who has told the doctor and his wife to come to the Ogowe, and that white people in Europe give them the money to live here and cure the sick negroes. Then I have to answer questions as to who these white people are, where they live, and how they know that the natives suffer so much from sickness. The African sun is shining through the coffee bushes into the dark shed, but we, black and white, sit side by side and feel that we know by experience the meaning of the words: "And all ye are brethren" (Matt. xxiii, 8). Would that my generous friends in Europe could come out here and live through one such hour!

6 LUMBERMEN AND RAFTSMEN IN THE PRIMEVAL FOREST

CAPE LOPEZ, *July 25th-29th*, 1914.

AN abscess, for the opening of which the help of the military doctor at Cape Lopez seemed to be necessary, compelled me about this time to go down to the coast, but we had scarcely got there when it fortunately burst, and the risk of further complications was avoided. My wife and I were kindly entertained at the house of a factory employee called Fourier, whose wife had spent two months that summer at Lambaréné, awaiting her confinement at our house. Monsieur Fourier is a grandson of the French philosopher Fourier (1772-1837), in whose social theories I was much interested when a student in Paris. Now one of his great-grandchildren has entered the world under our roof.

I cannot yet move about, so spend the whole day in an armchair on the verandah with my wife, looking out over the sea and inhaling with enjoyment the fresh sea breezes. That there is a breeze at all is a delight to us, for in Lambaréné there is never any wind except during the short storms, which are known as tornadoes. This time of leisure I will employ in writing something about the life of the lumbermen and the raftsmen on the Ogowe.

It was only about thirty years ago that attempts were first made to exploit the great forests of West and Equatorial Africa, but the work is not as easy as might be thought. Magnificent timber is there in any quantity, but how fell and transport it? At present the only timber on the Ogowe that has any commercial value is that which is near the river. The most magnificent tree a kilometre from the water is safe from the axe, for what is the good of felling it if it cannot be taken away?

Why not build light railways, then, to convey the logs to the water? That question will be asked only by those who do not know what a forest in Equatorial Africa is like. The ground on which it stands is nothing but a mass of gigantic roots and swamp. To prepare the ground for even 200 or 300 yards of light railway means cutting down the trees, getting rid of their roots, and filling up the swamp; and that would cost more than a hundred tons of the finest timber would fetch at Cape Lopez. It is, therefore, only at the most favourable spots that light railways can be built cheaply enough. In these forests one learns how impotent man is when pitted against Nature!

Work, then, has as a rule, to be carried on in a primitive way, and this for the further reason, also, that only primitive men can be got for labourers, and not a sufficient number even of them. The introduction of Annamites and Chinese has been talked of, but it is a hopeless proposal. Foreigners are of no use in the African forest, because they cannot endure the heat and the camp life in it, and, moreover, cannot live on the foods produced locally.

The first thing to be done is to choose the right place for work. In the virgin forest the trees grow in the most capricious fashion, and it pays to fell them only where there is near the water's edge a considerable number of the kind of trees required. These places are generally some distance within the forest, but when the river is high, are usually connected with the latter by some narrow watercourse, or by a pond, which at such times becomes a lake. The natives know well enough where these places are, but they keep the knowledge to themselves, and make a point of misleading any white man who comes into their neighbourhood to look for them. One European told me that the natives of a certain village kept taking from him for two months liberal presents of brandy, tobacco, and cloth while they went out with him every day on the search for such a place, but not a single one was discovered which seemed to promise profitable exploitation. At last, from a conversation which he happened to overhear, he learnt that they purposely took him past all the favourable spots, and then their friendly relations came to a sudden end. Of the timber that stands near enough to the river to be easily transported, nearly the whole has already been felled.

About half the forest area has been put, through concessions, into the hands of big European companies. The rest is free, and any one, white or black, can fell timber there as he pleases. But even in the woodlands covered by the concessions the companies often allow the natives to fell trees as freely as they can in the other parts, on the one condition that they sell the timber to the company itself, and not to other dealers.

The important thing, after all, is not to own woods, but to have timber for sale, and the timber which the negroes cut down on their own account and then offer to the company works out cheaper than what the latter get through their contract labour. On the other hand, the supply from the free natives is so uncertain that it cannot be relied upon for trade purposes. They may take it into their heads to celebrate a festival, or to have a big fishing expedition just when the demand for timber is greatest, so the companies, while they buy all

they can from the natives, also keep their own labourers
constantly at work.

*　　*　　*

When a suitable spot has been discovered, there come to
it either the men of a village who have agreed to exploit it together, or the white man with his labourers, and huts are
erected to live in. The great difficulty is food. One is faced with
the problem of securing supplies for from sixty to one hundred men for weeks and months together, and that in the
middle of the virgin forest. The nearest village and the nearest
plantations are perhaps twenty-five miles away, and only to
be reached by a weary struggle through jungle and swamp.
Unfortunately, too, the staple foods of banana and manioc[1]
are bulky, and therefore troublesome to transport; moreover,
they only keep good for a few days. The great drawback
attaching to Equatorial Africa is that none of its food products
keep long. Bananas and manioc ripen the whole year through,
now freely, now sparingly, according to the time of year, but
bananas go bad six days after gathering, and manioc bread
ten days after it is made. The manioc root by itself is unusable,
as there are poisonous species which contain cyanic acid,
to get rid of which the roots are soaked for some days in
running water. Stanley lost three hundred carriers because
they too hastily ate manioc root which had not been washed
long enough. When it is taken out of the water it is crushed
and rubbed, and undergoes fermentation, and this produces
a kind of tough, dark dough, which is moulded into thin sticks
and wrapped in leaves for preservation. Europeans find this
a very poor food.

Since, then, the regular provision of local foodstuffs is so
difficult, these native timber workers have to reconcile themselves to living on rice and preserved foods from Europe. This
means mostly cheap tins of sardines, prepared specially for
export to the inland regions of Africa, and of these the stores
always have a big supply in stock. Variety is secured by
means of tinned lobster, tinned asparagus, and Californian

---

[1] Manioc, better known perhaps to English readers as cassava, belongs to
the Euphorbiaceæ. The two chief kinds are *Manihot utilissima*, the bitter,
which contains the hydrocyanic acid, and *Manihot aipi*, the sweet, which is
harmless. The roots are 3 feet long and 6 to 9 inches in diameter, filled with
milky juice. The startch as prepared for food is known first as Brazilian
arrowroot, and this, when further prepared, as the tapioca of commerce.
(*Encycl. Brit., s.v.*)

fruits. The expensive tinned stuff which the well-to-do European denies himself as too expensive, the negro, when felling timber, eats from necessity!

And shooting? In the real forest shooting is impossible. There is, indeed, wild life in plenty, but how is it to be discovered and pursued in the thick jungle? Good shooting is only to be had where grassland or treeless marshes alternate with the forest, but in such places there is usually no timber to be felled. Thus, paradox though it seems, it is nowhere easier to starve than amid the luxurious vegetation of the game-haunted forests of Equatorial Africa!

How the timber-workers manage to get through the day with the tsetse fly, and through the night with the mosquito, it is hard to tell. Often, too, they have to work for days together up to the hips in water. Naturally they all suffer from fever and rheumatism.

The felling of the trees is very troublesome work because of the thickness of the trunks. Moreover, the giants of the forest do not grow up out of the earth round and smooth; they are anchored to the ground by a row of strong, angular projections, which as they leave the stems become the main roots, and acts as buttresses. Mother Nature, as though she had studied under the best architects, gives these forest giants the only sort of protection which could be effective against the forces of the tornadoes.

In many cases the hewing of the trees at ground level is not to be thought of. The axe can begin its work only at the height of a man's head, or it may even be necessary to erect a scaffold on which the hewers can then stand.

Several men must toil hard for days before the axe can finish its work, and even then the tree does not always fall. It is tangled into a single mass with its neighbours by powerful creepers, and only when these have been cut through does it come, with them, to the ground. Then begins the process of cutting up. It is sawn, or hewn with axes, into pieces from 12 to 15 feet long, until the point is reached at which the diameter is less than 2 feet. The rest is left, and decays, and with it those portions also which are too thick, that is, which are more than 5 to 5½ feet in diameter, as such huge pieces are too awkward to handle.

The felling and cutting up of the trees takes place as a rule in the dry season, that is, between June and October. The next work is to clear the track by which these mighty logs, weighing sometimes as much as three tons, are to be rolled to the nearest piece of water. Then begins a contest with the roots which have been left in the ground and the huge tree-tops which are lying upon it, and not infrequently the mighty trunk itself has in its fall embedded itself three feet in the soil. But in time the track is got fairly ready, the portions which run through swamp being filled up with wood. The pieces— spoken of as "billets" (French, *billes*)—are rolled on to the track, thirty men, with rhythmical shouts, pushing and shoving at each one and turning it slowly over and over on its axis. If a piece is very large, or not quite round, human strength may not suffice, and the movement is effected by means of jacks. Then a hillock in the way may present a difficulty to be overcome; or, again, the wood-packing in the swamp may give way! The thirty men in an afternoon's work seldom move one of these "billets" more than eighty to ninety yards.

And time presses! All the timber must be got to the pond to be ready for the high water at the end of November and the beginning of December, since it is only just then that the pond is in connection with the rivers. Any timber that misses this connection remains in the forest, and is reduced to such a condition by the parasitic wood-insects—especially by a species of Bostrichid beetle—that it is not worth buying. At best it can be saved when the spring high water comes, but that is often not high enough to connect all the ponds, and if the timber has to stay there till the next autumn flood it is assuredly lost.

Occasionally, once perhaps in ten years, even the autumn flood does not rise high enough, and then the season's work is wholly lost on many timber-working sites. This happened last autumn (1913), and many middle-sized and small trading firms are reported to have been nearly ruined. The male populations of many villages, too, after labouring for months, did not earn enough to cover their debts for the rice and tinned foods that they had had to buy.

At last the timber is in the river, moored to the jungle on the bank with ropes of creepers, and the white trader comes to buy what the negroes of the different villages have to offer him. And here caution is necessary. Is the timber really of the kind desired, or have the negroes smuggled in among it pieces of some other tree with a similar bark and similar veining which stood at the water's edge? Is it all freshly cut, or are there some last year's logs, or even some of the year before last, which have had their ends sawn off to make them look new? The inventive skill of the negroes with a view to cheating in timber borders on the incredible! Let the newcomer be on his guard! For example: In Libreville Bay a young English merchant was to buy for his firm some ebony, a heavy wood, which comes into the market in short logs. The Englishman reported with satisfaction that he had secured some huge pieces of magnificent ebony, but no sooner had his first purchase reached England than he received a telegram saying that what he had bought and despatched for ebony was nothing of the kind; that his expensive stuff was worthless, and he himself responsible for the loss involved! The fact was that the negroes had sold him some hard wood which they had allowed to lie for several months in the black swamp. There it had soaked in the colour so thoroughly that at the ends and to a certain depth all over it seemed to be the finest ebony; the inner part, however, was of a reddish colour. The inexperienced white man had neglected to test his bargain by sawing one of the logs in two!

The dealer, then, measures and purchases the timber. The measuring is a difficult job, as he has to jump about on the logs, which turn over in the water with his weight. Then he pays up half the purchase money, keeping the rest till the timber, on which the trade mark of his firm is now cut, has been brought safely down to the coast. Sometimes, however, it happens that natives sell the timber four or five times over, pocketing the money each time and then disappearing into the forest till the transaction has been forgotten, or till the white man is tired of spending time and money in going after the swindlers, by whom, indeed, he is not likely to be indemnified, seeing that, long before he finds them, they will have spent the money in tobacco and other things.

*　　*　　*

Next comes the building of the rafts, or floats, for which neither rope nor wire is needed, as the supple creepers of the forest are cheaper and better than either, and can be had as thin as a finger or as thick as one's arm. From 60 to 100 of the 12 to 15 feet trunks are arranged one behind the other in two rows and bound together, so that the raft is from 25 to 30 feet broad, and about 130 feet long, and its weight may be as much as 200 tons. Long planks are also bound upon it on a regular plan, and these give it the necessary strength and firmness. Next huts of bamboo and raffia leaves are built upon it, and a special platform of logs is coated with clay to serve as a fireplace for cooking. Powerful steering-oars are fixed in front and behind in strong forks, so that the course of the raft can be to some extent guided, and as each of these needs at least six men to work it, there must be a crew of between fifteen and twenty men. Then when all the bananas and manioc sticks that can be procured have been placed upon it, the voyage begins.

The crew must know well the whereabouts of the continually shifting sandbanks, in order to avoid them, and these, covered as they are with brown water, are very hard to detect at any considerable distance. If the raft strikes one, there is no way of getting it afloat again but by releasing from it one by one the logs which have got fixed in the sand, and putting them back again afterwards. Sometimes the raft has to be taken entirely to pieces and re-made, a proceeding which under those conditions takes a week and involves the loss of a certain number of the logs, which the stream carries away during the work. Time, too, is precious, for provisions are usually not too abundant, and the further they get down the Ogowe, the harder it is to get more. For a few wretched bananas the people of the villages on the lower Ogowe exact from the hungry raftsmen a franc, or a franc and a half; or they may refuse to supply anything at all.

It happens not infrequently during the voyage that the crew sells some of the good logs on the raft to other negroes, and replace them with less valuable ones of exactly the same sizes, putting the firm's trade mark upon these with deceptive accuracy. These inferior pieces that have been thrown away in the forest have been lying in dozens ever since the last high water, either on the sandbanks or in the little bays on the river banks, and there are said to be villages which keep a big store of them of all possible sizes. The good timber which has been taken from the raft is later made unrecognisable, and is sold over again to a white man.

Other reasons, too, the white man has for anxiety about his raft on its way down. In so many days the ship which is to take the timber will be at Cape Lopez, and the rafts have till then to come in: the crew have been promised a handsome bonus if they arrive in good time. But if the tomtom is sounded in a river-bank village as they pass, they may succumb to the temptation to moor the raft and join in the festivities— for two, four, six days! Meanwhile the ship waits at Cape Lopez and the trader must pay for the delay a fine which turns his hoped-for profitable stroke of business into a serious loss.

The 200 miles (350 kilometres) from Lambaréné to Cape Lopez usually take such a raft fourteen days. The, at first, comparatively quick rate of progress slows down towards the end, for about fifty miles from the river mouth the tide makes itself felt in the river. For this reason, too, the river water can no longer be drank, and as there are no springs within reach, the canoe which is attached to the raft is filled in good time with fresh water. From now on progress can be made only with the ebb tide and when the flood tide sets in the raft is moored to the bank with a creeper as thick as a man's arm, so that it may not be carried back upstream.

*　　*　　*

The next step is to get the raft into a narrow, winding side stream about twenty miles long which enters the sea through the southern shore of Cape Lopez Bay. If it is swept into any of the other arms which have their outlet in the middle of the bay it is lost, for the strong current of the rivers, which, after being dammed up by the flood tide, rushes down at five miles an hour, carries it right out to sea. Through the southern arm, however, it comes out into a strip of shallow water which runs along the coast, and over this it can be navigated with long poles to Cape Lopez. Here again, if the raft gets a few yards too far from the shore so that the punting-poles cannot touch bottom, it can no longer be guided and gets swept out to sea, and within these last ten miles a mighty contest often develops between the crew and the elements. If a land breeze gets up there is hardly anything to be done. If, indeed, the position of the raft is noticed at Cape Lopez, they try to send a boat to it with an anchor and a cable, and that may save it if the waves are not so strong as to break it up. But if that happens, there is only one thing for the crew to do, if they do not wish to be lost also, and that is to leave the raft, in the canoe—and at the right moment. For once out at the mouth of the bay, no canoe can make its way back to Cape Lopez in the teeth of the ebb tide and the regular current of the river. The flat, keelless vessels which are used in the river are useless in a contest with the waves.

In this way more than one raft has been lost, and more than one crew has disappeared in the waves. One of my white patients once found himself on one of these unlucky rafts. They were driven out to sea after dark by a breeze which got up quite unexpectedly, and the force of the waves made it hopeless to think of escaping in the canoe. The raft was beginning to break up when a motor longboat came to the rescue, someone on the shore having noticed the lantern which the despairing men had waved to and fro as they drove past, and sent the rescue boat, which happened fortunately to have its steam up, in pursuit of the moving light.

Brought safely to Cape Lopez, the raft is taken to pieces and the logs go into "the park." At the most sheltered part of the bay two rows of tree-trunks are bound together so as to form a sort of double chain. This is effected by driving into the trunks iron wedges which end in rings through which strong wire ropes are drawn. This double chain of logs protects the calm water from the movement of the sea, and behind this "breakwater," or boom, float as many logs as there is room for. The logs are further fastened together by other wire ropes, running through iron rings which have been driven into them, and every two or three hours a watchman goes round to see whether the boom is all right, whether the rings are still holding, and whether the continual rubbing in the rings and the frequent bending with the up and down movement of the water has not made the wire ropes worn and unsafe. But often the utmost foresight and care is useless. A rope in the breakwater gives way during the night without any one noticing it, and when in the morning the owner of the logs comes to inspect them, they have journeyed out to sea, never to return. Some months ago an English firm lost in this way, in a single night, timber worth something like £1,600 (40,000 francs). But if a tornado comes there is no controlling anything. The huge trunks in the park plunge about like dolphins bewitched, and finally make an elegant jump over the boom into the free water beyond.

* * *

Thus every day that the raft lies in the bay brings a risk, and anxiously is the ship awaited which is to take the logs away. No sooner has it arrived than the motor-boats tow raft after raft to its landward side, those that are to be shipped having been prepared first by having wire ropes run through a line of rings at each end. Negroes jump about on the tossing raft, and knock the two rings out of the log that is to be shipped next, so that it floats free of the raft, and then they slip round it the chain with which it is to be hoisted on board. This needs a tremendous amount of skill, for if a labourer falls into the water from the wet and slippery surface of a rolling log he will probably get his legs crushed between these two- or three-ton masses of wood which are continually dashing against one another.

From the verandah I can watch through my glasses some negroes occupied with this work, which is made much harder for them by the delightful breeze I am enjoying, and I know that if a tornado comes, or even a really stiff breeze, the rafts which are lying along the ship's side will certainly be lost.

The losses in timber, then, between the places where it is felled and its successful hoisting on board ship, are tremendous, and the lagoons near the mouth of the Ogowe are veritable timber graveyards. Hundreds and hundreds of gigantic tree-trunks stick out of the mud there, the majority being trees which could not be got away at the right time and were left to rot, till a bigger flood than usual carried them out to the river. When they got to the bay, wind and tide carried them into the lagoons, from which they will never emerge. At this present minute I can count, with the help of my glasses, some forty trunks which are tossing about in the bay, to remain the plaything of ebb and flood and wind till they find a grave either in the lagoons or in the ocean.

As soon as the raft has been safely delivered the crew make haste to get back up the river, either in their canoe or in a steamer, in order that they may not starve in Cape Lopez, for all the fresh provisions in the port town have to be brought some 125 miles down the river from the interior, since nothing of the kind can be grown in the sands of the coast or the marshes of the river mouth. When they have got back home, and have been paid off by the purchaser of the timber, quantities of tobacco, brandy, and all sorts of goods are bought by them at the latter's store. As rich men, according to native notions, they return to their villages, but in a few weeks, or even earlier, the whole of the money has run through their fingers, and they look out for a new place at which to begin their hard work over again.

The export of timber from Cape Lopez is increasing steadily; at the present time (1914) it amounts to about 150,000 tons a year. The chief sorts dealt in are mahogany, which the natives call *ombega,* and okoume (*Aucoumea klaineana*), the so-called false mahogany. The latter is softer than real mahogany, and is used mostly for making cigar-boxes, but it is employed also for furniture, and has a great future before it. Many species of it are almost more beautiful than the real mahogany.

If the timber is left too long in the water it is attacked by the boring mollusc, the *teredo navalis* (French *taret*). This is a small worm-like creature, really a kind of mussel, which eats a passage for itself straight to the centre of the log. For this reason any timber that has to wait a long time for the ship is rolled on to the shore, and advantage is usually taken of this to hew off the sap wood, so that the trunk becomes a square beam.

But besides the okoume and mahogany there are many other valuable kinds of wood on the Ogowe. I will mention the *ekewasengo,* or rosewood (*bois de rose*), and coralwood (*bois de corail*), both of which have a beautiful red colour, and the ironwood, which is so hard that in the sawmill at N'Gômô there are cogwheels in use that are made of it. There grows here also a wood which, when planed, looks like white *moiré* silk.

The finest woods, however, are not exported, because they are not yet known in European markets, and are, therefore, not in demand. When they do become known and sought after, the Ogowe timber trade will become even more important than it is to-day. The reputation of being the best wood expert on the Ogowe belongs to Mr. Haug, one of the missionaries at N'Gômô, who has a valuable collection of specimens of every kind of it. At first I could not understand how it is that everybody here, even people who have nothing to do with the timber trade, is so interested in the different kinds of wood. In the course of time, however, and thanks to continual intercourse with timber merchants, I have myself become, as my wife says, a timber fanatic.

7 *SOCIAL PROBLEMS IN THE FOREST*

WRITTEN WHILE ON THE RIVER, *July* 30*th-August* 2*nd*, 1914.

I AM again fit for work, and the skipper of a small steamer, which belongs to a trading firm at N'Djôli, has been kind enough to take us with him to Lambaréné, but our progress is only slow, as we have a heavy cargo of kerosene. This comes in square tins, each holding four gallons (eighteen litres), straight from the U.S.A. to the Ogowe, and the natives are beginning to use it freely.

I am profiting by the long voyage to arrange and clear my ideas as to the social problems which, to my astonishment, I have come across in the forest. We talk freely in Europe about colonisation, and the spread of civilisation in the colonies, but without making clear to ourselves what these words mean.

But are there really social problems in the forest? Yes; one has only to listen for ten minutes to conversation between any two white men, and one will certainly hear them touch on the most difficult of them all, viz., the labour problem. People imagine in Europe that as many labourers as are wanted can always be found among the savages, and secured for very small wages. The real fact is the very opposite. Labourers are nowhere more difficult to find than among primitive races, and nowhere are they paid so well in proportion to the work they do in return. This comes from their laziness, people say; but is the negro really so lazy? Must we go a little deeper into the problem?

Any one who has seen the population of a native village at work, when they have to clear a piece of virgin forest in order to make a new plantation, knows that they are able to work enthusiastically, and with all their might, for weeks together. This hardest of all work, I may say in passing, is forced upon

86

every village triennially. The banana exhausts the soil with extraordinary rapidity, so that every three years they must lay out a new plantation, manured by the ashes of the jungle, which they cut down and burn. For my part I can no longer talk ingenuously of the laziness of the negro after seeing fifteen of them spend some thirty-six hours in almost uninterrupted rowing in order to bring up the river to me a white man who was seriously ill.

The negro, then, under certain circumstances works well, but—only so long as circumstances require it. The child of nature—here is the answer to the puzzle—is always a casual worker.

In return for very little work nature supplies the native with nearly everything that he requires for his support in his village. The forest gives him wood, bamboos, raffia leaves, and bast for the building of a hut to shelter him from sun and rain. He has only to plant some bananas and manioc, to do a little fishing and shooting, in order to have by him all that he really needs, without having to hire himself out as a labourer and to earn regular wages. If he does take a situation, it is because he needs money for some particular object; he wishes to buy a wife, or his wife, or his wives, want some fine dress material, or sugar, or tobacco; he himself wants a new axe, or hankers after rum or cheap spirits, or would like to wear boots and a suit of khaki.

There are, then, various needs differing in number with the individual, but all lying outside the regular struggle for existence, which bring the child of nature to hire himself out for work. If he has no definite object in view for which to earn money he stays in his village. If he is at work anywhere and finds that he has earned enough to supply his heart's desires, he has no reason for troubling himself any further, and he returns to his village, where he can always find board and lodging.

The negro, then, is not idle, but he is a free man; hence he is always a casual worker, with whose labour no regular industry can be carried on. This is what the missionary finds to be the case on the mission station and in his own house on a small scale, and the planter or merchant on a large one. When my cook has accumulated money enough to let him gratify the wishes of his wife and his mother-in-law, he goes off without any consideration of whether we still want his services or not. The plantation owner is left in the lurch by his labourers just at the critical time when he must wage war on the insects that damage the cocoa plant. Just when there comes from Europe message after message about timber, the timber merchant cannot find a soul to go and fell it, because the village happens at the moment to be out on a fishing expedition, or is laying out a new banana plot. So we are all filled with righteous indignation at the lazy negroes, though the real reason why we cannot get them is that they have not yet learnt to understand what we really mean by continuous work.

There is, therefore, a serious conflict between the needs of trade and the fact that the child of nature is a free man. The wealth of the country cannot be exploited because the native has so slight an interest in the process. How train him to work? How compel him?

"Create in him as many needs as possible; only so can the utmost possible be got out of him," say the State and commerce alike. The former imposes on him involuntary needs in the shape of taxes. With us every native above fourteen pays a poll tax of five francs a year, and it is proposed to double it. If that is done, a man with two wives and seven children will contribute £4 (100 francs) a year, and have to provide a corresponding amount either of labour or of products of the soil. The trader encourages voluntary needs in him by offering him wares of all sorts, useful ones such as clothing material or tools, unnecessary ones such as tobacco and toilet articles, and harmful ones like alcohol. The useful ones would never be enough to produce an amount of labour worth mentioning. Useless trifles and rum are almost more effective. Just consider what sort of things are offered for sale in the forest! Not long ago I got the negro who manages for a white man a little shop close to a small lake, miles away from civilisation, to show me all his stock. Behind the counter stood conspicuous the beautiful white painted cask of cheap spirits. Next to it stood the boxes of tobacco leaves and the tins of kerosene. Further on was a collection of knives, axes, saws, nails, screws, sewing machines, flat-irons, string for making fishing-nets, plates, glasses, enamelled dishes of all sizes, lamps, rice, tinned stuff of every variety, salt, sugar, blankets, dress material, muslin for mosquitoes, Gillette safety razors (!), collars and ties in rich variety, blouses and chemises trimmed with lace, corsets, elegant shoes, openwork stockings, gramophones, concertinas, and fancy articles of all sorts. Among the last named was a plate, resting on a stand, of which there were several dozen. "What is that?" I asked. The negro moved a lever in the bottom part and a little musical box at once began to play. "This is my best paying article," said he. "All the women in the neighbourhood want one of these plates, and plague their husbands till they have earned enough to buy one!"

It is true that taxes and new needs can make a negro work more than he used to, but they do not train him to work, or only to a small extent. They make him anxious for money and for enjoyment, but not reliable or conscientious. If he does take service anywhere, he only thinks how he can get most money for least work, and he works only so long as his employer is near. Just recently I engaged some day labourers to build a new hut for the hospital, but when I came in the evening to see the work, nothing had been done. On the third or fourth day I got angry, but one of the blacks—and one who was by no means the worst of them—said to me: "Doctor, don't shout at us so! It is your own fault. Stay here and we shall work, but if you are in the hospital with the sick folk, we are alone and do nothing." Now I have adopted a plan, and when I engage any day labourers I arrange to have two or three hours free. During this time I make them work till their dark skins glisten with sweat, and so I manage to get a certain amount done.

Increasing their needs does effect something, but not much. The child of nature becomes a steady worker only so far as he ceases to be free and becomes unfree, and this can be brought about in several ways. The first step to be taken is to prevent him for a certain time from returning to his village. Planters and forest-owners never, on principle, hire labourers from the neighbourhood, but engage for a year young men from strange tribes who live at a distance, and then bring them where they are wanted by water. The agreements are drawn up by the Government, and, like many other things in French colonial administration, are calculated to effect their object with due regard to humanity. At the end of each week the labourer is paid half, but only half, of his wages; the rest is put by and is handed over to him at the end of the year when the white man has to send him home. He is thus prevented from spending his money as quickly as he earns it, and from going home with empty hands. Most of them hire themselves out in this way to get money enough to buy a wife.

And what is the result? They have to hold out for the year, because they cannot get back to their village, but very few of them are really useful workers. Many get homesick. Others cannot put up with the strange diet, for, as no fresh provisions are to be had, they must as a rule live chiefly on rice. Most of them fall victims to the taste for rum, and ulcers and diseases spread rapidly among them, living, as they do, a kind of barrack life in overcrowded huts. In spite of all precautions they mostly get through their pay as soon as the contract time is up, and return home as poor as they went away.

The negro is worth something only so long as he is in his village and under the moral control of intercourse with his family and other relatives; away from these surroundings he easily goes to the bad, both morally and physically. Colonies of negro labourers away from their families are, in fact, centres of demoralisation, and yet such colonies are required for trade and for the cultivation of the soil, both of which would be impossible without them.

*　*　*

The tragic element in this question is that the interests of civilisation and of colonisation do not coincide, but are largely antagonistic to each other. The former would be promoted best by the natives being left in their villages and there trained to various industries, to lay out plantations, to grow a little coffee or cocoa for themselves or even for sale, to build themselves houses of timber or brick instead of huts of bamboo, and so to live a steady and worthy life. Colonisation, however, demands that as much of the population as possible shall be made available in every possible way for utilising to the utmost the natural wealth of the country. Its watchword is "Production," so that the capital invested in the colonies may pay its interest, and that the motherland may get her needs supplied through her connection with them. For the unsuspected incompatibilities which show themselves here, no individual is responsible; they arise out of the circumstances themselves, and the lower the level of the natives and the thinner the population, the harder is the problem. In Zululand, for example, agriculture and cattle raising are possible, and the natives develop naturally into a peasantry attached to the land and practising home industries, while, at the same time, the population is so thick that the labour requirements of European trade can also be met; there, then, the problems of the condition of the natives and the promotion of civilisation among them are far less difficult than in the colonies where the country is mostly virgin forest and the population is at a really primitive stage of culture. Yet even there, too, it may come about that the economic progress aimed at by colonisation is secured at the expense of civilisation and the native standard of life.

What, then, is the real educational value of the much discussed compulsory labour as enforced by the State? What is meant by labour compulsion?

It means that every native who has not some permanent industry of his own must, by order of the State, spend so many days in the year in the service of either a trader or a planter. On the Ogowe we have no labour compulsion. The French colonial administration tries, on principle, to get on without any such measure. In German Africa, where labour compulsion was enforced in a humane but effective manner, the results were, according to some critics, good; according to others, bad. I myself hold labour compulsion to be not wrong in principle, but impossible to carry through in practice. The average colony cannot get on without having it on a small scale. If I were an official and a planter came to tell me that his labourers had left him just as the cocoa crop had to be gathered, and that the men in the neighbouring villages refused to come to his help at this critical time, I should think I had a right, and that it was even my duty, to secure him the labour of these men so long as he needed it for the saving of his crop, on payment, of course, of the wages usual in the locality. But the enforcement of general labour compulsion is complicated by the fact that under it men have practically always to leave their village and their families and go to work many miles away. Who provides their food on the journey? What becomes of them if they fall ill? Who will guarantee that the white man does not call on them for their labour just when their village has to set about its own planting, or when it is the best time for fishing expeditions? Will he not, perhaps, keep them longer than he is entitled to, on the plea that they have done no work? Will he treat them properly? There is always the danger that compulsory labour may become, secretly but really, a kind of slavery.

Connected to some extent with the question of compulsory labour is that of the management of colonies by the method of "concessions." What is meant by a "concession"? A company with plenty of capital has a large stretch of territory assigned to it, which it is to manage for so many years, and no other trader may establish himself there. Competition being thus excluded, the natives become very seriously dependent on the company and its employees. Even if the sovereign rights of the State are reserved to it on paper, the trading company does in practice come to exercise many of them more or less completely, especially if the taxes which are owed to the State can be paid to the company in the form of natural products or of labour, to be handed on by it to the State in the form of cash. The question has been much discussed at times, because the system of large concessions led in the Belgian Congo to great abuses, and I do not ignore its dangers; it can, if taken advantage of wrongly, lead to the native belonging to the trader or planter as a creature that has no rights. But it has also its good points. The upper course of the Ogowe has been granted as a concession to the "Company of the Upper Ogowe," and I have discussed the question thoroughly with employees of this company who were with me for considerable periods for medical treatment, thus getting to know the arguments of both sides. When a company has not to fear competition, it can—as the "Company of the Upper Ogowe" does—banish rum and cheap spirits from its district, and provide for sale in its stores only things that are worth buying, without any rubbish. Directed by men of intelligence and wide views, it can exert much educational influence, and since the land belongs wholly to it for a long period, it has a real interest in seeing that it is managed properly; and it is little tempted to exhaust the soil.

On the whole, then, the general principle of labour compulsion in the sense that the State puts the natives at the disposal of private individuals, is to be rejected. The State has to apply it to a quite sufficient extent in the work it has to exact from the natives for generally necessary public objects. It must have at its disposal boatmen and carriers for its officials when they travel; it must have men in its service for the construction and maintenance of roads, and under certain circumstances it must exact contributions of foodstuffs for the support of its troops and its staff generally.

There are two things which are terribly difficult in Africa:

one is to provide any place which has a large population with fresh provisions, and the other is to maintain roads through the forest; and both of these become proportionately more difficult where the population is thin and the distances great. I speak from experience. What trouble I have to secure food for my two assistants and for those of the sick in my hospital who live too far away to get what is necessary sent to them regularly from home! There come times when I have to resort to compulsory measures, and say that every one who comes for treatment must bring a contribution of so many bananas or manioc sticks. This leads to endless wranglings with the patients, who say either that they do not know about the order, or that they have not enough for themselves. Of course, I do treat the serious cases and those who come from long distances, even if they have not brought the modest tribute demanded, but, however strongly I insist on this contribution being made, it does sometimes happen that I have to send sick people away because I no longer have the means of feeding them. The head of the mission station, who has to provide food for the 100 or 150 children in the school, is sometimes in the same position, and the school has to be closed, and the children sent home, because we cannot feed them.

The labour levies and the food requisitions naturally affect chiefly the villages which lie nearest the white settlements. However considerate and just the action of the Government is, these natives feel it, nevertheless, as a burden, and endeavour to migrate to more distant parts, where they will be left in peace. Hence, in the neighbourhoods where there are only primitive tribes, and these not in great numbers, there comes into existence round the settlements of the white a zone which is uninhabited. Then the compulsion has to be applied in another way. The natives are forbidden to move their villages, and those at a distance are ordered to come near the white settlements, or to move to specified points on the caravan routes or on the river. This must be done, but it is tragic that it should be necessary, and the authorities have to take care that no change is enforced beyond what is really needful.

In the Cameroons the forest has been pierced with a network of roads, which are kept in splendid condition and are the admiration of all visitors from other colonies. But has not this great achievement been brought about at the cost of the native population and their vital interests? One is forced to ask questions when things have gone so far that women are impressed for the maintenance of the roads. It is impossible to acquiesce when, as is often the case, the colony itself prospers, while the native population diminishes year by year. Then the present is living at the expense of the future, and the obvious fatal result is only a question of time. The maintenance of the native population must be the first object of any sound colonial policy.

* * *

Close on the problem of labour comes that of the educated native. Taken by itelf, a thorough school education is, in my opinion, by no means necessary for these primitive peoples. The beginning of civilisation with them is not knowledge, but industry and agriculture, through which alone can be secured the economic conditions of higher civilisation. But both Government and trade require natives with extensive knowledge whom they can employ in administration and in the stores. The schools, therefore, must set their aims higher than is natural, and produce people who understand complicated figures and can write the white man's language perfectly. Many a native has such ability that the results of this attempt are, so far as intellectual knowledge goes, astounding. Not long ago there came to me a native Government clerk, just at the time that there was also a missionary staying with me. When the clerk went away, the missionary and I said to each other: "Well, we could hardly compete with him in essay writing!" His chief gives him documents of the most difficult sort to draw up and most complicated statistics to work out, and he does it all faultlessly.

But what becomes of these people? They have been uprooted from their villages, just like those who go off to work for strangers. They live at the store, continually exposed to the dangers which haunt every native so closely, the temptations to defraud and to drink. They earn good wages, indeed, but as they have to buy all their necessaries at high prices, and are a prey to the black man's innate love of spending, they often find themselves in financial difficulties and even in want. They do not now belong to the ordinary negroes, nor do they belong to the whites either; they are a *tertium quid* between the two. Quite recently the above-mentioned Government clerk said to the wife of a missionary: "We negro intellectuals are in a very uncomfortable position. The women in these parts are too uneducated to be good wives for us. They should import wives for us from the higher tribes in Madagascar." This loss of class position in an upwards direction is the misfortune which comes to many of the best of the natives.

Emancipation from the savage state produced by the accumulation of wealth plays no part here, though it may do so in other colonies. It is a still more dangerous method than that of intellectual education.

Social problems are also produced by imports from Europe. Formerly the negroes practised a number of small industries; they carved good household utensils out of wood; they manufactured excellent cord out of bark fibre and similar substances; they got salt from the sea. But these and other primitive industries have been destroyed by the goods which European trade has introduced into the forest. The cheap enamelled ware has driven out the solid, home-made wooden bucket, and round every negro village there are heaps of such things rusting in the grass. Many minor crafts which they once practised are now almost forgotten; it is now only the old women who know how to make cord out of bark, and sewing cotton out of the fibres of the pineapple leaves. Even the art of canoe-making is dying out. Thus native industries are going backwards instead of forwards, just when the rise of a solid industrial class would be the first and surest step towards civilisation.

*   *   *

One first gets a clear idea of the real meaning of the social danger produced by the importation of cheap spirits, when one reads how much rum per head of the population comes every year to the port towns, and when one has seen in the villages how the children drink with their elders. Here on the Ogowe officials and traders, missionaries and chiefs are all unanimous that the importation of cheap spirits should be stopped. Why, then, is it not stopped? Because it is so profitable to the revenue. The import duty on rum produces one of the biggest items in the receipts of the colony, and if it ceased there would be a deficit. The financial position of the African colonies is well known to be anything but brilliant, and the duty on spirits has a second advantage, that it can be increased every year without diminishing by a litre the quantity consumed. The position here, as in other colonies, is that the

Government says: "Abolish cheap spirits? Willingly—to-day rather than to-morrow; but tell us first what we can find to cover the deficit which that will cause in the budget." And the strongest opponents of alcohol have not been able to make any practicable proposal. When shall we find some way out of this idiotic dilemma? The one hope is that some day a governor will come who will put the future of the colony above the financial worries of the present, and have the courage to banish rum at the price of having to carry on for some years with a deficit[1].

It is often asserted that alcoholism would prevail among the natives even if there were no importation of spirits. This is mere talk. Of alcoholic drinks produced in the country itself palm wine is the only one which has to be considered in the forest, and that is no great danger. It is simply the sap of the palm tree allowed to ferment, but the boring of the trees and the taking the necessary vessels to them needs a good deal of labour, for the work has to be done on the quiet at a distance from the village, the boring of the trees being expressly forbidden. Moreover, palm wine will not keep. Its existence makes it possible, therefore, for the people of a village to get drunk several times a year, on the occasions of their festivals, but it is not a continual danger like the cheap spirits sold in the stores. Fresh palm wine tastes when it is fermenting, very like the must of grape wine, and by itself it is not any more intoxicating than the latter; but the natives are accustomed to put various species of bark into it, and then it can produce a terrible kind of drunkenness.

Polygamy is another difficult social problem. We Europeans come here with our ideal of monogamy, and missionaries contend with all their resources against polygamy, in some places even urging the Government to suppress it by law. On the other hand, all of us here must allow that it is closely bound up with the existing economic and social conditions. Where the population lives in bamboo huts, and society is not so organised that a woman can earn her own living, there is no room for the unmarried woman, and if all women are to be married, polygamy is a necessary condition. Moreover, there are in the forest neither cows nor nanny goats, so that a mother must suckle her child for a long time if it is to be reared. Polygamy

---

[1] In the year 1919 the Governor actually ventured to try this policy to the great joy of the whole colony.

safeguards the claims of the child, for after its birth the woman has the right, and the duty, of living only for her child; she is now no longer a wife, but only a mother, and she often spends the greater part of this time with her parents. At the end of three years comes the weaning, which is marked by a festival, and then she returns to her husband's hut to be a wife once more. But this living for her child is not to be thought of unless the man has another wife, or other wives, to make a home for him and look after his banana plots.

Here is another point for consideration. Among these nature-peoples there are no widows unprovided for and no neglected orphans. The nearest male relative inherits the dead man's widow, and must maintain her and her children. She enters into enjoyment of all the rights of his other wives, even though she can later, with his consent, take another husband.

To agitate, therefore, against polygamy among primitive peoples, is to undermine the whole structure of their society. Have we the right to do this if we are not also in a position to give them a new social order which suits their own circumstances? Were the agitation successful, would not polygamy still continue to exist, with the single difference that the later wives would be illegitimate ones? These questions naturally cause missionaries much anxious thought.

But, as a matter of fact, the more developed the economic condition of a people becomes, the easier becomes the contest with polygamy. When men begin to live in permanent houses, and to practice the rearing of cattle, and agriculture, it disappears of itself because it is no longer demanded by their circumstances, and is no longer even consistent with them. Among the Israelites, as their civilisation advanced, monogamy peacefully drove out polygamy. During the prophetic period they were both practised side by side; the teaching of Jesus does not even hint at the existence of the latter.

Certainly mission teaching should put forward monogamy as the ideal and as what Christianity demands, but it would be a mistake for the State to make it compulsory. It is also a mistake, so far as I can judge, to identify the fight against immorality with that against polygamy. Under this system the relation of the wives to each other is usually good. A negress does not, in fact, like being the only wife, because then she has the care of the banana plot, which always falls to the wives, all to herself, and this is a laborious duty, as the plots are usually at a distance from the village in some well-concealed part of the forest.

What I have seen in my hospital of life with many wives has not shown me, at any rate, the ugly side of the system. An elderly chief once came as a patient and brought two young wives with him. When his condition began to cause anxiety, a third appeared who was considerably older than the first two; this was his first wife. From the day of her arrival she sat continually on his bed, held his head in her lap, and gave him what he wanted to drink. The two young ones behaved respectfully to her, took orders from her, and looked after the cooking.

One can have the experience in this land of a fourteen-year-old boy announcing himself as a *paterfamilias*. It comes about in the following way. He has inherited from some deceased relative a wife with children, and though the woman has contracted a marriage with another man, that does not touch his rights over the children nor his duty towards them. If they are boys, he will some day have to buy wives for them; if they are girls, he will get the customary purchase price from those who wish to marry them.

Should one declaim against the custom of wife-purchase, or tolerate it? If it is a case of a young woman being promised, without being herself consulted, to the man who bids most for her, it is obviously right to protest. If it merely means that in accordance with local custom the man who is courting a girl must, if she is willing to marry him, pay to the family a sum mutually agreed upon, there is no more reason for objecting than there is in the matter of the dowry, customary in Europe. Whether the man, if the marriage comes off, pays money to the family or receives money from it, is in principle the same thing; in either case there is a definite money transaction which has its origin in the social views of the period. What has to be insisted on, both among ourselves and among "natives," is that the money transaction must remain subordinate, and not so influence the personal choice that either the wife is bought, as in Africa, or the husband, as in Europe. What we have to do, then, is not to fight against the custom of wife-purchase, but to educate the natives up to seeing that they must not give the girl to the highest bidder, but to the suitor who can make her happy, and whom she is herself inclined to take. As a rule, indeed, the negro girls are not so wanting in independence as to let themselves be sold to any one who offers. Love, it is true, does not play the same part in marriage here as with us, for the child of nature knows nothing of the romantic, and marriages are usually decided on in the family council; they do, however, as a rule, turn out happily.

Most girls are married when they are fifteen, even those in the girls' schools. Those in our mission school are mostly already engaged to some husband, and marry as soon as they leave school. They can even be promised to a husband before they are born, as I learnt through a case of most unprincipled wife-purchase, which took place at Samkita, and was related to me by a missionary. A man owed one of his neighbours £16 (400 fr.), but, instead of repaying it, he bought a wife and married her with the usual ceremonies. While they were at the wedding feast, the creditor made his appearance, and overwhelmed the bridegroom with abuse for having bought a wife instead of paying his debt. A palaver began which ended in an agreement that the debtor should give his creditor the first girl born of the marriage for a wife, on which the latter joined the guests and took his part in the festivities. Sixteen years later he came as a wooer, and so the debt was paid!

My opinion is, and I have formed it after conversation with all the best and most experienced of the white men in this district, that we should accept, but try to improve and refine, the rights and customs which we find in existence, and make no alterations which are not absolutely necessary.

*   *   *

A word in conclusion about the relations between the whites and the blacks. What must be the general character of the intercourse between them? Am I to treat the black man as my equal or as my inferior? I must show him that I can respect the dignity of human personality in every one, and this attitude in me he must be able to see for himself; but the essential thing is that there shall be a real feeling of brotherliness. How far this is to find complete expression in the sayings and doings of daily life must be settled by circumstances. The negro is a child, and with children nothing can be done without the use of authority. We must, therefore, so arrange the circumstances of daily life that my natural authority can find expression. With regard to the negroes, then, I have coined the formula: "I am your brother, it is true, but your elder brother."

The combination of friendliness with authority is therefore the great secret of successful intercourse. One of our missionaries, Mr. Robert, left the staff some years ago to live among the negroes as their brother absolutely. He built himself a small house near a village between Lambaréné and N'Gômô and wished to be recognised as a member of the village. From that day his life became a misery. With his abandonment of the social interval between white and black he lost all his influence; his word was no longer taken as the "white man's word," but he had to argue every point with them as if he were merely their equal.

When, before coming to Africa, I heard missionaries and traders say again and again that one must be very careful out here to maintain this authoritative position of the white man, it seemed to me to be a hard and unnatural position to take up, as it does to every one in Europe who reads or hears the same. Now I have come to see that the deepest sympathy and kindness can be combined with this insistence on certain external forms, and indeed are only possible by means of them. One of our unmarried missionaries at N'Gômô—the story belongs to a period some years back—allowed his cook to be very free in his behavior towards him. One day the steamer put in with the Governor on board, and the missionary went to pay his respects to the high official. He was standing on deck in an elegant suit of white among a group of officials and military men, when a negro, with his cap on his head and a pipe in his mouth, pushed himself into the group and said to him: "Well, what are we to have for supper to-night?" The cook wanted to show on what good terms he stood with his master!

The prevention of unsuitable freedom is, however, only the external and technical part, so to say, of the problem of authority. A white man can only have real authority if the native respects him. No one must imagine that the child of nature looks up to us merely because we know more, or can do more, than he can. This superiority is so obvious to him that it ceases to be taken into account. It is by no means the case that the white man is to the negro an imposing person because he possesses railways and steamer, can fly in the air, or travel under water. "White people are clever and can do anything they want to," says Joseph. The negro is not in a position to estimate what these technical conquests of nature mean as proofs of mental and spiritual superiority, but on one point he has an unerring intuition, and that is on the question whether any particular white man is a real, moral personality or not. If the native feels that he is this, moral authority is possible; if not, it is simply impossible to create it. The child of nature, not having been artificialised and spoilt as we have been, has only elementary standards of judgment, and he measures us by the most elementary of them all, the moral standard. Where he finds goodness, justice, and genuineness of character, real worth and dignity, that is, behind the external dignity given by social circumstances, he bows and acknowledges his master; where he does not find them he remains really defiant in spite of all appearance of submission, and says to himself: "This white is no more of a man than I am, for he is not a better one than I am."

I am not thinking merely of the fact that many unsuitable, and not a few quite unworthy men, go out into the colonies of all nations. I wish to emphasise a further fact that even the morally best and the idealists find it difficult out here to be what they wish to be. We all get exhausted in the terrible contest between the European worker who bears the responsibility and is always in a hurry, and the child of nature who does not know what responsibility is and is never in a hurry. The Government official has to record at the end of the year so much work done by the native in building and in road-maintenance, in service as carrier or boatman, and so much money paid in taxes; the trader and the planter are expected by their companies to provide so much profit for the capital invested in the enterprise. But in all this they are for ever dependent on men who cannot share the responsibility that weighs on them, who only give just so much return of labour as the others can force out of them, and who, if there is the slightest failure in superintendence, do exactly as they like without any regard for the loss that may be caused to their employers. In this daily and hourly contest with the child of nature every white man is continually in danger of gradual moral ruin.

My wife and I were once very much delighted with a newly arrived trader, because in the conversations we had with him he was always insisting on kindness towards the natives, and would not allow the slightest ill-treatment of them by his foremen. The next spring, however, he had the following experience. Lying in a pond some sixty miles from here he had a large quantity of mahogany, but he was summoned to Lambaréné to clear off some urgent correspondence just as the water began to rise. He ordered his foremen and labourers to be sure to use the two or three days of high water to get all the timber, if possible, into the river. When the water had fallen he went back to the place and found that nothing whatever had been done! They had smoked, and drunk, and danced; the timber which had already lain too long in the pond was almost completely ruined, and he was responsible to his company for the loss. His men had been thoughtless and indifferent because they did not fear him enough. This experience changed him entirely, and now he laughs at those who think it is possible to do anything with the natives without employing relentless severity.

Not long ago the termites, or white ants, got into a box which stood on our verandah. I emptied the box and broke it up, and gave the pieces to the negro who had been helping me. "Look," I said to him, "the ants have got into it; you mustn't put the wood with the rest of the firewood or the ants will get into the framework of the hospital building. Go down to the river and throw it into the water. Do you understand?" "Yes, yes, you need not worry." It was late in the day, and being too tired to go down the hill again, I was inclined to break my general rule and trust a black—one who was in fact on the whole intelligent and handy. But about ten o'clock I felt so uneasy that I took the lantern and went down to the hospital. There was the wood with the ants in it lying with the rest of the firewood. To save himself the trouble of going the twenty yards down to the river the negro had endangered all my buildings!

The greater the responsibility that rests on a white man, the greater the danger of his becoming hard towards the natives. We on a mission staff are too easily inclined to become self-righteous with regard to the other whites. We have not got to obtain such and such results from the natives by the end of the year, as officials and traders have, and therefore this exhausting contest is not so hard a one for us as for them. I no longer venture to judge my fellows after learning something of the soul of the white man who is in business from those who lay as patients under my roof, and whose talk has led me to suspect that those who now speak savagely about the natives may come out to Africa full of idealism, but in the daily

contest have become weary and hopeless, losing little by little what they once possessed of spirituality.

That it is so hard to keep oneself really humane, and so to
be a standard-bearer of civilisation, that is the tragic element
in the problem of the relations between white and coloured
men in Equatorial Africa.

8 *CHRISTMAS, 1914*

A WAR CHRISTMAS in the virgin forest! When the candles on
the little palm which served us as Christmas tree had burnt to
half their length I blew them out. "What are you doing?" asked
my wife. "They are all we have," said I, "and we must keep
them for next year." "For next year?" . . . and she shook
her head.

On August 4th, two days after our return from Cape Lopez,
I had prepared some medicine for a lady who was ill there,
and sent Joseph to a store to ask that their steamer might take
the packet down there on its next journey. He brought back a
short note: "In Europe they are mobilising and probably already at war. We must place our steamer at the disposal of
the authorities, and cannot say when it will go next to Cape
Lopez."

We needed days to realise that Europe was at war, though
it was not that we had failed to take the possibility of it into
account; indeed, following the advice of an experienced merchant, I had brought with me a considerable sum in metal
money in case it should come about. But since the beginning of
July we had received no news from Europe, and we knew
nothing of the entanglements which finally brought on the
fatal explosion.

The negroes had, at first, very little understanding of what
was going on. The Catholics among them were more really interested in the papal election than in the war, during the
autumn. "Doctor," said Joseph to me during a canoe journey,

"how do the Cardinals really elect the Pope; do they take the oldest one, or the most religious, or the cleverest?" "They take one kind of man this time, and another kind the next, according to circumstances," was my reply.

At first the black labourers felt the war as by no means a misfortune, as for several weeks very few were impressed for service. The whites did little but sit together and discuss the news and the rumours from Europe. By now, however (Christmas, 1914), the coloured folk are beginning to learn that the war has consequences which affect them also. There being a shortage of ships, no timber can be exported, and therefore the labourers from a distance who had been engaged for a year are being discharged by the stores, and as, further, there are no vessels plying on the rivers that could take them back to their homes, they collect in groups and try to reach the Loango coast, from which most of them come, on foot.

Again, a sudden rise in the price of tobacco, sugar, rice, kerosene, and rum, brings home to the negro's consciousness the fact that there is a war going on, and this rise is what gives them more concern than anything else for the moment. Not long ago, while we were bandaging patients, Joseph began to complain of the war, as he had several times done before, as the cause of this rise in prices, when I said to him: "Joseph, you mustn't talk like that. Don't you see how troubled the faces of the doctor and his wife are, and the faces of all the missionaries? For us the war means very much more than an unpleasant rise in prices. We are, all of us, anxious about the lives of so many of our dear fellow-men, and we can hear from far away the groaning of the wounded and the death rattle of the dying." He looked up at me with great astonishment at the time, but since then I have noticed that he now seems to see something that was hidden from him before.

We are, all of us, conscious that many natives are puzzling over the question how it can be possible that the whites, who brought them the Gospel of Love, are now murdering each other, and throwing to the winds the commands of the Lord Jesus. When they put the question to us we are helpless. If I am questioned on the subject by negroes who think, I make no attempt to explain or to extenuate, but say that we are in "front" of something terrible and incomprehensible. How far the ethical and religious authority of the white man among these children of nature is impaired by this war we shall only be able to measure later on. I fear that the damage done will be very considerable.

In my own house I take care that the blacks learn as little as possible of the horrors of war. The illustrated papers we receive —for the post has begun to work again fairly regularly—I must not leave about, lest the boys, who can read, should absorb both text and pictures and retail them to others.

Meanwhile the medical work goes on as usual. Every morning when I go down to the hospital I feel it as an inexpressible mercy that, while so many men find it their duty to inflict suffering and death on others, I can be doing good and helping to save human life. This feeling supports me through all my weariness.

The last ship which left Europe before the declaration of war brought me several cases of drugs and two of bandages, the last a gift from a lady supporter, so that I am now provided with what is necessary for carrying on the hospital for some months. The goods for Africa which were not sent by this vessel are still lying on the quays of Havre and Bordeaux. Who knows when they will arrive, or whether they will get here at all?

* * *

I am worried, however, about how to provide food for the sick, for there is something like a famine in the district— thanks to the elephants! People in Europe usually imagine that where "civilisation" comes, the wild animals begin to die out. That may be the case in many districts, but in others the very opposite happens, and that for three reasons. First, if, as is often the case, the native population diminishes, there is less hunting done. Secondly, what hunting is done is less successful, for the natives have forgotten how to trap the animals in the primitive but often extremely ingenious manner of their ancestors, and have got accustomed to hunting them with firearms. But in view of eventual possibilities it has been for years the policy of all Governments in Equatorial Africa to allow the natives only small quantities of gunpowder; nor may they possess modern sporting guns; they can only have the old flintlocks. Thirdly, the war on the wild animals is carried on much less energetically because the natives no longer have the time to devote to it. At timber felling and rafting they earn more money than they can by hunting, so that the elephants flourish and increase in numbers almost unhindered, and the results of this we are now beginning to experience. The banana plantations of the villages north-west from here, which provide us with so much of our food, are continually visited by elephants. Twenty of these creatures are enough to lay waste a whole plantation in a night, and what they do not eat they trample under foot.

It is not, however, to the plantations only that the elephants are a danger. The telegraph line from N'Djôle to the interior knows something about the damage they do. The long, straight clearing through the forest which marks its course is in itself a tremendous attraction to the animals, but the straight, smooth telegraph poles are irresistible. They seem to have been provided expressly for pachyderms to rub themselves against! They are not all very firm, and a very little rubbing brings one of the weaker ones to the ground, but there is always another like it not very far off. Thus, in a single night one strong elephant can bring down a big stretch of telegraph line, and days may pass before the occupants of the nearest guard station have discovered the damage and repaired it.

Although the elephants that roam the neighbourhood cause me so much anxiety about the feeding of my patients, I have not yet seen one, and very probably never shall. During the day they stay in unapproachable swamps in order to sally out at night and plunder the plantations which they have reconnoitred beforehand. A native who is here for the treatment of his wife, who has heart complaint, is a clever wood-carver, and carved me an elephant. Though I admired this work of primitive art, I ventured to remark that he seemed not to have got the body quite right. The artist, insulted, shrugged his shoulder. "Do you think you can teach me what an elephant looks like? I once had one on top of me, trying to trample me underfoot." The artist was, in fact, also a famous elephant hunter. Their method now is to go out by day and creep to within ten paces of the elephant, when they discharge their flintlock at him. If the shot is not fatal and they are discovered by the animal, they are then, of course, in a very unpleasant position.

Hitherto I have been able to help out the feeding of my

sick with rice if bananas were short, but I can do so no more. What we still have left we must keep for ourselves, for whether we shall get any more from Europe is more than questionable.

9 *CHRISTMAS, 1915*

CHRISTMAS again in the forest, but again a war Christmas! The candle ends which we saved from last year have been used up on our this year's Christmas (palm) tree.

It was a year of difficulties, with a great deal of extra work during the early months. Heavy rainstorms had undermined the spot on which the largest hospital ward stood, so that I had to decide to build a wall round it, and also to lay stone gutters throughout the hospital to carry off the water which streamed from the hill just above it. This needed a number of stones, some of them big ones, and these were either fetched by canoe or rolled down from the hill; but I had always to be on the spot, and often to lend a hand. Our next object was the wall, for which we got help from a native who knew something about building, and we fortunately had on the station a cask of half-spoilt cement. In four months the work was finished.

I was hoping now to have a little rest, when I discovered that, in spite of all our precautions, the termites had got into the chests where we kept our store of drugs and bandages. This necessitated the opening and unpacking of the cases, a work which occupied all our spare time for weeks. Fortunately, I had noticed them in good time, or the damage done would have been much greater; but the peculiar delicate smell, like that of burning, which the termites produce, had attracted my attention. Externally there was no sign of them; the invasion had been made from the floor through a tiny hole, and from the first case they had eaten their way into the others which stood by and upon it. They had apparently been attracted by a bottle of medicinal syrup, the cork of which had got loose.

Oh, the fight that has to be carried on in Africa with creeping insects! What time one loses over the thorough precautions that have to be taken! And with what helpless rage one has to confess again and again that one has been outwitted! My wife learnt how to solder, in order to be able to close up the flour and maize in tins, but it sometimes happens that you find swarms of the terrible little weevils (French *charançons*) even in the soldered tins. The maize for the fowls they soon reduce to dust.

Very much dreaded here, too, are small scorpions and other poisonous insects. One learns to be so careful that one never puts one's hand straight into a drawer or a box as in Europe. The eyes must precede the hand.

Another serious enemy is the traveller ant, which belongs to the genus *Dorylus,* and from it we suffer a great deal. On their great migrations they march five or six abreast in perfect order, and I once watched a column near my house which took thirty-six hours to march past. If their course is over open ground and they have to cross a path, the warriors form up in several rows on either side and with their large jaws form a kind of palisade to protect the procession, in which the ordinary traveller ants are carrying the young ones with them. In forming the palisade the warriors turn their backs to the procession—like the Cossacks when protecting the Czar— and in that position they remain for hours at a time.

As a rule there are three or four columns marching abreast of each other, but independently, from five to fifty yards apart. All at once they break up the column and disperse, though how the word of command is given we do not yet know. Anyhow, in the twinkling of an eye a huge area is covered with a quivering, black mass, and every living thing upon it is doomed. Even the great spiders in the trees cannot escape, for these terrible ravagers creep after them in crowds up to the very highest twigs; and if the spiders, in despair, jump from the trees, they fall victims to the ants on the ground. It is a horrible sight. The militarism of the forest will very nearly bear comparison with that of Europe!

Our house lies on one of the main routes of the traveller ants, which swarm mostly during the night. A peculiar scratching and clucking of the fowls gives us warning of the danger, and then there is no time to be lost. I jump out of bed, run to the fowlhouse, and open the door, through which the birds rush out. Shut in, they would inevitably be the prey of the ants, which creep into their mouths and nostrils until they are suffocated, and then devour them, so that in a short time nothing is left but their white bones. The chickens usually fall victims to the robbers; the fowls can defend themselves till help comes.

Meanwhile my wife has taken the bugle from the wall and blown it three times, which is the signal for N'Kendju and some men from the hospital to bring bucketfuls of water from the river. When they arrive, the water is mixed with lysol, and the ground all round the house and under it is sprinkled. While we are doing this we get very badly treated by the warriors, for they creep over us and bite us vigorously; I once counted nearly fifty on me. They bite themselves so firmly in with their jaws that one cannot pull them off. If one tries to do so the body comes away, but the jaws remain in the flesh and have to be taken out separately afterwards. At last the ants move on, leaving thousands of corpses in the puddles, for they cannot stand the smell of the lysol; and so ends the little drama which we have been playing in the darkness, with no light but that of the lantern which my wife has been holding. Once we were attacked by them three times in one week, and Mr. Coillard, the missionary, records in his memoirs, which I am just now reading, that he, too, suffered severely from them in the Zambesi district.

The most extensive migrations of these ants take place at the beginning and end of the rainy season, and between these two periods there is much less reason to expect an attack. As to size, these ants are not much bigger than our European red ones, but their jaws are much more strongly developed, and they march at a much greater speed, a difference which I have noticed as being common to all species of African ants.

*   *   *

Joseph has left me. Being cut off from Strasbourg, the source of my funds, and obliged to contract debts, I found myself compelled to reduce his wages from 70 francs to 35 francs, telling him I had decided on this only from extreme necessity. Nevertheless, he gave me notice, adding that "his dignity would not allow him to serve me for so small a sum." He lives with his parents on the opposite bank of the river, and had been keeping a money-box with a view to the purchase of a wife. This had now to be opened, and it contained nearly £8 (200 francs), but in a few weeks it had all been frittered away.

Now I have to depend only on N'Kendju's help. He is quite handy and useful, except on the days when he is out of temper, when nothing can be done with him; but in any case I have to do a good many things that Joseph used to do.

In the treatment of ulcers and suppurating wounds I have found pure methylen-violet most useful. This is a drug which is known to the trade as Merk's Pyoktanin. The credit of having made the decisive experiments regarding the disinfecting power of concentrated dyestuffs belongs to Professor Stilling, of Strasbourg, a specialist in diseases of the eye. He placed at my disposal a quantity of Pyoktanin which had been prepared under his superintendence—so that I might test it here —and it reached me not long before the outbreak of war. I began its use with some prejudice against it, but the results are such that I gladly put up with the unpleasant colour. Methylen-violet has the peculiarity of killing the bacteria without affecting or injuring the tissues or being in the least degree poisonous; in this respect it is much superior to corrosive sublimate, carbolic acid, or tincture of iodine. For the doctor in the forest it is indispensable. Besides this, Pyoktanin does, so far as my observation goes, promote in a striking way the growth of new skin when ulcers are healing.

Before the war I had begun to make a small charge for the medicine to those patients who seemed not to be absolutely poor, and this brought in something like 200 francs (£8) a month. Even though it was only a fraction of the real value of the medicines dispensed, it was something. Now there is no money in the country, and I have to treat the natives almost entirely for nothing.

Of the whites, many who have been prevented by the war from going home have now been four or five years under the Equator and are thoroughly exhausted, so that they have to resort to the doctor "for repairs," as we say on the Ogowe. Such patients are sometimes with us for weeks, coming often two and three together. Then I let them use my bedroom and sleep myself in a part of the verandah which has been protected from mosquitoes by wire-netting. That is, however, no great self-denial, for there is more air there than inside. The recovery of the patients is often due much less to my medicines

than to the excellent invalid diet provided by the doctor's wife
—fortunately we still have a good supply of tins of condensed milk for our patients—and I have for some time had
to take care that sick people do not come up here from Cape
Lopez for the sake of the diet instead of letting themselves be
treated by the doctor there—when there is one. With many
of my patients I have become quite intimate, and from conversation with those who stay here a long time I am always
learning something fresh about the country and the problem
of its colonisation.

*   *   *

Our own health is not first-class, though it is not really bad;
tropical anæmia has, indeed, already set in. It shows itself
in the way the slightest exertion tires one; I am quite exhausted,
for example, after coming up the hill to my house, a matter of
four minutes' walk. We also perceive in ourselves a symptom
that accompanies it, an excessive nervousness, and besides
these two things we find that our teeth are in a bad condition.
My wife and I put temporary fillings into each other's teeth,
and in this way I give her some relief, but no one can do for
me what is really necessary, for that means the removal of two
carious teeth which are too far gone to be saved. What stories
could be told of toothache in the forest! One white man whom
I know was in such pain, a few years ago, that he could hold
out no longer. "Wife," he cried, "get me the small pincers
from the tool-chest." Then he lay down, his wife knelt on his
chest and got hold of the tooth as well as she could. The man
put his hands on hers and together they got out the tooth,
which was kind enough to let this treatment be successful.
My mental freshness I have, strange to say, preserved almost completely in spite of anæmia and fatigue. If the day has
not been too exhausting I can give a couple of hours after
supper to my studies in ethics and civilisation as part of the
history of human thought, any books I need for it and have not
with me being sent me by Professor Strohl, of Zürich University. Strange, indeed, are the surroundings amid which I study;
my table stands inside the lattice-door which leads on to the
verandah, so that I may snatch as much as possible of the light
evening breeze. The palms rustle an *obbligato* to the loud
music of the crickets and the toads, and from the forest come
harsh and terrifying cries of all sorts. Caramba, my faithful

dog, growls gently on the verandah, to let me know that he is there, and at my feet, under the table, lies a small dwarf antelope. In this solitude I try to set in order thoughts which have been stirring in me since 1900, in the hope of giving some little help to the restoration of civilisation. Solitude of the primeval forest, how can I ever thank you enough for what you have been to me? . . .

The hour between lunch and the resumption of work in the hospital is given to music, as is also Sunday afternoon, and here, too, I feel the blessing of working "far from the madding crowd," for there are many of J. S. Bach's organ pieces into the meaning of which I can now enter with greater ease and deeper appreciation than ever before.

Mental work one must have, if one is to keep one's self in moral health in Africa; hence the man of culture, though it may seem a strange thing to say, can stand life in the forest better than the uneducated man, because he has a means of recreation of which the other knows nothing. When one reads a good book on a serious subject one is no longer the creature that has been exhausting itself the whole day in the contest with the unreliability of the natives and the tiresome worry of the insects; one becomes once more a man! Woe to him who does not in some such way pull himself together and gather new strength; the terrible prose of African life will bring him to ruin! Not long ago I had a visit from a white timber merchant, and when I accompanied him to the canoe on his departure I asked him whether I could not provide him with something to read on the two days' journey in front of him. "Many thanks," he replied, "but I am already supplied," and he showed me, lying on the thwart of the boat, a book, which was Jacob Boehme's *Aurora*. The work of the great German shoemaker and mystic, written at the beginning of the seventeenth century, accompanies him on all his journey. We know how nearly all great African travellers have taken with them solid matter for reading.

* * *

Newspapers one can hardly bear to look at. The printed string of words, written with a view to the single, quickly-passing day, seems here, where time is, so to say, standing still, positively grotesque. Whether we will or no, all of us here live under the influence of the daily repeated experience that nature is everything and man is nothing. This brings into our general view of life—and this even in the case of the less educated—something which makes us conscious of the fever-ishness and vanity of the life of Europe; it seems almost something abnormal that over a portion of the earth's surface nature should be nothing and man everything!

News of the war comes here fairly regularly. Either from N'Djôle, through which passes the main telegraph line from Libreville to the interior, or from Cape Lopez, telegraphic news comes to us every fortnight, a selection from the various daily items. It is sent by the District Commandant to the stores and the two mission stations by means of a native soldier, who waits till we have read it and give it back to him. Then for another fortnight we think of the war only in the most general way. What the frame of mind must be of those who have to go through the excitement of reading war news every day we can hardly imagine. Certainly we do not envy them!

About this time it became known that of the whites who had gone home to fulfil their military duties ten had already been killed, and it made a great impression on the natives. "Ten men killed already in this war!" said an old Pahouin. "Why, then, don't the tribes meet for a palaver? How can they pay for all these dead men?" For, with the natives, it is a rule that all who fall in a war, whether on the victorious or on the defeated side, must be paid for by the other side.

Directly the post has come in, Aloys, my cook, stops me to ask: "Doctor, is it still war?" "Yes, Aloys, still war." Then he shakes his head sadly and says to himself several times: "Oh lala! Oh, lala!" He is one of the negroes whose soul is really saddened by the thought of the war.

Now we have to be very economical with our European foodstuffs, and potatoes have become a delicacy. A short time ago a white neighbour sent me by his boy a present of several dozen, from which I inferred that he was not well and would soon be needing my services, and so it turned out! Since the war we have trained ourselves to eat monkey flesh. One of the missionaries on the station keeps a black huntsman, and sends us regularly some of his booty; it is monkeys that he shoots most frequently, since they are the game he finds easiest to bring down. Their flesh tastes something like goat's flesh, but has a kind of sweetish taste that the latter has not. People may think what they like about Darwinism and the descent of man, but the prejudice against monkey flesh is not so easily got rid of. "Doctor," said a white man to me a few days ago, "eating monkeys is the first step in cannibalism"!

At the end of the summer (1916) we were able to join our missionary neighbours, Mr. and Mrs. Morel, of Samkita, in a visit of some weeks to Cape Lopez, where a trading company, several of whose employees had benefited by our treatment and hospitality during illness, placed three rooms in one of their stores at our disposal. The sea air worked wonders for our health.

10 THE MISSION

July, 1916.

It is the dry season. Every evening we go for a walk on the big sandbanks in the river bed and enjoy the breeze which is blowing upstream. The hospital is not so busy as usual at this season, for the villagers are occupied with their great fishing expeditions, and will not bring me any patients till they are over. So I will make use of these vacant hours to note down the impressions I have formed about the mission. What do I really think about mission work after three years on a mission station?

What does the forest dweller understand of Christianity, and how does he understand—or misunderstand—it? In Europe I met the objection again and again that Christianity is something too high for primitive man, and it used to disturb me; now, as a result of my experience, I can boldly declare, "No; it is not."

First, let me say that the child of nature thinks a great deal more than is generally supposed. Even though he can neither read nor write, he has ideas on many more subjects than we imagine. Conversations I have had in the hospital with old natives about the ultimate things of life have deeply impressed me. The distinction between white and coloured, educated and uneducated, disappears when one gets talking with the forest dweller about our relations to each other, to mankind, to the universe, and to the infinite. "The negroes are deeper than we are," a white man once said to me, "because they don't read newspapers," and the paradox has some truth in it.

They have, then, a great natural capacity for taking in the elements of religion, though the historical element in Christianity lies, naturally, outside their ken. The negro lives with a general view of things which is innocent of history, and he has no means of measuring and appreciating the time-interval between Jesus and ourselves. Similarly, the doctrinal statements which explain how the divine plan of redemption was prepared and effected, are not easily made intelligible to him, even though he has an elementary consciousness of what redemption is. Christianity is for him the light that shines amid the darkness of his fears; it assures him that he is not in the power of nature-spirits, ancestral spirits, or fetishes, and that no human being has any sinister power over another, since the will of God really controls everything that goes on in the world.

> "I lay in cruel bondage,
> Thou cam'st and mad'st me free!"

These words from Paul Gerhardt's Advent hymn express better than any others what Christianity means for primitive man. That is again and again the thought that fills my mind when I take part in a service on a mission station.

It is well known that hopes and fears about a world beyond play no part in the religion of primitive man; the child of nature does not fear death, but regards it merely as something natural. The more medieval form of Christianity which keeps anxiety about a judgment to come in the foreground, has fewer points of contact with his mentality than the more ethical form. To him Christianity is the moral view of life and the world, which was revealed by Jesus; it is a body of teaching about the kingdom of God and the grace of God.

Moreover, there slumbers within him an ethical rationalist. He has a natural responsiveness to the notion of goodness and all that is connected with it in religion. Certainly, Rousseau and the illuminati of that age idealised the child of nature, but there was nevertheless truth in their views about him—in their belief, that is, in his possession of high moral and rational capacities. No one must think that he has described the thought-world of the negro when he has made a full list of all the superstitious ideas which he has taken over, and the traditional legal rules of his tribe. They do not form his whole universe, although he is controlled by them. There lives within him a dim suspicion that a correct view of what is truly good must be attainable as the result of reflection. In proportion as he becomes familiar with the higher moral ideas of the religion of Jesus, he finds utterance for something in himself that has hitherto been dumb, and something that has been tightly bound up finds release. The longer I live among the Ogowe negroes, the clearer this becomes to me.

Thus redemption through Jesus is experienced by him as a two-fold liberation; his view of the world is purged of the previously dominant element of fear, and it becomes ethical instead of unethical. Never have I felt so strongly the victorious power of what is simplest in the teaching of Jesus as when, in the big schoolroom at Lambaréné, which serves as a church as well, I have been explaining the Sermon on the Mount, the parables of the Master, and the sayings of St. Paul about the new life in which we live.

*   *   *

But now, how far does the negro, as a Christian, really become another man? At his baptism he has renounced all superstition, but superstition is so woven into the texture of his own life and that of the society in which he lives, that it cannot be got rid of in twenty-four hours; he falls again and again in big things as in small. I think, however, that we can take too seriously the customs and practices from which he cannot set himself entirely free; the important thing is to make him understand that nothing—no evil spirit—really exists behind his heathenism.

If a child enters the world in our hospital its mother and itself are both painted white all over face and body so as to make them look terrifying, a custom which is found in practice among almost all primitive peoples. The object is to either frighten or to deceive the evil spirits which on such an occasion have a special opportunity of being dangerous. I do not worry myself about this usage; I even say sometimes, as soon as the child is born: "Take care you don't forget the painting!"

There are times when a little friendly irony is more dangerous to the spirits and the fetishes than zeal expended on a direct attack upon them. I venture to remind my readers that we Europeans, ourselves, have many customs which, although we never think about it, had their origin in heathen ideas.

The ethical conversion, also, is often incomplete with a negro, but in order to be just to such a convert one must distinguish between the real morality which springs from the heart, and the respectable morality of society; it is wonderful how faithful he often is to the former. One must live among them to know how much it means when a man, because he is a Christian, will not wreak the vengeance which he is expected to take, or even the blood revenge which is thought to be an obligation on him. On the whole I feel that the primitive man is much more good natured than we Europeans are; with Christianity added to his good qualities wonderfully noble characters can result. I expect I am not the only white man who feels himself put to shame by the natives.

But to give up the common habit of lying and the readiness to steal, and to become a more or less reliable man in our sense, is something different from practising the religion of love. If I may venture on a paradox, I would say that the converted native is a moral man more often than he is an honourable one. Still, little can be effected by condemnatory expressions. We must see to it that we put as few temptations as possible in the way of the coloured Christian.

But there are native Christians who are in every respect thoroughly moral personalities; I meet one such every day. It is Ojembo, the teacher in our boys' school, whose name means "the song"; I look upon him as one of the finest men that I know anywhere.

How is it that traders and officials so often speak so unfavourably of native Christians? On my very first journey up the river I learnt from two fellow travellers that they never, on principle, engage any Christian "boys." The fact is that Christianity is considered responsible for the unfavourable phenomena of intellectual emancipation. The young Christians have mostly been in our mission schools, and get into the difficult position which for the native is so often bound up with a school education. They think themselves too good for many kinds of work, and will no longer be treated as ordinary negroes. I have experienced this with some of my own boys.

One of them, Atombogunjo by name, who was in the first
class at N'Gômô, worked for me once during the school holi-
days. On the very first day, while he was washing up on the
verandah, he stuck up a school book, open, before him. "What
a fine boy! What keenness for learning!" said my wife. Ulti-
mately, however, we found that the open school book meant
something beyond a desire for knowledge; it was also a symbol
of independence intended to show us that the fifteen-year-old
youth was too good for ordinary service, and was no longer
willing to be treated as a mere "boy," like other "boys."
Finally, I could stand his conceit no longer, and put him un-
ceremoniously outside the door.

Now in the colonies almost all schools are mission schools—
the Governments establish hardly any, but leave the work to
the missions—so that all the unhealthy phenomena which accompany intellectual emancipation show themselves among the
scholars and are therefore put down as the fault of Christianity. The whites, however, often forget what they owe to the
missions. Once, when, on board the steamer, the manager of
a large company began to abuse the missions in my presence,
I asked him: "Where, then, did the black clerks and the black
store employees who work for you, get their education? To
whom do you owe it that you can find natives here on the
Ogowe who can read, write, and handle figures, and who are
to a certain extent reliable?" He had no reply to make to that.

*   *   *

But how is a mission carried on? With what must it be provided, and how does it work? In Europe many people picture
it as a sort of village parsonage set down in the virgin forest,
but it is something much more comprehensive than that, and
more complicated too; it may be said to be the seat of a bishop,
an educational centre, a farming establishment, and a market!

In an ordinary mission station there must be one missionary
as head, another for the mission work in the district, a man to
teach in the boys' school, and a woman for the girls' school,
with one or two practical workers, and, if possible, a doctor.
Only a mission station of that size can accomplish anything
worth mentioning; an incomplete one only uses up men and
money with no permanent result.

As an illustration of this take Talagonga, where at the beginning of my time here there was a splendid evangelist working,

Mr. Ford, an American, but the station had no practical workers. There came a time when it was absolutely necessary to repair the floor of the house, built upon piles, in which Mr. and Mrs. Ford and their children lived, because mosquitoes found their way in through the holes in it, and, as fever carriers, endangered the lives of the inmates. So Mr. Ford set to work at the job and finished it in about two months, during which time the neighbourhood was left without any spiritual direction. A practical worker would have done it all in three weeks and made a permanent job of it, not mere temporary patchwork. This is one example out of hundreds of the useless, unprofitable condition of insufficiently manned mission stations.

In the tropics a man can do at most half of what he can manage in a temperate climate. If he is dragged about from one task to another he gets used up so quickly that, though he is still on the spot, the working capacity he represents is *nil.* Hence a strict division of labour is absolutely necessary, though on the other hand, each member must be able, when circumstances demand it, to turn his hand to anything. A missionary who does not understand something of practical work, of garden work, of treatment of the sick, is a misfortune to a mission station.

The missionary who is there for the evangelistic work must as a rule have nothing to do with the carrying on of the daily work of the station; he must be free to undertake every day his longer or shorter journeys for the purpose of visiting the villages, nor must he be obliged to be back at the mission on a particular day. He may be invited while out on one of his journeys to go to this or that village which was not included in his plan, because the people there want to hear the Gospel. He must never answer that he has no time, but must be able to give them two or three days or even a whole week. When he gets back he must rest, for an unbroken fortnight on the river or on forest paths will certainly have exhausted him.

Too few missionary journeys, and those too hastily carried through, that is the miserable mistake of almost all missions, and the cause of it always is that in consequence of an insufficient number of workers or of unwise division of work, the evangelist takes part in the superintendence of the station, and the Head of the station goes travelling.

On the Head of the station falls the work of the services in the station and in the nearest villages, together with the superintendence of the schools and of the cultivated land. He ought really never to leave the station for a day; he must have his eyes everywhere, and anyone ought to be able to speak to him at any time. His most prosaic business is conducting the market. The foodstuffs which we need for the school children, the labourers, and the boatmen of the station, we do not have to buy with money. Only when the natives know that they can get satisfactory goods of all sorts from us, do they bring us regular supplies of manioc, bananas, and dried fish; so the mission must have a shop. Two or three times a week the natives come with the product of their plots and with fish, and barter what they have brought for salt, nails, kerosene, fishing materials, tobacco, saws, knives, axes, and cloth. We do not supply rum or spirits. This takes up the Head's whole morning, and then what a time it takes him in addition to send off his European orders correctly and at the right time, to keep the accounts accurately, to pay the boatmen and the labourers their wages, and to look after all the cultivated ground! What losses are entailed, too, if he fails to have necessary material in hand when it is wanted! A roof has to be put on, and there are no raffia leaves ready, dried and sewn into sheets; there is some building to be done, and there are no beams and no boards; or the best time for brickmaking has been allowed to pass unused; or he has postponed too long the re-smoking of the store of dried fish for the school children, and discovers one morning that it is all a mass of worms and good for nothing! It all depends on the Head whether the mission station does its work cheaply and successfully, or expensively and unsuccessfully.

On one of our stations, for example, there had been for several years a succession of Heads who knew but little about land cultivation, and had not pruned the coffee bushes properly. They had let them grow so tall that they no longer produced what they ought to have done, and ladders had to be used to gather the crop. Then it was necessary to cut them off just above the ground, and it will be years before they have produced new shoots which bear a normal crop.

Another of the Head's duties is to investigate the not infrequent cases of theft, in which matter he has more opportunity than he likes for developing whatever detective talent he may possess. He has also to straighten out all the disputes between the coloured inhabitants of the settlement, and in this he must never show any impatience. For hours together he must listen attentively to their barren argumentations, since otherwise he is not the upright judge according to their notions. If canoes come from another station he must entertain and feed the rowers. If the steamer's siren sounds, he must be off with canoes to the landing place to take charge of the mail and the cases of goods.

Again, it may happen that there has been too small a supply of foodstuffs brought in on a market day; this means that canoes must be sent off to the more distant villages to secure what is needed. The expedition may take two or three days; what work is to be left undone because of it? And then the canoes may come back empty, so that a similar expedition has to be made in another direction!

What a terribly unromantic business life for one who came out to preach the religion of Jesus! If he had not to conduct the morning and evening services in the schoolroom and to preach on Sundays, the Head could almost forget that he was a missionary at all! But it is just by means of the Christian sympathy and gentleness that he shows in all this everyday business that he exercises his greatest influence; whatever level of spirituality the community reaches is due to nothing so much as to the success of its Head in this matter of—Preaching without Words.

*   *   *

A word now about the schools. A school to which children come for instruction while they live at home is impossible here because of the distances; there are villages, for example, attached to the Lambaréné Station, which are sixty or seventy miles away from it. The children must therefore live on the station, and the parents bring them in October and take them away in July when the big fishing expeditions begin. In return for the cost of their living the children, both boys and girls, do some sort of work, and their day is arranged very much as follows: From 7 to 9 in the morning they are at work cutting down grass and bush, for the defence of the station against invasion by the forest is in the main their task. When they have done all the clearing that is necessary at one end of the settlement they can always go to some other part where the undergrowth will have shot up again as it was before. From 9 to 10 is a rest hour, during which they breakfast; from 10 to 12 is school. The recreation time between 12 and 1 is usually spent in bathing and fishing. From 2 to 4 there is school again, and after that, work again for about an hour and a half. Some help in the cocoa plantation; the boys often go to the practical worker to help him, and they prepare bricks, carry building material where it is wanted, or finish digging or other work on the soil. Then the food for the following day is given out; at 6 comes the evening service, and after that they get supper ready. There is a big shed under which the children cook their bananas in native fashion, and they divide into groups of five or six, each of which has a pot and a fire hole to itself. At 9 they go to bed, that is, they retire to their plank bedsteads under the mosquito netting. On Sunday afternoons they make canoe expeditions, the mistress going out with a crew of girls. In the dry season they play on the sandbanks.

The work of the boys' school suffers, unfortunately, in this way, that when the evangelist goes out on his preaching rounds, or when a canoe expedition is needed for any purpose, a crew of boys has to be taken for it, and they may be absent for as much as a week. When shall we reach such a stage of efficiency that every mission station has its motor-boat?

* * *

Should a missionary have a thorough education? Yes. The better a man's mental life and his intellectual interests are developed, the better he will be able to hold out in Africa. Without this safeguard he is soon in danger of becoming a nigger, as it is called here. This shows itself in the way he loses every higher point of view; then his capacity for intellectual work diminishes, and he begins, just like a negro, to attach importance to, and to argue at any length about, the smallest matters. In the matter of theology, too, the more thorough the training the better.

That under certain circumstances a man may be a good missionary without having studied theology is proved by the example of Mr. Felix Faure, who at the present time is the Head of our station. He is by training an agricultural engineer (*ingénieur agronome*) and came to the Ogowe first of all to manage the station's agricultural land. At the same time he proved to be such an excellent preacher and evangelist that he became in time more missionary than planter.

I am not quite in agreement with the manner in which baptism is practised here. The rule is that only adults are baptised, it being felt that only those should be received into the Christian community whose way of life has stood some amount of testing[1]. But do we thereby build up a church on a broad and safe basis? Is it essential that the communities shall be composed only of members of comparatively blameless life? I think we must further consider the question of how they are to make sure of a normal stream of new members. If we baptise the children of Christian parents, we have growing up among us a number of natives who have been in the Church and under its influence from their childhood upwards. Certainly there will be some among them who show themselves unworthy of the Christian name given them in their childhood, but there will be many others who, just because they belong to the Church and find within it support in the dangers that surround them, become and remain loyal members of it. Thus the question of infant baptism, which so disturbed the Church in the early centuries, comes up again to-day in the mission field as a live issue. But if we wished to decide for infant baptism in the Ogowe district we should have in opposition to us nearly all the native evangelists and elders.

* * *

The most difficult problem in the mission field arises from the fact that evangelistic work has to be done under two banners, the Catholic and the Protestant. How much grander would be the work undertaken in the name of Jesus if this distinction did not exist, and there were never two churches working in competition. On the Ogowe, indeed, the missionaries of both bodies live in quite correct, sometimes in even friendly, relations with one another, but that does not remove the rivalry which confuses the native and hinders the spread of the Gospel.

I often visit the Catholic mission stations in my capacity of doctor and so have been able to gather a fairly clear idea of the way in which they conduct their evangelistic work and their education. As to organisation, their missions seem to me to be better managed than ours in several ways. If I had to distinguish between the aims which the two keep before them, I should say the Protestant mission puts in the first place the building up of Christian personalities, while the Catholic has in mind before all else the establishment on solid foundations of a church. The former object is the higher one, but it does not

---

[1] Most Protestant missions practise infant baptism. There are some, however, who object to it. On the Ogowe, infant baptism is not customary, because the American missionaries, who founded the Protestant missions here, did not introduce it.—A. S.

take sufficient account of realities. To make the work of training permanently successful, a firmly established church, which
grows in a natural way with the increase in the number of
Christian families, is necessary. The church history of every
period teaches this. Is it not the weakness as well as the
greatness of Protestantism that it means personal religion too
much and church too little?

For the work which the American missionaries began here
and the French have continued, I feel a hearty admiration. It
has produced among the natives human and Christian characters which would convince the most decided opponents of
missions as to what the teaching of Jesus can do for primitive
man. But now we ought to have the men and the means to
found more stations further inland, and so exert an educational influence on the natives before they are reached by the
white man's trade and the dangers and problems which it
brings with it for the child of nature.

Will this be possible within a measurable time? What will be
the lot of mission work after the war? How will the ruined
peoples of Europe be able to contribute any longer the necessary means for the various spiritual undertakings in the world?
There is, also, this further difficulty—that mission work can
only flourish when it is to some extent international; but the
war has made anything international impossible for a long
time. And, lastly, missions throughout the world will soon feel
that, owing to the war, the white race has lost a great deal of
its spiritual authority over the coloured ones.

11 RESULTS AND CONCLUSIONS

FOR four years and a half we worked in Lambaréné, but in
the last of them we were able to spend the hot, rainy months
between autumn and spring at the seaside. A white man who
pitied my almost utterly exhausted wife put at our disposal, at
the mouth of the Ogowe, two hours from Cape Lopez, a house

which before the war had been the home of the man who watched his timber floats when they lay at anchor, but which had been empty since the trade came to a standstill. We shall never forget his kindness. Our principal food was herrings, which I caught in the sea. Of the abundance of fish in Cape Lopez Bay it is difficult for anyone to form an adequate idea.

Around the house stood the huts in which the white man's labourers had lived when the trade was in full swing. Now, half ruined, they served as sleeping places for negroes who passed through. On the second day after our arrival I went to see whether there was any one in them, but no one answered my calls. Then I opened the doors one by one, and in the last hut saw a man lying on the ground with his head almost buried in the sand and ants running all over him. It was a victim of sleeping-sickness whom his companions had left there, probably some days before, because they could not take him any further. He was past all help, though he still breathed. While I was busied with him I could see through the door of the hut the bright blue waters of the bay in their frame of green woods, a scene of almost magic beauty, looking still more enchanting in the flood of golden light poured over it by the setting sun. To be shown in a single glance such a paradise and such helpless, hopeless misery, was overwhelming . . . but it was a symbol of the condition of Africa.

On my return to Lambaréné I found plenty to do, but this did not frighten me. I was fresh and vigorous again. Much of the work was caused just then by men who were ill with dysentery. Carriers for the military colony of the Cameroons had been impressed in our district, and many of them had caught the infection, but subcutaneous injections of emetin proved very effective even in the oldest cases.

When this levy of carriers was made, one of my patients who had a bad ulcer on his foot wanted to join as a volunteer, so that his brother, who had been taken, might not have to go alone. I represented to him that in three or four days he would fall out and be left on the roadside, where he would assuredly die. However, he would not let himself be convinced, and I almost had to use violence to keep him back.

I happened to be present when a body of impressed carriers who were to be taken to the Cameroons by water were embarked on the river steamer at N'Gômô. Then the natives began to know by experience what war really is. The vessel had started amid the wailing of the women; its trail of smoke disappeared in the distance, and the crowd had dispersed, but on a stone on the river bank an old woman whose son had been taken sat weeping silently. I took hold of her hand and wanted to comfort her, but she went on crying as if she did not hear me. Suddenly I felt that I was crying with her, silently, towards the setting sun, as she was.

About that time I read a magazine article which maintained that there would always be wars, because a noble thirst for glory is an ineradicable element in the heart of man. These champions of militarism think of war only as idealised by ignorant enthusiasm or the necessity of self-defence. They would probably reconsider their opinions if they spent a day in one of the African theatres of war, walking along the paths in the virgin forest between lines of corpses of carriers who had sunk under their load and found a solitary death by the roadside, and if, with these innocent and unwilling victims before them, they were to meditate in the gloomy stillness of the forest on war as it really is.

* * *

How shall I sum up the resulting experience of these four and a half years? On the whole it has confirmed my view of the considerations which drew me from the world of learning and art to the primeval forest. "The natives who live in the bosom of Nature are never so ill as we are, and do not feel pain so much." That is what my friends used to say to me, to try to keep me at home, but I have come to see that such statements are not true. Out here there prevail most of the diseases which we know in Europe, and several of them—those hideous ones, I mean, which we brought here—produce, if possible, more misery than they do amongst us. And the child of nature feels them as we do, for to be human means to be subject to the power of that terrible lord whose name is Pain.

Physical misery is great everywhere out here. Are we justified in shutting our eyes and ignoring it because our European newspapers tell us nothing about it? We civilised people have been spoilt. If any one of us is ill the doctor comes at once. Is an operation necessary, the door of some hospital or other opens to us immediately. But let every one reflect on the meaning of the fact that out here millions and millions live without help or hope of it. Every day thousands and thousands endure the most terrible sufferings, though medical science could avert them. Every day there prevails in many and many a far-off hut a despair which we could banish. Will each of my readers think what the last ten years of his family history would have been if they had been passed without medical or surgical help of any sort? It is time that we should wake from slumber and face our responsibilities!

Believing it, as I do, to be my life's task to fight on behalf of the sick under far-off stars, I appeal to the sympathy which Jesus and religion generally call for, but at the same time I call to my help also our most fundamental ideas and reasonings. We ought to see the work that needs doing for the coloured folk in their misery, not as a mere "good work," but as a duty that must not be shirked.

Ever since the world's far-off lands were discovered, what has been the conduct of the white peoples to the coloured ones? What is the meaning of the simple fact that this and that people has died out, that others are dying out, and that the condition of others is getting worse and worse as a result of their discovery by men who professed to be followers of Jesus? Who can describe the injustice and the cruelties that in the course of centuries they have suffered at the hands of Europeans? Who can measure the misery produced among them by the fiery drinks and the hideous diseases that we have taken to them? If a record could be compiled of all that has happened between the white and the coloured races, it would make a book containing numbers of pages, referring to recent as well as to early times, which the reader would have to turn over unread, because their contents would be too horrible.

We and our civilisation are burdened, really, with a great debt. We are not free to confer benefits on these men, or not, as we please; it is our duty. Anything we give them is not benevolence but atonement. For every one who scattered injury someone ought to go out to take help, and when we have done all that is in our power, we shall not have atoned for the thousandth part of our guilt. That is the foundation from which all deliberations about "works of mercy" out there must begin.

It goes without saying that Governments must help with the atonement, but they cannot do so till there already exists in society a conviction on the subject. The Government alone can never discharge the duties of humanitarianism; from the nature of the case that rests with society and individuals.

The Government can send out as many colonial doctors as it has at its disposal, and as the colonial budgets are able to pay for. It is well known that there are great colonising powers which cannot find even enough doctors to fill the places of those already working in their colonies, though these are far from sufficient to cope with the need. So again, we see, the real burden of the humanitarian work must fall upon society and its individual members. We must have doctors who go among the coloured people of their own accord and are ready to put up with all that is meant by absence from home and civilisation. I can say from experience that they will find a rich reward for all that they renounce in the good that they can do.

Among the poor people out here they will not as a rule be able to collect the cost of their own living and work; men must come forward at home who will provide what is necessary, and that is something that is due from all of us. But whom shall we get to make a beginning, without waiting till the duty is universally recognised and acted upon?

* * *

The Fellowship of those who bear the Mark of Pain. Who are the members of this Fellowship? Those who have learnt by experience what physical pain and bodily anguish mean, belong together all the world over; they are united by a secret bond. One and all they know the horrors of suffering to which man can be exposed, and one and all they know the longing to be free from pain. He who has been delivered from pain must not think he is now free again, and at liberty to take life up just as it was before, entirely forgetful of the past. He is now a "man whose eyes are open" with regard to pain and anguish, and he must help to overcome those two enemies (so far as human power can control them) and to bring to others the deliverance which he has himself enjoyed. The man who, with a doctor's help, has been pulled through a severe illness, must aid in providing a helper such as he had himself, for those who otherwise could not have one. He who has been saved by an operation from death or torturing pain, must do his part to make it possible for the kindly anæsthetic and the helpful knife to begin their work, where death and torturing pain still rule unhindered. The mother who owes it to medical aid that her child still belongs to her, and not to the cold earth, must help, so that the poor mother who has never seen a doctor may be spared what she has been spared. Where a man's death agony might have been terrible, but could fortunately be made tolerable by a doctor's skill, those who stood around his death-bed must help, that others, too, may enjoy that same consolation when they lose their dear ones.

Such is the Fellowship of those who bear the Mark of Pain, and on them lies the humanitarian task of providing medical help in the colonies. Their gratitude should be the source of the gifts needed. Commissioned by them, doctors should go forth to carry out among the miserable in far-off lands all that ought to be done in the name of civilisation, human and humane.

Sooner or later the idea which I here put forward will conquer the world, for with inexorable logic it carries with it the intellect as well as the heart.

But is just now the right time to send it out into the world? Europe is ruined and full of wretchedness. With all the misery that we have to alleviate even under our very eyes, how can we think of far-off lands?

Truth has no special time of its own. Its hour is now—always, and indeed then most truly when it seems most unsuitable to actual circumstances. Care for distress at home and care for distress elsewhere do but help each other if, working together, they wake men in sufficient numbers from their thoughtlessness, and call into life a new spirit of humanity.

But let no one say: "Suppose 'the Fellowship of those who bear the Mark of Pain' does by way of beginning send one doctor here, another there, what is that to cope with the misery of the world?" From my own experience and from that of all colonial doctors, I answer, that a single doctor out here with the most modest equipment means very much for very many. The good which he can accomplish surpasses a hundredfold what he gives of his own life and the cost of the material support which he must have. Just with quinine and arsenic for malaria, with novarseno-benzol for the various diseases which spread through ulcerating sores, with emetin for dysentery, and with sufficient skill and apparatus for the most necessary operations, he can in a single year free from the power of suffering and death hundreds of men who must otherwise have succumbed to their fate in despair. It is just exactly the advance of tropical medicine during the last fifteen years which gives us a power over the sufferings of the men of far-off lands that borders on the miraculous. Is not this really a call to us?

For myself, now that my health, which since 1918 had been very uncertain, has been restored as the result of two operations, and that I have succeeded, by means of lectures and organ concerts in discharging the debts which I had to incur during the war for the sake of my work, I venture to resolve to continue my activity among the suffering folk of whom I have written. The work, indeed, as I began it, has been ruined by the war. The friends from two nations who joined in supporting us, have been, alas! deeply divided by what has happened in the world, and of those who might have helped us farther, many have been reduced to poverty by the war. It will be very difficult to collect the necessary funds, which again must be far larger than before, for the expenses will be three times as heavy, however modestly I replan our undertaking.

Nevertheless, I have not lost courage. The misery I have seen gives me strength, and faith in my fellow men supports my confidence in the future. I do hope that I shall find a sufficient number of people who, because they themselves have been saved from physical suffering, will respond to requests on behalf of those who are in similar need. . . . I do hope that among the doctors of the world there will soon be several besides myself who will be sent out, here or there in the world, by "the Fellowship of those who bear the Mark of Pain."

ST. NICHOLAS' CLERGY HOUSE,
STRASBOURG,
August, 1920.

PART II

MORE FROM
THE PRIMEVAL FOREST

INTRODUCTION

THE following sketches, which were put together in intervals of leisure during my second period of work at Lambaréné between April, 1924, and July, 1927, were not originally meant to appear in book form as a continuation of the volume entitled *On the Edge of the Primeval Forest,* which was published nearly ten years ago and describes my work in Equatorial Africa during the years 1913-17. They were meant to be just letters for circulation in print among the friends of my undertaking to tell them about what was happening in the hospital. But in compliance with requests from different quarters, I have now decided to let them appear, somewhat shortened, as a book.

Two things unfortunately hindered me from undertaking the labour necessary for this publication during the visit to Europe —from the Autumn of 1927 to November, 1929—which followed my second period of activity in Africa; these were first fatigue, and then the necessity of completing as soon as possible the work on the Mysticism of S. Paul, which was begun thirty years ago.

It is only now, when I am again in Lambaréné, where I arrived at Christmas, 1929, and again at work, that I can face it. During the first few months here, indeed, the claims of the hospital weighed so heavily on me, that doing anything with a pen was out of the question. Now, however, in the summer of 1930, when I have with me the young Alsatian doctor who came to relieve me of much of the work, and when I am again inured to the climate of the equatorial forest, I feel fresh enough in the evenings, when the hospital work is over, to devote myself to this different activity.

While I am writing and going again in memory over the activities of which this book is the record, I think with deep emotion of the kind friends in England who by their gifts have helped to make it possible for me to take up the work in Lambaréné again and to carry it further. I shall never forget what they have done for me, and I ask them to accept this book as dedicated to them in proof of my gratitude.

As with *On the Edge of the Primeval Forest* and the two first volumes of the *Philosophy of Civilisation,* my dear friend C. T. Campion is once more exercising for me his skill as a translator. I here offer him my hearty thanks.

LAMBARÉNÉ
August 8th, 1930.

12 *THE VOYAGE*

EARLY on Thursday, February 21st, 1924, while it is still dark, the Dutch steamer *Orestes* leaves the port of Bordeaux, carrying me to Africa for my second period of work there. As I have been busy all the night through, writing important letters so as to be able to get them to post, I go to bed and sleep till near midday, when I find the boat leaving the Gironde for the open sea in brilliant sunshine.

At first I can hardly realise that I am returning to Lambaréné. The whole time I have lived through since the shores of the Gironde rose into sight on my return in 1917, sweeps before my mind's eye, as the same stretch of coast now gradually disappears. First came the long tale of months after the war, filled with anxiety about health and even about life itself, months during which I could make no plans at all, because it was uncertain whether I should ever regain the vigour needed for work in the tropics. Then the year 1920, during which my strength steadily increased, I found that I was again fit to do something in science and in art. After delivering some lectures at the University of Upsala, in which, during the early summer of that year, I for the first time broached the ideas contained in my *Philosophy of Civilisation,* I ventured, with encouragement from Archbishop Nathan Söderblom, to give some concerts and public lectures in Sweden, in order to pay off the heavy debts still owing on my hospital. This effort was almost too much for my strength, but the success it met with decided me to return to Strasbourg, with a resolution to resume the work at Lambaréné. When we left Sweden my wife was ready for the great sacrifice of consenting to my plan, although owing to the state of her health she would be unable to accompany me. At last I was in a

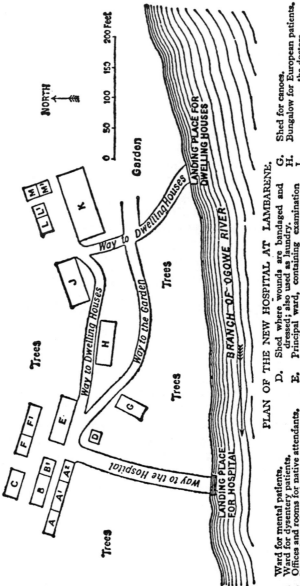

PLANTATION

PLANTATION

PLANTATION

Trees

Trees

Trees

Trees

Garden

NORTH

0   50   100   150   200 Feet

Way to Dwelling Houses

Way to the Garden

Way to Dwelling Houses

Way to the Hospital

LANDING PLACE FOR HOSPITAL

LANDING PLACE FOR DWELLING HOUSES

BRANCH-OF-OGOWE RIVER

A   A¹   A²   B   B¹   C   D   E   F   F¹   G   H   J   K   L   L¹   M   M¹

PLAN OF THE NEW HOSPITAL AT LAMBARENE.

A.   Ward for mental patients.
A1.   Ward for dysentery patients.
A2.   Offices and rooms for native attendants.
B.   Ward for native patients.
B1.   Store rooms for tools and provisions; the food rations are distributed from here.
C.   Ward for native patients with special accommodation for unaccompanied women and girls.
D.   Shed where wounds are bandaged and dressed; also used as laundry.
E.   Principal ward, containing examination and treatment rooms, surgery, operating theatre, laboratory, and store room for linen and bandages.
F.   Rooms for native attendants.
F1.   Ward with two divisions for operation cases.
G.   Shed for canoes.
H.   Bungalow for European patients.
J.   "   "   the doctors.
K.   "   "   the nurses.
L. & M. Store rooms for provisions.
L1.   Kitchen.
M1.   Fowl house.

position to promise what they wanted to the natives who had been bombarding me with entreaties to go out and be their doctor again. But the carrying out of the plan was still in the far distance. For more than two years I had to stay in Europe to give concerts and popular lectures in order to raise funds for the new work, as well as many academic lectures which I had promised to a number of Universities; there was also the task of getting ready for the press the manuscripts of *The Decay and Restoration of Civilisation* and of *Civilisation and Ethics.*

On all these things and on the many weeks devoted to buying and packing the necessary supplies I keep thinking, as the ship leaves the estuary for the open sea, and begins rocking on its waves. I can hardly realise that once more, as in 1913, it is carrying me and all my packing-cases towards the Equator.

Nor is my satisfaction unqualified. My thoughts sweep back to that first start, when my wife, as a loyal helpmeet, was travelling with me. Unceasingly I thank her in my heart that she rose to the sacrifice of acquiescence in my return under these circumstances to Lambaréné.

I think, too, of the many dear people whose friendship I won in almost every country in Europe during my lecture and concert tours. Again I feel overpowered by remembrance of the affection I had the privilege of winning from people with whom I could not speak in their own language, but who nevertheless welcomed me as if I were a friend of their own, and helped me to get together what has enabled me to go out to work among the sick and poor of the Ogowe district. What an abundance of friendship I met with in England alone during my two short visits to that country!

My companion on this voyage is an eighteen-year-old Oxford undergraduate, Noel Gillespie, who is ready to spend some months with me in Lambaréné, and help me in the heavy work of beginning afresh.

I have purposely chosen to travel by a cargo-boat which will have many stopping-places big and little. I want to get to know the West Coast as thoroughly as I can, and I hope to be able to work better than I should be able to on a mailboat, on which one is continually interrupted by the other passengers. Before we get to Lambaréné hundreds of letters must be dealt with, which on account of the pressure of work could not be answered in Europe. At Bordeaux a customs officer spent a whole hour and a half rummaging in trunks filled with these letters, because he could not fathom why anyone should be going off with so many letters addressed to himself! As the export of gold from France was at that time strictly prohibited, he supposed that some at least of the numerous envelopes must contain gold or banknotes, which I was hoping by this ingenious method to smuggle out of the country.

During the voyage we have a splendid north wind behind us.

The ship touches at Dakar, Conakry, Freetown, Sassandra, Grand Lahou, Grand Bassam, Secondee, Accra, Lome, Cotonou, Fernando Po, and Duala.

It has on board as passenger, the only one besides ourselves, a lady who is travelling to the Cameroons. When off Cotonou this passenger takes advantage of the presence of a doctor in the ship to bring into the world a baby which was not expected till she should be at Duala. As there is no other woman on board the care of her falls on me, and the care of the baby on Noel, who now learns what the temperature of a ship's galley is in the tropics. Eight times a day he has to visit the galley to prepare the milk for the feeding-bottle.

At Duala we leave the ship for a fortnight's expedition in order to visit an, at that time, abandoned station of the Basle Mission, named Nyasoso, in the English part of the Cameroons. I wanted to learn about its situation, and the conditions of life in that district, in case I should one day want to start another hospital, an offshoot from Lambaréné. This neighbourhood had been recommended to me in several quarters as suitable. So in order to discuss this quite nebulous plan with the Resident, Major Ruxton, we make our way to Buca, which is situated on the slope of the Cameroon Mountain, about 3,200 feet above the sea, and we enjoy there for two days the hospitality of the Resident and his wife. The plan of another hospital in Nyasoso I subsequently for various reasons allowed to drop.

The day after Palm Sunday we leave the Cameroons in the mail-boat *Europe* the vessel which had brought me to Africa in 1913, and in two days we are in Cape Lopez, or Port Gentil, as it is now called. On the beach I am recognised by natives, who can hardly contain themselves for joy at having "our doctor" back again.

During the afternoon of Maundy Thursday we leave Cape Lopez on board the *Alembe,* on which I went up the Ogowe in 1913. What a dirty old ramshackle boat it has become! But among the white timber-merchants on board I meet several old acquaintances, who give me a hearty welcome.

Through the quietness of Good Friday I travel once more along "the edge of the primeval forest," past the same antediluvian landscape, the same papyrus swamps, the same decaying villages, and the same ragged negroes. How poor this territory is compared with the Gold Coast and the Cameroons! And poor because . . . it is so rich in valuable timber! The exploitation of the forests goes on at the expense of the cultivation of the means of life, and these have to be imported. So wherever we stop we see the same sort of cargo unloaded: sacks of rice, cases of ship's biscuits, cases of dried fish, and, with these, casks of red wine.

At table, as soon as timber-prices and labour have been sufficiently discussed, the conversation turns to the bands of human leopards, whose depredations have much increased everywhere in recent years, and have spread over the whole of the West Coast. The missionaries at Duala told me how they sometimes visit districts which have been so terrorised by these creatures, that no one ventures out of his hut after dark. Two years ago they actually perpetrated a murder at the Lambaréné mission station.

They are men who are possessed by the delusion that they are leopards, and therefore must kill men, and when they are out to do this, they try to behave altogether like leopards. They go on all fours, fastening on their hands and feet real leopard's claws or iron imitations of them, so as to leave behind them a spoor like that of a leopard; and when they catch a victim, they sever his carotid artery, as leopards do.

The remarkable and uncanny fact is that most of them have become human leopards involuntarily, having been made members of one of the bands without being aware of it. The band prepares in a human skull a potion made out of the blood of one of their victims, and some man, on whom they have previously fixed, is secretly given some of it in one of his ordinary drinks. Then he is informed that he has drunk the potion, and therefore is from that time one of the band. Nor does any one of them resist. They are all alike dominated by the belief that a magic postion has some magic power against which no one can successfully fight, and so they obey unresistingly. The next step is a command to take one of their brothers or sisters to some place where he or she can be attacked and killed by the members of the band. Then they must themselves start killing.

An official in the hinterland of the Ogowe district, who a few months before had received orders to put an end to the depredations of the human leopards, captured ninety suspicious characters. They would, however, betray nothing, and poisoned each other in the prisons.

How far these bands of human leopards mean just a wave of pure superstition, and how far they have gone on to adopt the definite objects of revenge and plunder, it is impossible to decide. Like other secret associations they are signs of an uncanny process of fermentation which is going on in the heart of Africa. Reviving superstition, primitive fanaticism, and very modern bolshevism are to-day combining in the strangest way in the Dark Continent.

*   *   *

What a relief it is after conversation about such things to escape to the deck and lose oneself in the contemplation of nature! The boat moves slowly upstream along the dark bank. Wood and water are flooded with the soft light of the Easter full-moon, and one can hardly bring oneself to believe that under such a flood of light there can be so much misery and terror as we are assured exists.

At sunrise on Easter Eve, April 19th, we are at Lambaréné, but it is a long time before we see the canoes from the mission station which is on one of the side-streams of the Ogowe, and an hour's journey from the steamer's landing-place. Nor are they sufficient to take our numerous packages. Others belonging to natives have to be called for, and volunteer crews obtained. However, we do at last secure transport enough, and get it properly loaded. The paddles dip into the water, and we are soon at the bend where we enter the side-stream and the houses of the mission station on their three small hills become visible. How much I have lived through since in the autumn of 1917 my wife and I lost sight of them! How often I have been on the point of giving up all hope of ever seeing them again! Now, here they are once more, but I no longer have my helpmate with me. . . .

We get on shore about midday, and while Noel superintends the unloading I walk up to the hospital like one in a dream. It might be the Sleeping Beauty's place of concealment! Grass and brushwood are growing where once stood the wards which I constructed with so much trouble. Above what is still standing are stretched the boughs of big trees which I remember as little saplings. There are still standing the building of corrugated iron in which we had our operating room, consulting room, and dispensary, and another in which we housed some of the patients. These two are still in fairly good condition, though their roofs of palm-leaves are hopelessly damaged.

The path from the hospital up to the little Doctor's house on the hill is so overgrown with grass that I can scarcely follow its windings. "To-morrow, the first thing," says Missionary Herrmann, "the boys shall clear it." "Oh no," is my answer, "let me tread it clear again!"

Mons. Herrmann and Mons. Pelot, who are both from Switzerland, Madame Herrmann and the school mistress, Mademoiselle Arnoux, who at the present time form the staff of the mission, are dear acquaintances made during my first period here, and by the time we are seated together at the table I feel myself quite at home again in Lambaréné.

Mons. Herrmann and Mons. Pelot have tried to keep my leaf-roof in a state of repair, but had to abandon the task more than a year ago. There are no more stitched-leaf tiles to be had. In view of two international exhibitions in Europe and America the demand for timber is so great that the Ogowe merchants are quite unable to fulfil the orders that are showered in on them. Anyone who can handle the axe finds well paid work in the forest. Anyone who knows anything about rafts takes rafts down the river. The few natives who have learnt a trade no longer work at it, since they can earn more in the forest.

Of the carpenters who wrote to me, either themselves or through others, that they were ready to help me with my repairs, not one is near, and no one even knows where they are. Moreover, for months no one has given a thought to stitching raphia leaves over bamboos to make leaf-tiles, except those who have to supply them, as compulsory service, to the Government. The natives have not even for themselves any material for roofing their huts; the roofs of their huts are as ruinous as the roofs of our buildings.

All this is bad news, and the state of things is worse than I expected. With holes as big as one's fist in the roofs I cannot put away my belongings or begin work, so there is nothing for it but to find some leaf-tiles as soon as possible and at any price. By three o'clock, therefore, although it is Easter Eve, I am seated in a canoe with Noel to visit a village an hour and a half away where I am well known. There is handshaking and an exchange of compliments, and I go from hut to hut peering about in hopes of finding some stitched-leaf tiles somewhere. An old negro to whom I complain about my pressing needs, leads me behind one of the huts, and there are twenty lying on the ground. I make a few more similar discoveries and end with sixty-four!

But the flattery and the presents I had to distribute in order to be able to take the leaf-tiles away with me I should like to forget! I even go so far as to threaten that if the people will not meet my requests, I will never treat any sick person from that village. But such threats, coming from "our Doctor," were only greeted with laughter. To conclude, however—as darkness falls Noel and I return to Lambaréné in pouring rain but in possession of sixty-four leaf-tiles.

I can, therefore, keep Easter with a contented mind, for the worst holes can be mended. But how very differently had I pictured to myself the first days after our return! As it is, the prose of Africa has got hold of me, and it will be a long time before it releases its grip.

We can have, at first, only two rooms in the small doctor's house the other two being occupied by Mons. Pelot, and in one of ours a swarm of wild bees has established itself. Some months before, in consequence of a heavy storm, the house had threatened to collapse, so at a height of six feet Mons. Pelot has protected it with a kind of breastplate of strong oak planks.

For our meals we remain the guests of Madame Herrmann.

13 *THE FIRST MONTHS IN LAMBARÉNÉ*

EASTER MONDAY sees our first patients arrive, among them several old people with heart complaints and in very poor condition, for whom scarcely anything can be done. We therefore get many deaths in the first weeks. With one of these bad cases I sat up a whole night hoping to save him by means of injections of caffein, ether, and camphor, with the result that a small native girl in the mission station believes me to be a human leopard. She runs away in terror every time she sees me, and though the schoolmistress tries to talk her out of her fear, it is of no use. "I saw them," she says, "take the man into the hospital in the evening, and he was alive. Then came the doctor and was alone with him the whole night. In the morning they brought him out dead. Evidently the doctor killed him. He is a white human leopard who is allowed to go about freely, while they shut up the black ones in prison."

For our rebuilding operations help comes from a black timber-merchant, Emil Ogouma, who puts at my disposal five labourers and a foreman. These undertake the most urgent repairs, while I look after the sick and unpack the cases of drugs and other things which are still here, left over from my first period of work.

In a fortnight's time we have the dispensary and the con-suting-room ready with the absolutely necessary fittings, and then the big ward for the patients is taken in hand. But for that our supply of leaf-tiles is not sufficient, although I have meanwhile secured another two hundred. And we are still in the rainy season; there are heavy storms every night, and in the morning I find my patients lying on the floor wet through. The result is a number of chills, two of which end fatally.

I am quite in despair, and many an afternoon which I wanted urgently for the sick or for getting things straight at home, I spend going about in a canoe, hunting for leaf-tiles! Many a journey, too, does Noel make in my stead for the same purpose.

By Ascensiontide the roof of the big ward has been fairly well repaired, and the building of a second can be taken in hand. Under the same roof there will be rooms for the stocking of bottles and tins, for the storage of the washing-boiler, the building materials, and our stuff generally. While this work is going on Emil Ogouma's men leave me, their contract-year being up, and go home, no offer of high pay being of avail to persuade them into staying for even a month longer. Their employer will not succeed in recruiting others in their place, and I am making no attempt to do so. The call for labour is so incessant in the district that I know it would be useless. I am therefore thrown back upon volunteers who have come with the patients as their attendants, and have to play myself the part of building-superintendent, routing the people out every morning from behind their cooking-pots, flattering them, promising them food and presents, forcing the tools into their hands, and in the evening seeing that all the axes, hatchets, bush-knives, and all unused material have been brought back.

Sometimes I have half a dozen workers, sometimes a couple; often when I come down in the morning I cannot find a single one. They have gone fishing, or have left to visit their village and get a supply of food, or they had to go somewhere to take part in a great palaver. Then the work is at a standstill for days. The zeal of my coloured folk to provide for those who will come after them better quarters than they have themselves is very small. They do not work for those they do not know.

The indifference of primitive man towards persons he does not know is beyond anything we can conceive. One day, towards evening, a wounded man had to be brought hastily from the ward to the consulting room to have his dressings renewed. I asked a man who was sitting by the fire, and whose sick brother I was nursing, to lend a hand with the stretcher. He pretended not to hear, and on my repeating the request somewhat more pressingly, he answered quite calmly:

"No. The man on the stretcher is of the Bakele tribe; I am a Bapunu."

Thus I have to divide myself between doctoring and building, the latter being made specially laborious because I have no big canoe. Nor does the mission possess one; it manages with two middle-sized ones, which have had the necessary minimum of repairs. I therefore have great difficulty in getting the bamboos which are to provide the rafters. And time presses. One cannot just go into the forest and cut them; the big bamboos that can be used for this position grow only in certain places in the swamps, and within a radius of many kilometres in this district there is only one place where they are to be found, and from which they can be brought away. For places which lie far away in the swamps, inaccessible either by land or by water, must be left out of account. It is just the same with the raphia palms which provide the materials for the stitched-leaf tiles, and with the plants from the bark of which is made the cord that binds the bamboos to the walls and the leaf-tiles to the bamboos. To get this bark I have to send a canoe something like twenty kilometres.

For the possession of places from which bamboos, raphia, and bark can be easily brought away the tribes used in former days to wage war on each other, just as white nations do for the sake of deposits of metal or coal.

Between Easter and Whitsuntide, when the water reaches its spring high level, I manage with toil and trouble to secure four hundred of the five hundred bamboo stems which I really need.

About Whitsuntide we get the help of a hospital attendant whom Madame Morel has engaged for us at Samkita. His name is G'Mba; he can read and write well and enjoys the reputation of not being dishonest. He knows nothing at all at present about medicine, although it is a real taste for the work that has made him wish to become an orderly. So I have still to do, with Noel's help, all the work, not being able to entrust to G'Mba even the cleaning of the instruments we use every day.

After Whitsuntide a regular stream of patients begins to come in. The thunderstorms have somewhat abated, and people have learned that the rain no longer drips through on to the patients.

The number of the sleeping-sickness and leprosy cases that are brought for me to see gives me the impression that these two plagues have been increasing since my last residence here. In Whitsun week I have under treatment as many as twenty-five patients with sleeping-sickness, and about the same number with leprosy. Those with sleeping-sickness I keep here for six weeks; then the treatment stops for eight weeks. They go home and come back again. Unfortunately I have many cases in the last stage of the disease; they give a great deal of trouble and can hardly ever be saved.

The lepers are sent home at the end of ten days with a supply of Chaulmoogra oil and instructions to come again six weeks later. Intensive treatment with the modern preparations for intramuscular injection I cannot employ till there is more room and I have no longer to be doctor and builder at the same time.

Two thirds of the hospital inmates are there on account of ulcers. Those caused by syphilis or frambœsia I now always treat with intravenous injections of neosalvarsan, which I never had the means of doing before. The treatment requires about a month. I am also trying new preparations of bismuth, and, as it seems to me, with good results.

For children with frambœsia, who are often covered all over with sores, I do not as a rule rely on the intravenous injections of salvarsan. I have no need to subject them with their tiny arm veins, to this often long and tedious torment. The new drug called stovarsol saves me from that. It is given in the form of easily swallowed pastilles. In four days the scabs over the sores begin to dry up; in eight or ten they fall off, and the child is permanently cured of the disease. Unfortunately this drug is very expensive.

I allow the rumour to spread everywhere that my principle is to give stovarsol only in return for stitched raphia leaves, though I am unable to enforce the restriction. Many a poor mother is not in a position to obtain stitched leaves with which to secure from the doctor the treatment of her child. Still, I have been able, thanks to stovarsol, to get some square yards of roof covered. Chaulmoogra oil, too, it is my principle to give only in return for stitched leaves or bananas, at least to the people in the neighbourhood. Those who come from a distance cannot load their canoes with such things. They must be thankful if they are able to bring with them their sleeping mats, their cooking pot, their supply of food, and whatever else they will need for the journey, or while they are camping at the hospital.

On the whole, the patients and their companions are really grateful, especially the lepers, those with heart complaints, those whose ulcers have been treated with neosalvarsan, and those who came on account of accidents or wounds. Only I must not be too eager to get tangible proofs of gratitude. If the son of a convalescent father is to help for four or five days at our building or other efforts at improvement, or even to go into the forest to fetch timber, I must encourage his impulse to gratitude with a few presents to prevent its disappearing like an expiring lamp-flame.

The chief of a little village in the Samkita district is with me just now for treatment of a damaged hand, the result of the bursting of the gun with which he was trying to shoot a wild pig. This kind of accident happens much more frequently now than it used to. Down to ten years ago they used to sell to the natives flintlock muskets which had come down from the military stores of the good old times. Now that these honestly-made weapons are sold out, there come to Africa similar muskets of the worst possible make, the barrels of which have more lead than steel in their compositon. These treacherous weapons are used with the same heavy charges that were safe with the old style. And a black sportsman, let me add thinks he can never cram enough powder into the barrel. Moreover, he likes best to use as bullets fagments of cast-iron cooking pots. Such charges as that are too much for the modern factory musket; hence the many injuries caused by bursting guns.

My little chief, for all the gratitude he feels toward us, takes care to let Noel and me feel from the very first day that he is a chief, while we are only ordinary mortals. When I begin to bandage him only once a day instead of examining his wound both morning and evening, I must humbly explain to him the reason for it. His authority, however, is not far-reaching enough to bring his relatives, who spend the whole day in the hospital, to show their gratitude by doing a little public work for us. To get from him one hundred and fifty stitched leaves I have to threaten to stop dressing his hand and to let it "go bad," and as no danger is involved I do, in fact, carry out my threat by not looking at his hand for three or four days. Of the five hundred of which I got a promise if his hand got healed, I have as yet seen nothing. But, nevertheless, I think kindly of him. He is in his own way a fine man. There are many things about which one must not argue with a primitive.

That the sufferers from sleeping-sickness and ulcers have to be treated with intravenous injections means a vast amount of work. There are often twenty such injections to be made in one day, and to make them for black people is much more difficult than to make them for white. There is no such bluish tint as shows through the skin of the latter the position of the veins. Moreover, in many cases scratches and cutaneous eruptions have turned our patients' skins into a coat of mail through which the most practised finger can no longer find any blood vessel. Many sleeping-sickness victims, too, are mere skeletons whose miserable little veins make intravenous injections terribly difficult. Repeated trials are therefore necessary before the needle can find the right way for itself. These difficult cases, a single one of which may sometimes demand an hour's work, are always left to take their turn when the "good veins" have been dealt with. One little girl with sleeping-sickness, Zitombo by name, is the patient we most dread. Many a lump of sugar must be put into her mouth to stop her tears while the needle goes again and again into her poor little arm in search of the vein. And when it is all over, she is carried out of the hospital on the doctor's arm. Saturday is the great day for sleeping-sickness injections, and on that day Madame Herrmann knows that we shall be an hour or two late to meals. But she is very forebearing with us.

Luckily, Noel has acquired very quickly the technique of intravenous injections, so he is able to spare me much work.

Among the natives Noel is known as "the lieutenant." Ever since the military administration of the colony began, it has been the rule to have an official called a lieutenant, in addition to the district captain, and as the people have known army surgeons only, I too have in their eyes something of a military character. Thus it comes easily to them to regard my white colleague as the doctor's lieutenant. Noel has become quite accustomed to the soubriquet, and no one calls him anything else at the mission station.

The praiseworthy habit of dumping sick persons at my hospital and then making themselves scarce has not been lost by the Ogowe people. I have been here barely a fortnight when I find lying in front of it an old man with heart disease, almost naked, and without either blanket or mosquito net, no one knowing how he got there. He himself claims to have a large number of influential relations near Samkita, some of whom will very soon be coming to bring a good supply of food for him and a handsome present for me. I give him a blanket and a mosquito net and some food, and he is with us for several weeks until death releases him. Even when he can hardly speak he continues to refer to his rich relations who will certainly come, and the last service I can do for him in life is to listen to his assurances as if I believed them! The patient next to him, who was deposited here in just the same way, is waiting for his death in order to have the use of his mosquito net and blanket, for the supply of these, which came with my personal baggage, is exhausted, and the seventy-three cases which were sent off from Strasbourg, in February, are still undelivered.

A woman, too, from a village not far from Lambaréné, as ragged and as near death as the men, has been deposited here. She has no one at all belonging to her, so no one in the village troubles about her. A neighbour's wife, so I am told, asked another woman to lend her an axe that she might get a little firewood for the old woman to keep her warm during the damp nights. "What?" was the answer, "an axe for that old woman? Take her to the doctor, and leave her there till she dies." And that was what happened.

The prospect of people getting accustomed to depositing here sick or old neighbours whom they want to get rid of is a dangerous one, for it means a heavy burden on the hospital, such persons being sometimes on our hands for months. It means also a great increase in our death-rate, and this depresses the other inmates, especially as the deaths take place before their eyes. For I have not yet got any separate room for hopeless cases.

With the medicine-men, my native colleagues, it never happens that a patient dies. They reject hopeless cases at once, acting in this respect like many doctors in European hospitals, who do not want to have their statistics spoilt. And if a medicine-man does unexpectedly lose a patient, he protects his reputation by finding out at once who bewitched the dead man so that he could not escape dying. The view of the natives is that the very first proof of medical skill is for the doctor to know whether his patient will die or not, so that he may not waste his skill on one who, to speak accurately, is already dead. If he does treat one who afterwards dies, that only proves that he does not even know whether the illness will be fatal or can be cured. Even during my first stay here Joseph was always urging me to get rid of the obviously doomed so as not to damage my reputation. And the same question is still facing us to-day.

Three such foundlings have recently died one after another, and there was grumbling in the hospital. One man with a phagedenic ulcer, on whom I had spent much time and trouble, had himself fetched home by his relations, and two others followed his example. It is not the first time that I have had this experience, but I do not let it modify my ideas. My hospital is open to all sufferers. Even if I cannot save them from death I can at least show them love, and perhaps make their end easier. They are welcome, therefore, to come at night and lay such poor creatures at my door. If I succeed in bringing one of them through, I have no need to trouble about how I am to get him home. The news that he is capable of working and therefore can be made use of again, will reach his village at once, and any night they may come and fetch him away as secretly as they brought him.

At the grave of the poor woman for whom they would not provide even a little firewood, Mons. Herrmann spoke in touching words of how she was cast off by her own people, but met with tenderness among strangers, because through Jesus love had come into the world. And beautiful was the sunlight as it streamed through the palm trees upon the poor grave, while the school children sang a funeral hymn.

A burial gives us a great deal of trouble. The procedure is not so easy as putting a pick or a spade into the hands of three or four of those who have come here with the patient, promising them a present, and getting them to dig the grave. If there is a death, every man who can use a spade has generally disappeared, ostensibly to fish, or to go home to fetch food. The native will have nothing to do with a dead stranger, and primitive religious ideas about "uncleanness" play their part in producing this refusal. If, for example, a birth is expected in a family, no member of it may have anything to do with a corpse. Often, too, the parents have vowed at the birth of a child that it shall never come into contact with a corpse, and this vow it must observe.

Once I succeeded in concealing the fact of a death during the night, and so surprising with the request that they would dig a grave two young men whose ulcers were well on the way to healing, that they could not escape. But when I put the tools into their hands with the promise of a handsome present, they knelt before me with tears in their eyes, and besought me not to compel them to do what they ought not to do. And I could not bring myself to compel them. In the Epistle to the Romans (chapter xiv) S. Paul orders us to respect weak consciences, and the command holds good to-day in Africa as well as elsewhere. The Catholic Mission has the same difficulty to contend with. A native woman belonging to Catholic circles once died with us, on which I informed the Father Superior, and asked whether he would bury her in the Catholic cemetery. "Yes," he replied, "if people come to dig a grave for her. We have had to give up expecting this work to be done by our schoolboys."

Our digging is generally done by those who are being trained at the mission station to be evangelists; but when they are not at hand, we have to do it ourselves. Noel has often officiated as sexton and bearer. That G'Mba in these cases rises above all prejudices and gives valuable help, I reckon as very much to his credit.

* * *

The midday hour is the worst of the whole day, for then every creature who can crawl comes to the consulting-room and asks for a "ration." This food-ration consists of about 600 grams (*c.* 21 oz.) of rice with some salt, or seven to ten big bananas, or three to six sticks of manioc. For fat we distribute palm-oil, or, if that is not to be had, tinned vegetable fat imported from Europe. Sometimes there is dried fish, either carp from the Ogowe, which, after the big fishing expeditions in the dry season, is dried over big fires and stored in sacks, or sea-fish from the coast waters of Angola. The patients do their own cooking.

My principle is to give the ration only to those who have come a long distance, or are really poor and have to stay here a considerable time, though I give it also to those who have been working for me on that particular day. These, however, receive at midday only half the ration; the rest they get in the evening, for if they got it at noon they might refuse to do any more work.

But every day there are cases which invite me to abandon my principle, and give rations which were not foreseen as needed. A man who was working for me the previous day is unwell to-day, but hopes to work again to-morrow; he therefore demands a ration to-day. Or sick people who have hitherto received bananas and manioc from their villages come up because for two days none have arrived. The people at home have perhaps no canoe at their disposal, they say; or they cannot beat up a crew; or the men in the canoe have been taken up by black soldiers because they have not paid their taxes for the gear; or wild pigs have devastated the plantation. . . . I am worked upon with a score of such possible explanations of the stoppage of supplies, till at last I yield, and instruct G'Mba, who is standing behind the rice-trough, to put the petitioners on the list of those to be fed till further notice. But how often the result is that their names are there permanently! If the people in the village get to know that I do not let their relatives starve because their supply of food is delayed, their zeal for supplying it cools down very considerably.

Here is another case. A patient arrives who has some money and with his attendants receives his daily rations from me in return for a reasonable payment. The village is much too far away for supplies to be brought to him, or it is perhaps in a famine district. The illness is protracted, and his money gives out, so he stands in the crowd at midday and begs to be fed with them till further notice. His condition is not such that I can send him away. So what am I to do? I have to feed him and his, and screw myself up to the belief that he will some day make good his promise to reimburse me for my expenditure.

How often, on hearing the Strasbourg cathedral clock strike midday, have I said to myself: "This is just the time when, in Africa, you'll have the palaver about rations, and be lucky if it does not last more than an hour."

Still, I must not be too strict with the petitioners. Not long ago I began to treat with narcotics a man who was getting his food from home, and when I asked him whether he had obeyed my instructions for such cases, not to eat anything in the morning before treatment, he replied: "I've had nothing at all to eat for two days." Because I always show myself so incredulous of the reasons given for the non-arrival of food supplies, he and his wife had not ventured to say anything about their hunger. Of course they were at once put on the list of recipients.

When I am unable to get away from other work, G'Mba distributes the rations and decides with Solomon-like wisdom whether to give ear to new entreaties or not. And he is much harder than I am. The fact that, driven by necessity, I am compelled to leave the control of it all to him is a great temptation. I can only hope that he does not succumb to it.

The usual number of rations given out daily is between twenty and thirty, though it is often larger. What a number of sacks of rice we have already got through!

Directly after Whitsuntide we have to stop for a time the rebuilding of the second sick-ward, and work with all haste at a strong cell for the mental cases. One of the sleeping-sickness patients, a young woodcutter, N'Gonde by name, has what is often incidental to that disease, viz., fits of excitement, and becomes dangerous. Half a dozen planks are all that I have available. These are nailed to posts fixed in the ground and form the frame-work of the cell. The spaces between are filled with lengths of hard wood in the round, as thick as one's arm, which are nailed to the planks. The constructor of this provisional cell is Noel, and for more than ten days the posts and N'Gonde together make his life a misery; the former because they are of magnificent African hardwood, so hard that the nails always bend while being hammered into it, and the latter because he always manages to find the weak spots in Noel's work and to break out either at dinner time or during the night. To enable Noel to work, I have to keep the patient quiet for hours together with scopolamia and morphia. We have no place in which to put him except the cell under construction, for all the living rooms in the hospital are, of course, constructed just of bamboos and stitched-leaf tiles.

Scarcely is the cell finished, when the floor of our rotten fowl-house falls in under Noel's weight as he is counting the fowls one evening, and that brings about a sympathetic collapse of the walls. Repairs are out of the question, for no nail would hold in the rotten wood, so all other work has to be abandoned and a new fowl-house built as quickly as possible—yes, as quickly as possible, because the old one affords not the slightest protection against snakes or leopards.

Meanwhile, I have discovered, very fortunately, that the husband of a sleeping-sickness patient knows something about carpentry. As his wife is improving, Monenzalie—that is his name—agrees to work regularly for me in return for food and presents.

* * *

At last, on June 21st, the steamer brings my seventy-three packing-cases. On the same day there arrives a strong motor-boat for the mission station, and with it a new twenty-three-year-old missionary, Mons. Abrezol, from Switzerland. He has learnt in Europe how to manage a motor-boat, and at once places himself and the boat at our disposal for towing canoes which must bring my cases from the steamer's landing-place. There they must be on the grass in the open, exposed to rain and thieves unless we succeed in bringing them over before nightfall. The Catholic Mission lends us a big canoe which can take my eight biggest cases at once, and the motor-boat makes it possible for the canoes to make two journeys in the afternoon. Finally, about sundown, there actually arrives by chance a small steamer belonging to a Dutch timber-merchant, who has been under my care for weeks. Of course, his steamer is requisitioned for help with the transport, and by eight o'clock all the cases, except that containing the cooking-stove, are lodged in the open canoe shed. There they will have to stay for two or three weeks protected from rain so far as the holes in the roof allow, and from thieves so far as is ensured by the wakefulness of the two patients whom I install there as watchmen.

Meanwhile the departure of Mons. Pelot leaves the doctor's house free, and we can now use all its four rooms. The most urgent repairs are hastily effected, and then the cases are unpacked. We have no cupboards yet, but they are to be provided from the big cases, which have been specially made so that they can be fitted with handles and fixed one upon the other. This work can only be done bit by bit, but the cases must be unpacked at once; the open canoe shed is a very dangerous place for them. So we can do nothing but pile their contents higgledy-piggledy in the corners of the rooms; linen and kitchen apparatus, surgical instruments and curtains, boots and medicine bottles, books and bandages. To find any particular thing needed, we have to excavate, and tunnel into the piles, like those who want to desecrate the royal tombs in Egypt. This nomadic misery is slightly more tolerable because, having foreseen it while in Strasbourg, I got friendly hands to sew together by the dozen sacks of different sizes, into each of which, as we unpack, we can stuff things of the same category.

From our third week here onwards we have always had two or three white patients, room for them being provided by Noel taking up his quarters on the verandah.

*　*　*

On July 18th we welcome Mademoiselle Mathilde Kottmann from Strasbourg as nurse. Now the clouds are beginning to lift. Never again will our white patients find their beds made with tablecloths instead of sheets. Noel will no longer be responsible for the filling of the lamps, the boiling of the drinking water, or for getting the weekly washing done. Nor will he, in future, have to go in the evening and count the fowls, or conduct a search for possible eggs. I myself shall be relieved of the superintendence of the kitchen and all that is in it. And the piles of goods into which we had to tunnel are disappearing, if slowly, into the cupboards that we have made out of piled up packing-cases.

At first, indeed, Mademoiselle Kottmann had for weeks so much to do in the house, and in looking after the white patients, that she hardly counted for anything in the hospital. For that, Joseph has at last come back and taken up his work again. How long he will stay I do not know. The timber-trading fever has attacked him too, and he and a few friends have rented a big area of forest which they mean to exploit with workmen engaged for a year. I have to promise that he can absent himself at any time to look after his business. At first his wife takes his place as foreman at the timber site, which is three days' journey from here. But I am afraid that Joseph, like so many natives who engage in the timber-trade on their own account, will lose money instead of making it.

It gives me great pleasure that some of the few native timber-merchants who have been fairly successful, mean to give me, at the suggestion of Emil Ogouma, some considerable donation for the upkeep of the hospital. They wish to contribute as nearly as they can the cost of Mlle. Kottmann's voyage, but I am not sure that such a sum will be collected.

For a good many weeks after Whitsuntide I feel unwell. I have to drag myself to work and I am scarcely back from the hospital at midday and in the evening when I have to lie down. I cannot even manage to make out the order for the necessary drugs and dressings. It is the roof of the hospital that is chiefly to blame for this. I had not noticed that it showed again a number of holes, and I no doubt got several slight sunstrokes. A roof of stitched leaves should really be examined every day. The slightest blast of wind is enough to push the rotten leaves up against one another in such a way that another hole is made.

* * *

At the end of May the dry season begins here, and it lasts to the middle of September. This year, however, it does not begin at all. Rainstorms come continually one after another.

That there should be no dry season is something that the natives have never experienced or heard the old people talk of. This gives a shock to many Christians, because, since the native languages have no words for summer and winter, the missionaries have translated the promise of God in Genesis, made after the Flood: "While the earth remaineth, wet season and dry season, day and night, shall never cease." So now they want to be told why it is that the weather does not go on as the Bible says it will.

In July we are greatly upset by the death of the latest missionary recruit, Mons. Abrezol. Although an exceptionally good swimmer, he was drowned while bathing at dawn in a lake near N'Gômô, before the eyes of Mons. Herrmann and Noel, with whom he was on a journey[1]. His body was found, but could not be brought to Lambaréné, since the motor-boat had been damaged by grounding on a sandbank. So he was buried on the hill at N'Gômô. He was a lovable and extraordinarily good all-round man and had won all hearts.

---

[1] Since then several people have been drowned in the same body of water or similar ones, in a quite unaccountable way, and we assume that they were paralysed by being stung by an electric fish.

At the beginning of August Mons. and Madame Morel came to us for a fortnight in order to start for Alsace from here. They have to take the river-steamer here, since it is uncertain whether, with the lower water-level, it will be able to go up as far as Samkita.

Mons. Morel had not long before killed a boa-constrictor near the girls' school. As it was shot with my gun, I got, as was fitting, half of it for the hospital. Unfortunately, it was only five-and-a-half feet long, and not very fat. The patients very nearly came to blows over the distribution of this dainty.

In the third week of August Noel left us, at the same time as Mons. Morel. I do not know how to thank sufficiently this good comrade for all the help he gave me. His typewriter, which he used like a practised typist, will be sorely missed by my poor tired hand. But he himself, amid his lectures at Oxford, will remember as if it were a dream, how once he was, in Africa, doctor's assistant, carpenter, foreman, sexton, and other things besides.

The doctor's house is never without a white patient as an inmate, and some of these remain for several weeks. Just after Noel's departure four came in about the same time. Those of them who come fresh after several months of camp life at a timber site, can hardly realise at first that they are now lying in a proper clean bed. The wife of one of them, who had been sharing the loneliness of the forest with her husband, had first of all to get accustomed to seeing several white people together.

Now at last I have my permanent cook, viz., Aloys, who was in my service during my first period here. He is quite clever, under Mlle. Kottmann's direction, at providing from very limited resources attractive and well varied diets for the patients. One of them had had for several weeks, during a severe attack of fever, nothing to eat but tinned foods, which he was not even able to warm.

The white patients belong to all nationalities. In my little Visitors' Book there are names of English, Swiss, Dutch, Swedish, Canadian, and American patients. Most of them come because of ulcers on the feet or malaria, but I have had two cases of blackwater fever, one of them serious, the other at a very early stage of it. Blackwater fever is a sequela of malaria, producing, under conditions which are not yet understood, a general destruction of the red blood-corpuscles.

The resulting débris blocks the kidneys and thus endangers life. The red pigment set free by the destruction of the corpuscles appears in the urine and gives it a dark red colour; hence the name of the disease. The treatment has for its object the arrest of this process of destruction, and this is best attained by eight-hourly injections of half a litre (about three-quarters of a pint) of a sterilised three per cent solution of common salt. This is very painful, but effective, and, if begun fairly early in the course of the disease, usually saves the patient. One gives at the same time a subcutaneous injection of 20 c.c. of serum. We use for this the anti-snake-bite serum of the Pasteur Institute, which we always keep in stock.

I am having a great deal of trouble with a Canadian who came with numerous deep-seated muscle abscesses. No sooner was one opened than another showed itself. Up to now my lancet has operated on eight. How long the patient can hold out under the discharges of pus, and the constant accompanying fever, weakened as he is by five years in the tropics and exhausting work on timber sites, I cannot predict.

Such abscesses, which are always multiple, are common here, with whites and blacks alike. The latter, however, never suffer from blackwater fever.

A sailor who wanted to try his luck at timber-dealing as well, was recently brought to me suffering, after only a few weeks in the district, from pneumonia, and already with the death-rattle in his throat. He died almost immediately, and I found the words, "No luck," tattoed on his chest.

Just at present we have to call up daily at bandaging-time "the leopard man." This is a quiet young fellow who was attacked by a leopard while asleep in his hut. The animal seized his right arm with its paw, but released him on people hurrying up with a light. As the natives know by experience what terrible infection is caused by a leopard's claws, they put the man into a canoe at once to bring him to me. On his arrival twelve hours later the arm was already swollen and hard to the touch, and extremely painful. Fever had set in too. In the skin itself no sign of injury could be seen except four tiny marks which might have been made with a needle. But when the place was opened with a lancet it could be seen that the claws had torn the flesh right down to the bone. Our leopard man will very soon be fit to return home, and meanwhile he makes himself useful by helping to iron the linen.

N'Gonde, too, the sleeping-sickness patient for whom the isolation-cell had to be built, is cured. As he has neither home nor relatives, he will remain in service here as general *factotum*. His chief task will be roof-mending, at which he is an expert. No sooner was he really better than he said to me: "Now that you have cured me, buy me a wife." That was a job at which I did not jump, but he now has a money-box for savings towards the purchase of a wife. Since becoming roof-mender, he has renounced the name of N'Gonde, and calls himself Ambrosius.

Madame Herrmann and Mlle. Arnoux are kind enough to hold a short service every evening about sunset in among the smoky fires and the seething cooking pots, and the conversation about the Bible passages read out is often lengthy. On one occasion a native, and one of the real savages, too, took Mlle. Arnoux to task because she read out that no one had ever seen God. That, he said, was untrue; he himself had once caught sight of God in the forest.

*　　*　　*

The rainstorms continue, and it is a great misfortune for the country. From May to August is the period when vegetation should be cut down and burnt so that fresh land, manured with wood-ash, may be used for banana plantations. But since this year it is always raining, the people have no heart for cutting down anything, for it will never get dry enough to burn. So we shall have to face a year of famine.

Moreover, since the water keeps at a high level, the natives cannot make any big fishing expeditions, and there are nowhere to be found those supplies of smoked fish which, as a rule, satisfy for months in the year the demand for flesh-food. The Catholic Mission, which usually has a good supply of everything, has only about five hundred small carp in store for their children. The Father Superior, therefore, who is an excellent shot, goes out hippo-hunting with twelve boys, a whole day's journey away. That means that they must pass the night on a sandbank, or in a swamp in the rain. Then they will return two or three weeks later, perhaps empty-handed, perhaps with the canoe full of smoked hippotamus flesh, and the latter means that the schoolwork will go on satisfactorily all through the winter. A negro-boy who gets meat to eat two or three times a week is willing and eager to learn; without meat he is a listless creature who, even if he is well stuffed with rice, is always complaining of being hungry. The inhabitants of the primeval forest have an almost diseased hunger for flesh meat.

And now I cannot help fearing that my narrative has given my readers far too much of the prose of Africa, but whatever one gets drowned in fills the mouth. Our life is so filled with this prose that I cannot but write about it. Anyone who wants to do good under our African conditions must fight any tendency in himself to let his nerves and temper be upset by all the big and little difficulties of daily life, and must retain his full joy in his work. So it is all to the good that our far-away friends should experience with us something of the prose of Africa. They are thus in a position to estimate what good it does us here to receive proofs of their affection.

14 LATE AUTUMN TO CHRISTMAS, 1924

EARLIER than I had ventured to hope has come the fulfilment of my dream of having a doctor to help me. On October 19th, a countryman of my own, Victor Nessmann, began work here. He is the son of a pastor in Alsace, who, when qualifying for the profession, was my fellow-student in Strasbourg.

And his help came in the very nick of time. Not a day longer could I have supported the double burden of builder and doctor. How I had suffered from being unable to make my examinations of patients as thorough as they should have been, because in spite of all my efforts I could not summon sufficient energy for the task! And how it had disquieted me that with the strong and risky remedies that so many tropical diseases demand, I could not give sufficient time to each patient! How often ought microscope and test-tube to have been called upon for guidance and were not! In surgery, too, only the necessary minimum was undertaken.

So the hoot of the river-steamer which is bringing my countryman, means my release from the distress of medical work which, in spite of the best of good will has to be too superficial. The canoes are quickly manned, and very soon, amid the gently falling rain of the just beginning wet season, we lay to at the side of the steamer, and my young countryman, who does not know yet what fatigue is, signals me from the deck. "Now you shall rest, and I will take over all the work," are his words when we shake hands. "Good," I answer; "then begin at once, and look after the loading of the canoes with your trunks and cases." Here is already a test of fitness for life in Africa. Piled on the deck in fine disorder are the trunks and cases. Each passenger has to collect his own from the various heaps and see that his men leave none behind; also that they carry off nothing belonging to someone else, that they let nothing fall into the river, and that they distribute the weight properly in the canoes. The new doctor, who is regarded with astonishment by the natives on account of his youthful appearance, shows himself to be a skilful stevedore. During the passage to shore I can hardly get a word out, so overcome do I feel by the fact that I now have a professional colleague. It is blissful to be able to confess to myself how tired I am.

What was indicated in the transport job is confirmed again and again in the next few days; the new doctor seems to have been made for Africa! He is of a practical turn of mind, has the gift of organisation, and knows how to tackle the natives. Moreover, he has a sense of humour, without which no one can get on properly out here. In spite of his well-developed body he is called by the natives "the little doctor," "little" meaning in the language of this district "young."

He is soon quite accustomed to our medical routine, though during the first few weeks he does occasionally betray himself as a newcomer. Having, for example, with much trouble spelt out the quite impossible name of a quite raw native for entry in the register of patients, he goes on, unconsciously following the practice in Europe, to ask for his Christian name!

About the middle of November we lose, through death,

our loyal second orderly, G'Mba. Having with leave of absence spent All Saints' Day and All Souls' Day (November
1st and 2nd) with relatives, he returned through heavy rain,
and caught cold. Fever supervened, and with all our drugs
we could not master it. He himself was quite aware of the
seriousness of his condition. By the end of the second week
the fever had quite broken down his power of resistance, and
his last days were passed in a state of coma. The anxious be-
seeching looks which he directed at us whenever we were
treating him I can never forget, and his death affected us all
deeply.

G'Mba was born to be a hospital orderly, and he loved his
work, only we could never get him to recognise that care for
order and cleanliness in the hospital was one of his duties. He
would look on unperturbed while patients' wives threw their
slops and kitchen refuse on the ground in front of the wards
instead of taking them to the rubbish-heap. On one occasion
when, not for the first time, I called him to account for this,
he answered: "Well, what am I to say to them? My own wife
doesn't obey me. How can I expect the other women to listen to me?"

Joseph, too, does not like having anything to do with the
non-medical side of the hospital work, because it means having to argue with the sick and their relatives; nor can I
feel really annoyed with him. It is very difficult for any native,
whatever his position, to secure obedience from his fellows.
At the timber camps the work is made very much harder
because it is impossible to find any black foremen who can
exert authority. The new doctor and I have, therefore, to
undertake the duty of supervision in the hospital and everywhere else, and waste far too much time in argumentations
big and little instead of being able to leave such things to
our staff. So it may happen that the new doctor, who relieves
me as much as he can in this matter, has to spend a couple of
hours trying to discover which woman it was who threw the
kitchen-refuse into the path. As examining-magistrate also
he is showing himself to be first-class!

G'Mba's place is taken by Dominic, one of our convales-
cents, and he shows himself to be fairly adaptable, though
unfortunately he can neither read nor write.

It means a great lightening of our work that Joseph has
mastered fairly well the technique of intravenous injections,

which play such an important part in the treatment of tropical diseases. With a sufficient amount of supervision, this work can be left almost entirely to him, and it often takes up a whole morning.

* * *

The presence of the new doctor allows me to give, if necessary, almost the whole day to the building work. The first thing to be done is to provide the two completed buildings with beds, for hitherto I have had enough to do in making and mending roofs. When I say beds, of course I do not use the word in the European sense.

I myself put the frames together with the help of Minkoë, a seventeen-year-old native, whom Madame Morel sent to me from Samkita at the beginning of the summer in pitiable condition with a huge ulcer on one of his feet. Having been cured with neosalvarsan he makes himself as useful as he can. Towards evening the new doctor generally comes to join me, so as to get some change and relief from his medical work by handling hammer and saw.

I want to fit up my hospital with bed-frames of hardwood, which will rest upon posts in the ground, but can be lifted from the posts and taken out into the sun to be cleaned. In order to make full use of the space protected by the roofs, I put a second tier of beds above the first, as one finds in railway sleeping-cars. The inner part consists of a layer of strips of hardwood of uniform thickness, over which thin bamboos are bound with small vine stems.

Quite the simplest way of making the beds would be to use planks, but I have none available, nor any prospect of securing a sufficient number in the near future. I have, therefore, to make them with hardwood strips and bamboos, which works out more expensively than the dearest planks would be and costs me far more toil. What a number of days have to be spent in collecting the materials! What a number of presents and rations I have to distribute to the people who, under the leadership of Minkoë, undertake the many necessary journeys into the forest and the swamps!

At last about forty beds are ready. Next there is needed a hut which can be locked, for the storage of paddles and tools. There is urgent need, too, for a room where we can store bananas and sacks of rice, and for a big chest with partitions for the sorting and piling together of the tins and big and little bottles in which we give the patients their medicines. How easy everything would be if we had planks! How complicated and troublesome it is if one has to work with wood in the round, especially if it has to be fetched from a distance! And what a task it is to build with such material something which will be safe against thieves!

Often the work ceases for a whole day because the men refuse to go off into the forest. They want first to have a thorough rest from their last expedition. Or it is raining, and then no one can get the natives of Equatorial Africa to work. A day of rain they take as a God-given day of rest. Still, in this objection to getting wet they are not far wrong. Since all natives here are more or less infected with malaria germs, the slightest chill may start an attack of fever, and I myself always take care to give them as little as possible to do in rainy weather.

When these store-rooms are ready, another ward is taken in hand, calculated to hold thirty beds, for the number of our patients is always growing. Every evening now it falls to us to offer shelter to sixty or seventy sick folk without counting those who accompany them. We must also, some day, have a special room with fifteen beds for those who have undergone an operation. If we ever get to practising surgery to the extent that is called for here, it will no longer do for the subjects to be placed among the other sick, just where there happens to be room.

While I give up a great part of my time to these various works, Monenzalie, the carpenter who came here with his wife suffering from sleeping-sickness, is busy constructing a small house of three rooms. It will be built on piles, with a floor of planks and the usual roof of leaf-tiles, and will be for the new doctor and the white patients. To its construction are devoted all the beams and planks I can get hold of. In answer to pressing entreaties I get some old beams offered to me from various quarters. Planks are sawn for me from time to time in small quantities at the saw-pit of the Mission at N'Gômô, but then there is the task of getting the wood here. They have to be brought more than twenty-five miles upstream, and some of the beams that have been given me nearly sixty-five miles. Moreover, navigation may be made more difficult by a period of flood. Too often, then, the work on the house for the new doctor and the white patients comes to a stop because there are neither beams nor planks at hand. It is often interrupted, too, because the black carpenter must give all his time to his wife, who is already quite helpless. And he looks after her with touching patience.

He does his work fairly well, but cannot use the foot-rule properly, because he has never put himself on familiar terms with printed figures. If I tell him that one door must be four inches wider than the rest, he looks at me with embarrassment, and asks me to show him on the foot-rule how much that is. Consequently, I have to visit the work frequently, give him the measurements, and see that he keeps to them. All the problems, too, which arise from the differences in length and thickness between the beams which our begging has collected require my presence.

Till the new house is ready the young doctor lives in the roomy dwelling of the missionary, Mons. Herrmann. There the white patients also receive kind hospitality, if there is no room in my house.

* * *

The stream of black patients that comes to us now is much stronger than it was during my first residence here, but they are people of a quite different class, and I have regretfully to confess that my hospital is no longer what it was then. This is the result of economic changes in the Ogowe district.

When I was here before, the people who sought my help belonged with few exceptions to the settled population of the country. To-day a large proportion of my patients are savages who have moved hither from the interior, and now work in groups fifty to a hundred together, at the white man's timber-felling centres in the forest. They are homeless proletarians in the saddest and worst sense of that word.

This migration of the population from the interior to the region of the lower Ogowe creates serious social and economic problems. In itself it is natural, and it is hardly possible to stop it, for the population here is diminishing in number, and it is far from large enough to provide the timber trade with the amount of labour-power which is needed for the exploitation of the forests. There must, therefore, be migrations from the interior, if industry and commerce are not to be crippled.

In our district the immigrant proletarians are, so far as I can judge, a fifth at any rate of the population; they may be more.

But to what extent is it permissible that the interior be depopulated for the benefit of the Ogowe forests, and our district burdened with proletarians? For a depopulation of the interior is already setting in of itself, in consequence partly of the epidemic of influenza which raged after the war, and partly of the famine which prevailed during the same period, not to mention the ravages of sleeping-sickness. The subsequent movement of so many of its capable workers means for each district not only a further diminution of the population, but also a perpetuation of the famine. Who is to clear away the forest and lay out the plantations, if none but women, children, and old men are left in the villages? For our district, too, the influx of these men means likewise perpetuation of the famine, for being engaged on nothing but the obtaining of timber, they can lay out no plantations and they increase the consumption of the already short supply of the foodstuffs which are produced here.

In view of these circumstances attempts are made to regulate the migration from the interior, and to limit it so far as it is bound up with the labour needs of the timber trade. Decrees have been issued that only a fixed proportion of the men of a village may enlist to work in the Ogowe forests. It is also laid down that no one may stay here for a long period. Settlement here is absolutely forbidden. At the expiry of their labour contract, that is at the end of one or two years, these workers have to return to their villages.

The recruiting of labourers, therefore, is not carried on just as the European employers would like; it is regulated down to the smallest details. The timber-merchant who wants lumbermen must make his wants known to the authorities. Then he gets permission to go into the interior and secure a definite number of men. The district from which he may get them, and the date by which the recruiting must be finished, are definitely laid down. He often has to travel some 250 miles through forest, swamp, or open country before reaching the villages named. When the contract period is ended, he cannot just let his labourers go; he must take the whole gang back to their homes. It is hoped that with these measures the evil will be controlled.

There are, however, people with knowledge of the situation, some of them Government officials, who were once in favour of allowing labourers from the interior to bring their wives and children and settle in the Ogowe forests, which offer them permanent employment. These settlers would then themselves lay out plantations and find themselves living under far more favourable conditions in every way than they do at present, when they just camp here without homes. Then, too, they would not make such demands on the foodstuffs produced by the resident natives as they do now.

I am myself inclined to agree with this theory, but have to admit that it takes no account of one important fact. At the end of two or three years, sometimes even sooner, a timber site, however large it is, has to be abandoned. That does not mean that all the timber in the neighbourhood has been felled, but only that there is none left which can be rolled, without excessive trouble, into the water, or can be removed without too much expense in laying down a temporary line of iron rails. When spots are reached where there is not a recognised proportion of okoumé (false mahogany) trees to the hectare, that being the only kind of tree which is considered worth exporting, the exploitation of that patch of forest is not worth while. The camp has therefore to be transferred elsewhere to a spot, perhaps thirty or sixty miles away, where there is a good supply of okoumé trees, growing on level ground and near the water. This would bring the labourers into the position of having to abandon their plantations just when they were beginning to be productive, which is not till between two and three years after the laying out. On the new site, again, not only the labourers but their families would have to live for over a year on the food produced in the district at the expense of its original population, or, if there were no food for them, would have to be supplied with rice imported from Europe or India.

Far-sighted Europeans try to solve the problem of the timber trade's food supply by having plantations laid out beforehand in the neighbourhood of sites marked out for future exploitation, so that they will be producing just when the tree-felling begins. But this planting for the future is very expensive. First of all, a body of labourers has to be maintained on this far-off spot, and they, since there is no European supervision, generally do nothing at all. The plan is often made impossible anyhow by the shortage of labour, every available man being employed on the cutting and rolling of timber.

I take this opportunity of correcting the mistaken idea that the timber-merchants here all get rich through the sweat of the natives whose labour they hire. If any of them does once in a way make a huge profit, he generally owes it to a stroke of luck which is not likely to be repeated for some time. That was the case this year, for example, with a young man who ventured into the timber trade without any previous experience. In his unsuspecting simplicity he undertook the exploitation of some fine growths which his rivals seemed to have overlooked. They were, however, in portions of forest from which the timber could be moved only when the water was abnormally high. He was therefore on the high road to losing all the money and trouble which he was putting into the job. But this year the autumn flood reached a height to which it had not risen for years. The timber, which according to ordinary estimates had been cut down entirely in vain, could be got into the water with ease and without any extra expense. The river itself came up to fetch it away. The contractor returned home with a fine balance of profit, and—will come back, enticed by the primeval forest, to make a similar venture when the water is less obliging, to lose everything, and to finish heavily in debt!

Generally speaking, the profits made in the timber trade cannot be called more than modest considering the amount of money invested and the hard, comfortless conditions of life on a timber site. If anyone works on credit advances, and is consequently so tied down as to the sale of his timber that he cannot make full use of any favourable chance that meets him, he must often feel relieved if he ends his business year free from debt. I have had Europeans with me for treatment, hard-working business men too, who were not in a position to repay the hospital the cost of their food and medicine, but had to ask that the debt might stand over till better times came.

It is absurd to talk of exploitation by the timber merchants of the labourers who come down from the interior, if that means that wages are too low. The work that these primitive humans do often bears no relation to the wage which has to be handed out to them at the end of their contract period. During the first months of it many of them are almost wholly useless, because they have never held an axe in their hands and have first of all to learn how to use one. Nowhere in the world, probably, strange as the statement may seem, is the total cost of labour higher in proportion to the work done than in the primeval forest.

And yet, if not in the ordinary sense victims of exploitation, these savages who have become lumbermen are creatures who must excite pity. Coming down from the open country and the hills of the interior, they cannot stand the trying climate of the Ogowe depression. They are always homesick, and all the time. The forest is to them something uncanny; still more so the water, to which they are unaccustomed. Though unable to swim, they have to deal with tree-trunks floating in lakes or rivers. Many do soon become used to it, but many more have to go on from day to day never losing their dread of the work in the water. Moreover, the regular daily work demoralises these children of nature. They always have gnawing at their hearts a longing for those intervals of *dolce far niente*, which when they were at home made up for the periods of hard work.

On the top of all this come health disturbances, which result from a change of diet. On the long laborious journey they have already begun to suffer from having to eat rice. Many arrive already half-ill as the result of it. At the timber site, indeed, so far as my experience goes, all that is possible is done for them in the matter of food. It is, of course, to the interest of the timber merchant to keep his labourers as fit as possible. A native who does not get enough to eat shirks his work, untroubled about the consequences that may follow. But with the best of will in the matter, the European is often unable to offer his men anything but perpetual rice and salted fish, the two foodstuffs which it is easiest to procure and transport, and which keep in good condition longest. Rice, however, is a food which the savage of Equatorial Africa finds, in general, much less adapted to his constitution than other people do, though why that is so I cannot say. It is certainly to some extent a result of his being too impatient to cook it for more than half the time it needs. The employers have tried to help them by distributing rice ready cooked, and prepared with fat and salt. But they will not have it. They are just savages, who will eat only what they have cooked themselves in their small pots over a smoky fire. The rice, then, plays havoc with them. They lose weight, they contract stomach and bowel troubles, and beri-beri develops among them, sometimes in a mild, sometimes in a serious form.

The harm done by the rice diet would certainly be less if they could obtain instead of the polished stuff, rice which had lost only the outer husk and had retained the inner coat. This, as is now well known, contains the vitamins, and if it is removed, the native gets a vitaminless diet which, if it is used for any considerable time as his sole foodstuff, must cause beri-beri.

I too have to feed my patients on this polished, vitaminless stuff because in spite of repeated attempts I have never yet been able to procure the other sort in sufficient quantities. Science has proved that the polished rice is a dangerous foodstuff, yet the trade delivers to its customers everywhere only this kind. Are we really living in a progressive age?

To the damaging of the bowel by this rice diet I attribute the fact that dysentery is especially frequent among the black lumbermen just at times when the shortage of bananas and manioc compels them to live on it exclusively. The bowel is then no longer capable of protecting them, as it could if they had their normal diet, from the standing infection produced by the dirty water which these savages of ours drink day after day.

Malaria too, as well as dysentery, lies in wait for these immigrant lumbermen. In their own hinterland, in the open country and on the elevated plateaux, they know nothing of mosquitoes or malaria. But on the timber sites these two evils are a serious plague.

Then there are colds and chills. These savages are very susceptible to the damp atmosphere of the forest. Then why do they not spend part of their wages on mosquito nets and blankets? Because mosquito nets are expensive, and being real savages they would rather buy tobacco and trifles than useful things. "Then their masters should be obliged to provide them with mosquito nets and blankets!" Quite right. But they would soon barter the blankets and nets for bananas or baubles of any sort which were offered them by a native from the neighbourhood, just as they dispose of their master's axes and bush knives for a trifle, and then declare that they are lost.

These labourers from up-country are attacked also in a terrible way by ulcers on their feet. It often happens that a few weeks after their arrival a large proportion of them become incapacitated for work and, as a rule, by the tropical phagedenic ulcer, the worst kind of all. First comes a small spot which festers and discharges, but of which they take no account. Then in the course of days or weeks it develops into a sore as large as one's hand, and is terribly painful. And living, as they do, overcrowded in dirty huts without even a pretence of hygiene, they of course infect each other. Sometimes I get a dozen of them at once from the same timber site, who have developed these phagedenic ulcers all by infection from one single case.

And so we can explain why my hospital, in spite of a big diminution of the population, nevertheless shows a much bigger stream of patients than before. There are fewer people, but more sick, because from the lumbermen of the hinterland a very heavy toll is exacted by the change of climate, their new diet, and the diseases already prevalent here.

* * *

What a tragedy it is when half-starved creatures like that, betrayed by their physiognomy as savages from up-country, are deposited, with their miserable little bundles of belongings, at our gate! However often one has to go through the experience, it always moves one to fresh pity. One is seized by an indescribable sympathy with these poor strangers. And how often the sympathy is quite hopeless, since it is evident at the first glance that the visitor will draw his last breath here, far away from his own people, who are waiting for his return and for the money that he ought to bring with him.

These poorest and most numerous of our guests we call "Bendjabis," because a large proportion of them belong to the Bendjabi tribe.

But the complete absence of any discipline among them makes the work of the hospital so much harder that the sight of them arouses in our hearts a complex feeling of sympathy and despair. Hence I must repeat—to my sorrow—that my hospital is no longer what it used to be.

Of order and subordination we require in the hospital only the minimum amount necessary. If a Bendjabi appears of his own accord each morning for his bandaging or his injection or to get his medicine, and does not run away because his turn does not come at once; if when the horn sounds for rations he does not wait more than half an hour before appearing with his plate; if he throws all refuse in its proper place; if he does not steal fowls from the missionary or let the latter catch him plundering his fruit trees or his banana plants; if at clean-ing-up time on Saturday afternoon he helps without too much outcry; if when the lot falls upon him and his condition allows it, he jumps into the canoe ready to paddle it; if when there are cases and sacks of rice to be unloaded he lends a hand, even if fate has willed that he has first to be routed out from be-hind his cooking-pot as fit for the job—anyone who does these things and a few others like them, passes with us for a virtuous and rational being in whom we gladly overlook many short-comings in other directions.

The Bendjabis, however, are alas! far below this ideal, modest as it is. Being real savages they are a painful distance "beyond good and evil." The rules which govern life for the hospital inmates are to them mere words which do not con-cern them. In this matter, indeed, they can appeal to the fact that these rules have never been put before them. The daily proclamation of them as described in my book, *On the Edge of the Primeval Forest* was given up long ago; the language difficulty had made it useless. Formerly we could manage with a knowledge of the Galloa and Pahouin languages; to-day there are some ten languages spoken in our wards. Dominic, G'Mba's successor, who has lived for some time in the interior, can express himself in several of them, but not in all, so that we have to deal with many patients with whom we cannot ex-change an intelligible word.

What this means was brought home to us in a tragic fashion one day by the case of a poor savage who came to us with a strangulated hernia. We had to place him on the operating-table without being able to explain to him what we were go-ing to do, and while he was being fixed in position horror painted itself on his face; he certainly believed that he had fallen among cannibals! But with the anæsthetic there came an end to his terror, and when he woke, free from his torturing pain, an understanding look spread over his face, and he gave us a smile of gratitude. But alas! it was impossible to save his life. Never have I used the operating-knife with such deep emotion as I did that day.

That we can trouble them so little with talk is an encouragement to these Bendjabis to rise superior to everything that
can be expected of a guest in our hospital.

Anyone who gives a Bendjabi an order has to wait in vain
for any sound or movement which may indicate whether he
has been understood or not, and whether or not the order will
be obeyed. He might as well give it to a log of wood.

Of what is meant by property they have no notion, and they
steal from the other inmates whatever they can, even robbing
of his food a patient who cannot leave his bed.

Hence I live in a state of perpetual anxiety as to when these
savages will cause us difficulties with the Mission. Only a few
days ago Mons. Herrmann brought me two who had been
caught in the act of carrying off nuts from one of the Mission
station palm-trees. They were two miserable dysentery patients who could scarcely walk about, and into whose hands we
should not have ventured to put a broom for the Saturday
clean-up. Yet they climbed the palm-tree, and managed successfully the troublesome job of freeing the nut with a bush-
knife from the thorny growth around it. Fortunately, Mons.
Herrmann smoothes over all such difficulties with Solomon-
like wisdom and Christian kindness.

But we are not tried only by the entire absence of discipline
in our savages; we suffer from their absolute inability to understand that anything can be valuable. The hospital being so
near the forest it is really not at all hard for them to get firewood. But, as it is rather less trouble, they prefer to burn the
beams and planks which I procure with so much trouble and
such heavy expense, and having no place which I can make
secure with lock and key, I am quite at a loss for a way of
keeping my precious timber safe from them.

This unsuccessful struggle, repeated day after day, to produce in these savages some notion of what is meant by value,
is a trial of patience and nerves as severe as any that anyone
could imagine.

My poultry is, of course, no safer from the Bendjabis than is
that of the missionaries. Many a fowl has already ended its
days in a cooking-pot to provide an evening banquet.

I am describing only the worst of our Bendjabis, but the
worst are many in number. If they remain some time, they do,
through the example of others, get somewhat accustomed to
regularity and order, but fresh ones are continually coming

with whom we have to begin again at the beginning, and this uses up our nervous vigour much more than the work does. We are learning the full meaning of the interesting fact that we are allowed to spend our life among savages.

And yet, however often we groan over the Bendjabis—and one of our household sayings is: "How beautiful Africa would be without its savages!"—we do feel that there is a link between them and us. When the new doctor launches out into angry denunciation of them, I point out to him with what regret and affection he will look back upon them when he is again in Europe. Many of them are, indeed, men who have become human animals, not merely savages, but creatures who, through living far from their homes and coming under so many injurious influences, have sunk even below the level of savages. They do not even feel any gratitude for what we do for them. Their interpretation is that we behave in this way because it is a sure way to get rich, and they tell this to their comrades on the timber site, as I know from those who have heard them do so.

There are others, however, who do become attached to us. How many a savage of whom we had unpleasant reminisences and of whom we were confident that after the numerous scoldings he had received he would have taken away no good report of us, has run to greet us with a beaming face when one of our journeys has brought us close to his timber site! How often, as a canoe is passing, a hearty greeting floats over to us from someone in the row of paddling Bendjabis!

I daresay we should have fewer difficulties with our savages, if we could occasionally sit round the fire with them and show ourselves to them as men, and not merely as medicine-men and custodians of law and order in the hospital. But there is no time for that. All three of us, we two doctors and Nurse Kottmann, are really so overwhelmed with work that the humanity within us cannot come out properly. But we cannot help it. For the present we are condemned to the trying task of carrying on the struggle with sickness and pain, and to that everything else has to give way.

* * *

Sometimes I have to deal with natives who were in Europe as soldiers during the war. The one with whom I get on best is a Pahouin who never boasts of any heroic deeds. Coming home safe and sound he entered the service of a white man, three hours above Lambaréné, as cook. Then, while playing one day with his master's sporting gun, he got his right elbow shattered, partly through his own fault, partly through that of the boy who was handling it with him. He was brought to us during the night and by the light of a lantern I staunched the blood-flow and removed the splinters.

Through questions which I put to the man about the gold crowns on some of his teeth, I learnt that my patient had been in Europe and in military service, though he had said nothing about it. These crowns did not imply any damage to the teeth, but the black soldiers made a practice of getting them put on in order to make an impression on their people at home. Otherwise the warrior from Europe had in clothing and behaviour become a native again like his neighbours, except that his experience had made him really serious; it weighed him down like a burdensome secret.

"In the village (he said to me) they are always asking me to tell them about the war, but I can't do it. And they wouldn't understand if I did. It was all so horrible, so horrible!"

The whole time that the wounded man spent in the hospital I kept with us the boy who had let off the gun, for fear lest the relatives should do him a mischief, or even carry him off so as to extort a big ransom for him. He was told off to assist in the kitchen and with the washing boiler, and he gave useful help to Nurse Kottmann. To my great joy, too, I was able to bring about an agreement as to compensation between him and his victim. The former was to pay a sum of money worth about one hundred shillings in monthly instalments of ten shillings, and give a goat as well. Custom demands that in every case of possibly fatal injury something living must be handed over. If the victim had lost his arm, the other would have had to buy him a wife.

Many a serious conversation did I have with this native who was suffering thus from his experience of the war. Madame Herrmann also won his regard, and whenever she came into the hospital for the evening prayers, he was one of the first to take his place.

In December, a Bendjabi is brought to us from a timber site on Lake Azingo. He and his mates had devoured in three days a large elephant which had been killed in the neighbourhood, and he had got a lump of hard elephant flesh stuck in his throat.

The Canadian, who has been here since early in October, and for whom we had to open one abscess after the other, is now beginning to walk. He has become a skeleton, and I had almost given up all hope of saving him.

And I have been a patient myself for weeks. Ulcers on my feet from my first residence here, though perfectly healed over, have broken out again, because of repeated injuries received during building operations, and they give me much trouble. I hobble about as well as I can, but when they are very bad I get myself carried down to the hospital. I must be down below the whole day, else no building gets done. The worst of the ulcers is that the continual burning pain causes extreme nervous irritation.

On December 12th one room is ready for use in the little house meant for the doctor and white patients. I had worked on into the night with the black carpenters to get the doors and shutters fixed, and did well to refuse to listen to the new doctor and Nurse Kottmann, who wanted to forbid me all building work because of the condition of my feet, for the very next day in trooped together six European patients, who had to be housed. Among them was a lady with a small child, the condition of both of whom gave cause for much anxiety. Her husband was ill also. One of the men, as soon became clear, was in the first stage of sleeping-sickness. A few days later another European came in, so that at Christmas we had, with the Canadian, eight white patients to provide for. Without that room, which was ready just in time to take four of them, I should not have known how to put them up. Two are taken in by Mons. and Madame Herrmann. The native carpenter, who wanted to leave me in the lurch because he did not like being hurried so much, is reconciled by a handsome present.

On Christmas Eve there is a general feeling of depression. The lady, who is lodged in our house, feels very miserable, and while we others sing carols round a decorated palm-tree, Nurse Kottmann sits on the edge of her bed and tries to stop her tears. On the hillside below there is a light burning far into the night, for the Canadian is celebrating his recovery with his room-mates. He can walk about again, and even help me with the building.

15 SPRING 1925 MORE BUILDING NEEDED

WE begin the new year badly, for all three of us are unwell. The new doctor is in bed with boils; Mlle. Kottmann feels miserably out of sorts; and I am suffering more than ever from the ulcers on my feet, which are spreading. I cannot get a shoe on, so I drag myself about in wooden ones. We get through the work after a fashion, but that is all.

But we are immensely cheered by the condition of the sleeping-sickness patient, who is improving every day. His fever has gone, and his torturing headaches are lessening. His case shows us once more that in every case of illness which begins with fever or headaches or rheumatism, the first thing to do is to examine the blood microscopically. Without the information that affords, an incipient case of sleeping-sickness might pass for one of malaria and be treated with quinine, which would do no good and would lose valuable time. Moreover, the new remedies work with certainty only in the first and second stages. Of course, the patient first learns what his illness is when he is on the way to recovery.

And now there comes a piece of news which gives us all fresh courage. A third doctor, Dr. Mark Lauterburg, of Berne, will be here in a few weeks. Dr. Nessmann and I are already convinced that we two cannot manage alone. The surgical work still has to be curtailed; to do what is needed would mean operating on three mornings a week, and that is impossible. The ordinary work keeps us so busy that we should not know how to get three mornings for it. And here, moreover, there falls on the surgeon all the petty attendant work, before and after an operation, which in Europe can be left to the nurses and the orderlies. For this we have not sufficient strength, nor would our exhausting activities allow us to come to the actual operation fresh enough. The new doctor already knows, alas, how closely connected are Africa, fatigue, and nervous irritation.

On the other hand, I am more strongly convinced than ever that a hospital in the primeval forest achieves its object only if surgery occupies its proper place in the work. In a land where hernia and elephantiasis are so common, the help that the knife can give must not be wanting. A successful operation conveys a message into the remotest districts, and gives sufferers confidence in the ability of the white doctor. We must therefore, so we decided, get a medical man here whose work will be chiefly surgery. And now he is actually on the point of embarking!

The third doctor, who must bring with him (so logic demands!) a second, possibly even a third, nurse, compels me to think of more building. The three-roomed cottage which was meant for the second doctor and the white patients, can now be considered as possibly a house for doctors only. Anyhow, the two rooms provided for the white patients would in the long run not have been sufficient, as I saw at Christmas. How sorry I felt for the four patients, who had to be quartered together in the small and low room which had just enough space for four camp beds! If there had been a dying man among them, where else could I have put him?

I have also to think about providing some rooms in which our reserves of household things, linen, bedding, and foodstuffs, can be stored, together with bandages and drugs. All these supplies are at present kept in piled-up chests and packing-cases, many of which stand in a shed which is far from providing proper protection against either rain or thieves. To get out any object that is wanted at once, one has to summon some natives and shift a dozen heavy cases. And how Dr. Nessmann and I shudder when any drug has to be taken from our reserve!

People in Europe can hardly form an idea of the amount and variety of stores which must be provided for the regular conduct of a hospital in an African forest. Formerly I arranged to keep myself supplied for six months ahead. Now I calculate for a year.

Of the land belonging to the mission station, but placed at my disposal, there is still a piece vacant which has just room for a house about sixty feet long and twenty feet broad. I determine, therefore, to undertake a big building which will have room within it for the white patients, and also for our stores.

It must be built on piles with a corrugated iron roof, and contain ten rooms. The Canadian, Mr. Crow, who is now almost completely well again, goes with a good crew which is at my disposal for a few days, to fetch the hardwood piles from a small side-stream about eighteen miles up the river. Each evening the new doctor and I take spades and level a portion of the site. The people at the N'Gômô saw-pit promise to do their best to deliver the timber, so there is hope that all the preparations will be so far completed by the beginning of the dry season at the end of May that we can then begin building.

On January 17th the native carpenter's wife is released by death from her sufferings. By careful nursing we have at least managed to save her from getting bed-sores. That is what makes sleeping-sickness as an illness so especially pitiable. We all followed her body to its last resting-place.

But now for a long time her husband will do no work. Mourning means holiday, and there is no shaking that custom. For weeks the widower must sit in his hut in torn clothing and touch nothing. And this is a sacred duty. In their customs, at any rate, the negroes honour their dead more than we do.

It follows that I must finish the house for the two doctors without help, and for the present Dr. Nessmann remains dependent on the hospitality of Mons. and Madame Herrmann.

Mr. Crow, the Canadian, who was to have started for home on February 20th, got a bad sunstroke while on a journey to visit a friend, and this weakened his resisting power so much that his body succumbed to the infection over which, after months of struggle, he was on the point of triumphing. Persistent fever set in with new abscesses, and his life was once more in danger. What an amount of anxiety and work this one white patient has cost us!

*   *   *

On January 27th Mlle. Kottmann and I together just escape death by drowning. We were returning with a good crew after nightfall in a heavily-laden canoe from a factory where we had made many purchases. I gave an order not to keep too near the bank, because on our journey out I had noticed in the water a huge mass of foliage belonging to a fallen tree. We had travelled some distance when I began to suspect that we were after all too near the bank. The crew denied it, and I quieted my suspicions with the reflection that the eyes of these children of nature would certainly see better than mine. But I was suddenly seized with an inexplicable feeling of unrest. I jumped up and compelled the crew to turn the canoe towards the middle of the river. At that very moment there loomed up out of the water the huge mass of the tree, and we just managed to scrape past it. But for that turn we should have dashed into it at full speed, have been dazed by the impact, and have been thrown into the water. One can never rely on the natives here, not even in things which they understand from long practice. They are so thoughtless that you can never tell what they are going to do.

On the day following this adventure there arrives the long and eagerly awaited hospital motor-boat. It comes from kind friends in Sweden, who have been collecting money for it since 1922. We do not know how to express our gratitude for it. It means for us all travelling more safely, more quickly, and more comfortably. Completely covered by a canvas awning, it will protect us from both sun and rain, if the latter is not too heavy. Best of all, the travelling will cost not more than by canoe, as might have been thought, but less. What we have had to offer a crew in the way of food, wages, and presents is considerably more than the outlay on petrol and oil for the same length of journey.

Built with a fairly narrow hull, the motor-boat makes good way against the strong current, and it draws little water, so as to be all right in shallow water during the dry season. Its length is about 28 feet, its width 5 feet, and it can carry a ton weight. The extremely simple single-cylindered motor is of 3½ horse-power, and uses about 2½ pints of petrol per hour. Against the current and heavily laden it makes 7 to 8 kilometres (four and a quarter to five miles) per hour, in still water rather more than 12 (seven and a half miles).

This kind of motor-boat is used by almost all timber merchants here, and it has proved itself a reliable craft. Ours bears a Swedish name: *Tack sa Mycket,* i.e. "Many thanks."

On February 10th a large and well-appointed motor-boat brings an ailing Dutch lady up from Cape Lopez. Its owner, Mr. Drew, a friendly Englishman, is kind enough to take back with him the Canadian, who is now getting better. We think him fit for the journey, but, as he still needs bandaging, Dr. Nessmann goes with him to the coast.

For ten days I am again the only doctor. About this time we almost always have with us half a dozen white patients. One of them, a Pole named Rochowiack, who came on account of a wounded foot, goes down, while here, with blackwater fever. He gives himself up for lost, because he had seen, in Rhodesia, seven cases of it, all of which ended fatally. I, on the other hand, can comfort him with the assurance that I have never yet lost a blackwater fever patient.

Once more I have found corroboration of the statement that heavy doses of quinine taken suddenly by people not accustomed to the drug do in some way or other cause the outbreak of this fever. Mons. Rochowiack felt himself somewhat feverish, took some quinine, though he was not in the habit of using it, and a good deal of it, too, as exhorted to do by the patients who shared his room. The next morning he had blackwater fever. Under what conditions quinine produces that wholesale destruction of the red blood corpuscles, which we know to be the precursor of this fever, we cannot yet say, and, indeed, many points connected with this disease are still a mystery.

As soon as ever he was fairly well, Mons. Rochowiack began helping me with the building work. He is a joiner and carpenter, and I learnt many things from him. He instructed me in the simplified method of timber construction which is widely followed in S. Africa, where he had lived a considerable time.

Just now we have with us two natives who have wounds caused by human teeth. One of them got his while trying to arrest a dilatory debtor. Biting as a method of offence or defence is more frequent with Africans than with us. "The worst bite (says Joseph) is that of the leopard; worse still is that of a poisonous snake; worse still a monkey's bite, but quite the worst of all that of a man." There is some truth in this. I have had occasion in Africa to see about a dozen cases of the human bite, and all showed at once symptoms of severe infection. In two cases a general blood-poisoning seemed imminent although the victims came to me within a few hours. One of these two victims will have to lose the end joint of one finger.

Cases of leprosy are continually coming to us, though there would be many more if the treatment were not so tedious! For it is only at the end of several weeks, as a rule, that the sick person notices an improvement. Many find their patience exhausted before that, and will not let us keep them any longer.

They usually come only to obtain and take home with them some Chaulmoogra oil which has been prepared for drinking, that is, has been diluted with sesame and peanut-oil. They have been for a long time familiar with this treatment, but they are unwilling to learn that much better results can be obtained if this is followed by a series of injections of Chaulmoogra oil derivatives, because that requires too long a stay in the hospital. We hope, however, to get results which will convince them. I have, indeed, to allow that life in our overcrowded wards is not a pleasant experience.

*   *   *

On March 16th, on my return from a two-day journey in the motor-boat, I see standing by Dr. Nessmann on the landing-stage a slender figure in the elegantly careless attitude of a cavalry officer. It is the new doctor, Dr. Mark Lauterburg.

The beds in the wards for the surgical patients have just been finished, so he can begin work at once, and the first case which is entrusted to his knife is a sleeping-sickness patient with an empyema which requires a rib resection. The poor creature is a savage from the interior called Yezu, and he has been with us for months. The sleeping-sickness seems to have been mastered, but he, no doubt, lacks strength to get over the empyema. We like him because of his gentle nature. How grateful he is for the soups which are made for him! "When I am well (he says) I will stay with you forever."

During his second operation, at which we others are with him, Dr. Lauterburg is startled by a native, who rushes into the room crying out: "They are trying to kill the Doctor's chickens," "they" meaning the Bendjabi, who can just crawl about, and his accomplices. I should have been surprised if they had *not* used for the benefit of their cooking-pot the time when doctors and nurses were all engaged indoors!

In the small hours of March 19th a European patient died suddenly of sunstroke, though the day before he had been discussing plans for his voyage home. He was buried in the Catholic cemetery on the same afternoon as Joseph's mother, who was a fine old woman.

How difficult to write are the letters in which I have to tell the relatives of a European who has died here about his last days and his death!

Out of affection for me, Joseph appears again for work

after only three weeks of mourning for his mother, which I think very much to his credit. "The Doctor is a slave to his work, and Joseph is the Doctor's slave," he says. The native carpenter, Monenzalie, now a widower, returns at the same time. He is one of the best carpenters in the whole district, and could any day get a better-paid and much pleasanter post. If he decides in my favour, it is a result of personal attachment.

Since Dr. Lauterburg's arrival there have been operations three mornings a week. His name among the natives is "N'Tschinda-N'Tschinda," i.e., "The man who cuts boldly." Dr. Nessmann they call "Ogula," i.e., "The Captain's son," "the Captain" meaning me. The men tell each other that in return for his loyal service I am going to buy him a wife in Europe, so that he can marry as soon as he gets back.

In the matter of accident surgery, N'Tschinda-N'Tschinda has some difficulty in converting himself to acceptance of the principle on which I act, of non-amputation. We must, that is to say, here avoid amputation in cases when, in spite of some danger to the patient's life, it is done in Europe as a matter of course. Else the report would spread to the end of our world that the doctor at Lambaréné cuts people's arms and legs off, and that would frighten numbers from coming here for help.

Hitherto I have had no cause to repent of having aimed at the reputation of being a doctor who leaves arms and legs in their places, but my success in this I owe to methyl-violet. Every traumatic wound of a limb, however serious it may look —and most of them do look serious—is treated with this methyl-violet. My own experience is that it is successful only if the dressing is kept moist. Dry dressings, or wet ones which get dry, may actually be dangerous, because the methyl-violet, in its state of very fine division, may dry into a scab, and thus form a covering layer beneath which the infection can spread still further. Boils, whitlows, and all supporting foci which cannot drain easily may therefore give very poor results from treatment with methyl-violet. The dressing must be kept always moist, so as to avoid any dry deposit. Then only is the drug safe, and then only can the dye produce its full effect.

An open wound is therefore covered with gauze which has just been dipped in a weak solution of methyl-violet, and this is kept moist by constant application outside it of gauze which has been dipped in sterilised water. Moreover, owing to the simplicity of the remedy the dressing can be wrapped in waterproof material to prevent evaporation, and this can be done even with badly infected wounds on which a moist dressing would otherwise be a mistake. Methyl-violet also makes possible the use of a moist bandage when one would otherwise have to abstain from using it, and so lose the result it produces. In severe cases we also resort to long-continued sprinkling with a weak solution of methyl-violet. This drug has the great advantage of not causing irritation; it has, on the contrary, a decidedly soothing effect, as I have often observed.

Burns I treat from the third or fourth day with a 3 per cent methyl-violet ointment, after having applied to them, in the usual way, bandages with tannic ointment.

Dr. Lauterburg has been quite surprised by the results of our procedure in cases where amputation seemed to be demanded. The most convincing of them he found in a compound and septic fracture of the lower leg, which was brought to us with gas gangrene already beginning.

Thanks to our complete abstinence from amputation we can now resort to it in absolutely necessary cases without endangering our reputation. Occasionally it happens that natives even ask for it of their own accord.

Dr. Lauterburg has now operated on quite a number of hernia cases, and had ample opportunity of convincing himself that such operations do, as a rule, offer more difficulties here than in Europe, for the reason that one almost always meets with extensive displacements. These are produced by the various attempts which the natives make to reduce the hernia, and thereby the tissues get mishandled and pinched.

Elephantiasis, too, has its turn on the table. On April 1st we attack a growth weighing 72 lbs., on a man from near Samkita. The weight of it had for a long time condemned him to inactivity, and it is of such a size that he can use it as a cushion to sit upon. Although he is still fairly young, he looks like an old man. The operation lasts from ten o'clock till three in the afternoon, and the handling of such a mass makes heavy demands on the physical strength of all three of us. We follow in our procedure the method, first made public in 1913, by Dr. Ouzilleau, of cutting the tumour down the middle as if it were a pear. This facilitates the search for the blood vessels, and makes possible the complete prevention of hæmorrhage.

That very day there turns up unexpectedly a helper for the building operations, viz., a young Swiss, named Schatzmann. Having heard of my need in this direction, he embarked without any long correspondence with me and came to give me the most unselfish help. He is a skilled worker, both as carpenter and foreman, and he takes in hand the building of the ten-roomed house. What a relief for me! I have, though, some difficulty in providing him with accommodation; an unexpected arrival is, in Africa too, a serious event.

Although the new helper had ideas of building a complete hospital, that is certainly impossible, but when he has finished his work for me, some of the trading firms will certainly approach him about building for them. Building foremen are persons much sought after here, though only if, as is the case with Mons. Schatzmann, they can work themselves and get on well with the natives. I have already had some enquiries about him, as to when he will be free for another engagement.

There is a tragic happening just about this time. A dysentery patient who cannot stand upright kills his neighbour, who is as miserable a skeleton as himself; he thought he meant to steal his rations, for many dysentery patients have a good appetite up to the very end. We leave the murderer, who shows no sort of remorse for his act, undisturbed, as it is evident that he will soon follow his victim into the other world. And so he does.

At the end of April we lose close together two patients after operations, and there are not a few deaths to register among the medical patients. This so depresses us that we just drag ourselves about to our work.

At the beginning of the month the work on the ten-roomed house threatens to come to a standstill because we have no more beams, although some have been lying here for weeks. Mons. Mathieu, a Samkita timber-merchant, has sent me thirty fine hardwood beams in recognition of my having had under my care for a long time one of his European staff who was seriously ill. But the beams are 25 cm. square, while I want some of 8 cm., and it would be only a small job to saw each of these into four. That would give me 120 beams of the size I want, and enable me to make a beginning, but I can find no sawyers though I have been trying for weeks. If I wanted five-and-twenty native clerks, I should have fifty applying tomorrow. But sawyers? No.

How true it is, after all, that civilisation does not begin with reading and writing but with manual labour. Because we have no manual workers here, real progress is impossible. The natives learn to read and write without learning at the same time to use their hands. With these accomplishments they obtain posts as salesmen and clerks, and sit about in white suits. But manual work is despised.

Had I any say in the matter, no black man would be allowed to learn to read and write without being apprenticed to some trade. No training of the intellect without simultaneous training of the hands! Only so can there be a sound basis for further advance. How ridiculous it seems to me to read that Africa is being opened up to civilisation because a railway has been built to this place, a motor-car has got through to that, and an air service is being established between two other localities. That does not mean any real gain. "How far are the natives becoming efficient men?" That is the one thing that matters, and efficient men they can become only through religious and moral teaching combined with manual work. All other things have meaning only when this foundation has been well and truly laid. And of all handicrafts that of the sawyer is, once more, the most important, for he turns tree-trunks into beams and planks with which we can build houses to live in. Before there were any saw-mills, our ancestors sawed them by hand, and if the natives do not advance by that same road they remain just savages, even if one or another of them, as a commercial or a Civil Service clerk, earns money enough to get his wife silk stockings and high-heeled shoes from Europe. Both they and their descendants will continue, in that case, to live in bamboo huts.

For the sawing of beams and planks out of a tree-trunk the latter is fixed above a pit, about six feet wide, and twelve feet or more long. It is then taken in hand by two sawyers with a long, straight saw, one of them standing on the trunk, the other in the pit. The path the saw-blade must take is carefully marked beforehand with corresponding lines above and below, and the special skill is shown in keeping the saw perpendicular and on the lines. This requires some practice, but two good sawyers, working well together, can produce ten beams or planks a day. This kind of work, however, though for this district the most valuable of all, is held in least respect as being too simple and too fatiguing. Consequently the people live in miserable little huts when they might live in houses of mahogany, and I cannot get even a couple of sawyers to cut up some big beams into smaller ones!

In this difficulty help comes to me through an inflamed throat. The wife of a timber merchant whom I know to have two good sawyers in his service, comes to us in April to be treated for a rather severe attack. Her husband cannot but send the sawyers here, and place them at my disposal. A few days see the job finished, and I have 120 small beams. The new house can now have its roof put on.

On May 3rd I go with Dr. Nessmann to a timber site lying north of this place, where severe dysentery has broken out and claimed many victims. Our journey takes us first to the end of Lake Azingo, forty-four miles away, and there we leave the motor-boat. Then in two small canoes we travel fifteen miles up a small stream with a strong current, where we are plagued by tsetse flies. At the timber site we examine the whole body of workers, give advice as to the treatment of those who have mild attacks, and take the bad cases back with us. This is Dr. Nessmann's first visit to a timber-site. On May 5th we are back in Lambaréné, thanks to the motor-boat, which manages the forty-four miles upstream in well under a day.

On this journey I write my last letter to my father, but it never reaches him, for death called him home that very day, May 5th.

*   *   *

Through a series of new experiences N'Tschinda-N'Tschinda learns that surgery in Africa is not what it is in Europe. It fell out that in a quarrel with another man—about a woman—a native got a blow in his forearm with a bush-knife. His relatives, in a body, bring him to us, and it is found necessary to suture the wound, which our surgeon does in the most approved professional way. Now when a patient is so injured that he cannot cook for himself, our rule is that someone stops to wait on him, and this man's relatives appointed unanimously to the post one of their number, who accepted it as being a matter of course. But Dr. Lauterburg is never really satisfied with the state of his patient in spite of his faultless suturing. The wound seems to heal well, but the man himself begins to fall off in condition; he lurches about when coming to have the wound dressed, is confused, and loses the power of speech. N'Tschinda-N'Tschinda finds himself quite non-plussed by an infection which produces such general symptoms, but with no fever and the wound healing up so well . . . "Poison!" I ejaculate, as soon as he draws my attention to the case, for anyone who has worked here for a long time always assumes poison as a possible cause of any symptoms which are otherwise inexplicable. So on some honourable pretext the attendant who has hitherto cooked for the poisoned man is given work in the hospital, and his victim gets his food only from the hands of one of our orderlies. Then the disturbing effects pass slowly, very slowly, away.

A little later the matter is cleared up. The man left here was the man who had had the difference with the patient and had inflicted the wound, and he had been obliged to undertake the work as compensation. Then he succumbed to the temptation to misuse his opportunity and get rid of his rival. Although we breathed not a word of what was happening, the relatives became suspicious, so to prevent them from killing the poisoner and adding a second drama to the first, the latter was enlisted for personal service to Nurse Kottmann in the doctor's house, where he worked willingly and well at washing and water-carrying.

That there is an extensive use of poison in Equatorial Africa is only too true. One day—it is a story of several months ago—there came to us with his relatives a sick man in a most miserable condition. He, too, had lost his power of speech. At first I thought it might be a general blood-poisoning as a result of infection in some small injury, but the heart was all right, and the sick man was at times so thoroughly himself that the assumption seemed a very questionable one. Since he refused bananas and rice, I tried to feed him with milk, but the milk which his relatives offered he refused to take. That roused my suspicions. I therefore seized the opportunity one day, when his relatives were out of sight, to give him some milk myself. This he drank greedily, so after that he got all his food and drink from one of our orderlies, and these he never refused. The explanation we gave to the relatives was that he needed specially prepared food and drink. However, he was too far gone to be saved.

I remember, too, that once, when I was treating a European whose condition I could not explain, I found some excuse for getting rid of the black servants who had come with him.

That does not mean that I had any direct suspicions of the cook and the boy; they may have merely been too unobservant to prevent an attempt at poisoning by someone else through them.

For investigation of the nature of the poisons used I have never had time; but they are usually slow ones. Let it suffice to say that in a number of cases since 1913 I have tested animal charcoal as a remedy. Whenever I find myself suspicious, the patient gets animal charcoal in water to drink; if there is none to be had, ordinary charcoal will do. Joseph watches me knowingly when I prepare "the black medicine." Perhaps we shall some day have doctors enough here to let one of us devote himself to the investigation of poisons.

But there are also involuntary poisonings to be taken into account. Of the roots, bark, and leaves which the natives use for all sorts of diseases, many have the peculiarity of irritating the kidneys severely, others of attacking the heart. Some of them, if given in excessive quantities, endanger life itself. A number of cases of kidney disease, before which we have to confess ourselves powerless, can be traced back to some drink that was taken as medicine. If the heart beats too slowly, it may be assumed that the sufferer has been given seeds of the strophantus bush, which grows here in huge quantities. There are also cases of delirium which arise from poisoning.

Europeans who let themselves be treated with the medicines used by the natives, paying for this sometimes a heavy penalty, are not so few in number as one would like to think.

16 *SUMMER, 1925*

JUST when we had all our rooms occupied with white patients, there came an enquiry whether one of us could go to Cape Lopez to act as *locum tenens* for the doctor there, who was suffering from a suppurating wound in one of his hands. Dr. Lauterburg started for the coast on May 13th, and during the six weeks he was there sick people, both white and black, gave him plenty to do.

On May 14th an Italian arrived, a Signor Boles, who among the lagoons south of Cape Lopez, had had his arm badly mauled by a leopard. He had wounded the animal with a bullet and followed the blood-track, which led him into a small valley overgrown with reeds. Just as he got the leopard in view so that he could shoot again, the negroes, whom he had left in the rear while he followed the spoor, caught sight of it also, and the loud shout they raised to warn their master irritated the beast so that, instead of retreating, it sprang on the Italian before he could shoot again. He drew back, and used the butt end of his rifle to defend himself, but fell, and the leopard seized his arm and kept hold of it till the men despatched it with their spears. It was not till ten days later that he reached me; the arm was in a bad state, and his general condition such as to cause much anxiety, but methyl-violet dressings, used after a sufficient opening of the wounds, were, as usual, effective.

Yezu, the sleeping-sickness Bendjabi, who was operated on for empyema, is dying, and we are very sad at not being able to save him. We are affected also by the death of another Bendjabi, called N'Dunde, who has been here a long time and has cried over every patient whom we have had to carry out to his last resting-place. And just now there are many deaths. There have been days on which we have had to record as many as three, but that is because so many patients are brought to us in a dying condition.

The digging of the graves, which at first caused us so many difficulties because the natives would not undertake the work, is now done without our having to trouble about it, thanks to an arrangement made with Dominic. For each grave he receives a fixed bonus, for which he has to secure the necessary four workers and superintend the job. These four also act as bearers. After the burial they get a present and an extra big food ration, and are free from work for the rest of the day. We cannot, however, get the hospital inmates to come as mourners. The graveyard is to them such an uncanny place that they resist all pressure in the matter.

Yet what a charming place our forest graveyard is! It is overshadowed by beautiful palms, and no sound breaks its silence except the songs of the birds. Coffins for the bodies we cannot provide, having neither planks nor carpenter for them. The bodies are wrapped in linen, and laid in palm-leaves tied together. So they have a green coffin which is much more beautiful than one of boards.

At the end of May we have another death among our white patients, that of an employee of one of the timber merchants, who was brought to us in a state of coma.

Now at last the roof of our new house is finished, and far sooner than it would have been without Mons. Schatzmann. The flooring, the wall-panelling, and the doors can be finished, if necessary, by the black carpenter alone, provided there is wood for them.

The biggest commercial house in the Ogowe district now offers to put Mons. Schatzmann in charge of all their buildings, and he takes my advice to accept this important and interesting post, though, indeed, he would much prefer to stay and build me a complete hospital.

Early in June the leopard-bitten Italian is so far restored to health that he can return to his business at Cape Lopez, and I go with him to recruit for a short time at the seaside. For a whole year I have not had a day out of harness.

But my recruiting does not amount to much. N'Tschinda-N'Tschinda had made such a reputation for us down there, that I am called in again and again by sick people. In particular, some ships in the harbour, on which dysentery had broken out, give me a lot of work. It was the result of drinking polluted water obtained in some harbour away to the south.

Meanwhile we lose by death a man who was waiting for an operation on his large elephantiasis tumour. The cause is penumonia, a condition which is very frequent at the beginning of the dry season. We also have a fatal case of tetanus, but that condition is very rare here.

During my absence my two colleagues were extremely pleased that a woman who had been bitten by a fish and came to us with a badly poisoned arm, asked of her own accord for amputation. She belongs to the district where the Bendjabi, whose arm we could not help amputating, has preached the usefulness of such an operation. Her case, too, ended satisfactorily.

The two doctors also correctly diagnosed as sleeping-sickness the case of a white lady from near N'Gômô, who came to us with fever and headache. When I got back she was already on the road to recovery. We also took in another white lady for her confinement.

Still another, whom I had attended in similar circumstances

some months before, came from the interior with her baby, accompanied by her husband. She was now suffering from mental disease, but fortunately there were already some rooms in the new house finished, so that I could accommodate her till she left for Europe. It was a very serious case.

* * *

Towards the end of June the dysentery cases increased to an alarming extent, and we did not know where to put the sufferers. It is well known that there are two kinds of dysentery, amœbic and bacillary.

The former is caused by amœbæ, unicellular organisms which settle in the large intestine and bore into its walls, giving rise to hæmorrhage. The remedy for this kind is emetin, a drug which is obtained from ipecacuanha bark and has been in use since 1912. From eight to ten centigrammes of emetin dissolved in sterilised water is given for several days running by subcutaneous injection, and the injections are repeated after an interval of a few days. Unfortunately, this drug is terribly expensive.

The other kind of dysentery, that produced by bacteria, we are not so well prepared to deal with. Every possible remedy is being tried, but so far without satisfactory results.

Both kinds may occur together. Formerly it was the amœbic which was commonest here; now we often have cases of mixed infection, especially in men who come from the timber-sites.

What work is caused us by the dysentery patients who can no longer move about, and who dirty everything where they sit or lie! Many have to be fed by hand because they are too weak to carry a spoon to their mouths. And the care of them is all the more laborious because the natives will not stir a finger to help; to such disgusting work there is no bringing them. We therefore often have to do it all ourselves, and if there ever *is* a black man who will help, he is loaded with presents and smothered with praise.

Our great concern is to prevent the permanent infection of the hospital with dysentery germs. Anyone who tastes food or water that is polluted in any way with dysenteric excrement catches the disease. Anyone who has washed his hands in polluted water, or touched polluted earth with them, and then puts a finger in his mouth, may get dysentery. Anyone who washes his cooking utensils in polluted water may also become infected.

We have, therefore, to take the greatest care that the dysentery patients pollute nothing and do not mix with the others. I ought to have wards for them only, but I have not. Nor have I even a piece of ground on which I could build some. The only thing I can do is to build cubicles for them in the existing wards. To leave them permanently in these confined spaces where they get hardly any sun or air, is impossible. Yet if I leave them in the sun, they pollute in the most conscienceless way every place they visit. With them warnings are no help, and supervision is impossible. If only I could provide a room for them with a good fence round it!

It is useless for us to preach carefulness to the patients. They are told to use only water from the spring. But the river is only twenty paces away while the spring is a hundred so they fetch their water from the former. It is forbidden to do any cooking jointly with a dysentery patient, but they do cook with them and eat out of the vessel into which the latter have put their dirty fingers.

A Bendjabi, being treated for ulcers, discovered among the dysentery patients a man from his own district, and now he shares with him his ward-space and his cooking-pot. We drag him away and explain to him the risk he runs. In the evening he is again in the cubicle, and every time he is removed he manages somehow to get back. "Do you want to kill yourself?" Dr. Nessmann asked him. "Better be with my brother and die, than not see him," was the answer. Home sickness is with them stronger than fear of death. Of course the dysentery does not let this self-offered victim escape.

Since our number rose to three so that we can find time to make liberal use of the microscope, we have proved that angkylostomiasis is much more prevalent here than we believed. It is well known that attention was first drawn to this disease when many of those who were working on the S. Gotthard tunnel began to suffer from severe anæmia. The cause was discovered to be small worms about a centimetre long in the small intestine. Later on it was established as a fact that this disease occurs wherever men work in damp earth which is never exposed to cold, as is the case in tunnels, mines, and other hot places.

Infection comes in a remarkable way. The larva out of which the worm develops lives in water or in damp earth, and enters the human body, not through the mouth in drinking-water but through the skin. It stays for a time in the lung, but then settles in the small intestine, where it develops into the worm. There is no known protection against this disease and it can even be caught by washing one's hands in apparently clean water. The regular course of infection is indicated by bowel disturbances with increasing weakness and anæmia. The sufferer loses blood continually through the injuries caused by the worm to the mucosa of the intestine.

Whenever, therefore, a sick person, whether white or black, complains of anæmia and weakness, it must be settled whether or not he has any of these parasites, and this is done by searching his fæces with the microscope for the eggs. These are found in large numbers; the worms themselves much seldomer.

What a relief it is when his condition is found to be due to this parasite! That means that the mischief is comparatively simple to deal with. Repeated doses of thymol or carbon tetrachloride drive the worms out, and the patient recovers his healthy condition. Moreover, these drugs are not very expensive. They must be used carefully however. No alcohol or fat must be taken during their administration, as these dissolve the thymol. And thymol is a poison but, being insoluble in water, it passes through the intestine without being absorbed. If, however, it is dissolved in alcohol or ether, it gets absorbed and its poisonous qualities come into play. For that reason every patient who goes through the treatment here is isolated for two or three days, and carefully watched. Not even with Europeans can I be sure that they will of their own accord obey these instructions. One of them once disregarded them and got a very bad heart attack. Fortunately I had him, in accordance with my fundamental rule, constantly under observation, and was able to intervene in time.

With carbon tetrachloride the danger lies in the drug not being pure, and still containing traces of carbon bisulphide. During recent years chenopodium oil has also been used in treating angkylostomiasis.

The depression we feel at the increase of dysentery is made worse by news of there being severe famine further upstream. The districts most severely hit are those bordering on the Cameroons and crossed by the N'Djole-Boue-Makokou caravan route. The root cause of it was the rain which fell during the 1924 dry season and prevented the vegetation which had been cut down from getting dry and being burnt. The prevailing practice is to plant only where the vegetation has been burnt, a procedure which gets rid of the trees and undergrowth and also fertilises the ground with wood-ash. If rain makes this impossible, the people plant nothing, regardless of the consequences. That is how they acted in the districts mentioned above, and also in this one. In our neighbourhood, when the rain stopped, they had not even cut down the vegetation.

It must be added that the laying out of a new plantation is by no means made impossible by the rain, though it is made more difficult. Instead of burning the timber and brushwood, one need only collect them in heaps and then plant in the spaces between the stumps and the heaps. But the people would not make up their minds to do this, so now they have no plants from which they can get any fruit.

In our neighbourhood this fact does not make itself so painfully noticeable, because along the navigable portion of the Ogowe the provision of rice from Europe and India is possible. But in the interior to which the rice would have to be transported for hundreds of kilometres by porters, it can only to a very limited extent be reckoned on as a means of feeding the population. So in those parts there is severe famine, while here the famine is mild. If when the famine began maize had been planted at the right time, the worst stage of the calamity might have been avoided. Maize grows here splendidly, and within four months is ready for reaping. But when food began to run short the natives ate the maize which ought to have been sown. And the height of calamity was reached when the inhabitants of the hardest hit districts moved into neighbourhoods where there was still some food to be had, and there raided the plantations. Thus these places, too, were reduced to misery, and no one anywhere had the courage to plant anything. It would only have been for the profit of the raiders. So the people sit passively in their villages awaiting the end.

This inability to exert themselves and adapt themselves to difficult circumstances is typical of the natives of Equatorial Africa, and makes them pitiable creatures. There may be no vegetable food from the plantations, but they could secure animal food in the forest and in the open country. Twenty men armed with spears and bush-knives could surround a herd of wild pigs and bag one of them, for these animals are not so fierce as those of Europe. But the starving natives sit in their huts and wait for death just because it is famine time. One cannot say in this country: "Need stimulates invention." It has to be: "Need paralyses into idiocy."

*   *   *

At the end of July I manage to renew the roof of my dwellinghouse, which lets in sun and rain through countless holes big and little, for during the last few months we have collected the necessary three thousand stitched leaves. The merit of this belongs to Dr. Nessmann, who has the gift of bringing home to the hearts of our patients the need for this tribute of leaf-tiles much more convincingly than I can.

When the roof is finished, our canoes are beached to be repaired and re-tarred, all these things being work which must be done during the dry season, when "every day is worth three," as Frère Silvain says, the Catholic missionary who so kindly provides us with vegetables from his big garden. We have no place to make a garden, and should not just now have time to sow if we had one. It is, unfortunately, only for a few weeks that Frère Silvain can make us happy with beans, cabbage, and other vegetables. The garden produces only during the dry season; during the rains it must lie fallow, because cabbages and other vegetables do not flourish in the all-pervading damp heat.

At the beginning of August Dr. Nessmann goes down to Cape Lopez to recruit, a small river steamer taking him there. Wherever they put in, he is greeted by former patients and his services are claimed afresh. At Cape Lopez he visits the Norwegian whalefishers, who at this season of the year ply their trade there because the whales come from the southern seas to the Equator to escape the cold. In the southern hemisphere it is, of course, winter, and south winds bring us cool weather.

About this time there arrives from the interior a man who wants to be operated on for a big elephantiasis tumour. Tippoy is his name, and he has dragged himself here from his home over three hundred miles away, though he can walk only with quite tiny steps! Here and there he had to traverse the famine district.

Another man whom we had delivered from a similar tumour, gave the people of his village a regular fright on his return there. When he walked in among them with jaunty steps and looking quite rejuvenated, they thought it was his ghost and scattered in all directions! This he told us himself one day when he came to bring us a goat as a present and more patients for operations. Unfortunately, elephantiasis patients are not all as grateful as he was. One Sunday afternoon Dominic caught one trying to give us the slip, taking with him a blanket and a mosquito net.

At the beginning of September another European comes to us in the early stages of sleeping-sickness. It is an unusually interesting case because the patient has been only twenty-five days in the country, and has never before lived in any colony. It is therefore certain that the infection is quite recent. Nevertheless, he looks quite emaciated, and his face wears that permanent expression of suffering which is characteristic of the advanced stage. I have never watched a case in which the progress of the disease was so rapid, yet after three weeks of treatment he feels as if he had been born again.

Such a cure, which seems to border on the miraculous, gives us great encouragement, and we need it, for the hospital work is getting more and more exhausting through the ever-increasing amount of dysentery. We are all worn out and depressed, trying, as we do, in vain to arrest the growing infection of the hospital. Several patients who came for other complaints have caught dysentery, and some we could not save from death. Some who were on the point of being discharged after an operation have suffered the same fate. How anxiously we ask every morning in the ward where such patients sleep, whether anyone has been seized with dysentery! If anyone comes in complete confidence to entrust himself to our knife, I tremble. Will he not fall a victim to the dysentery?

In vain do we worry ourselves to death in acting as police and trying to ensure a certain amount of obedience to the rules which are directed against dysentery. The inability of our savages to comprehend anything of the kind makes mock of all our efforts. One evening I found a woman filling a bottle close to the landingstage, where the water is worst polluted. She was the wife of an operation patient, and was getting drinking-water for her husband, using the cover of darkness to get it from the forbidden place. The spring was too far away!

The worst of it is that the sick are beginning to conceal their dysentery, being unwilling to be under supervision and have their freedom curtailed. The other patients do not betray them, and even help them to keep us in ignorance. It was discovered the other day just after we had operated on him, that a man had dysentery, and had had it, too, for some time, but had concealed it because he knew that we do not operate on persons in that condition.

Through the extra work entailed by all this our staff is getting quite exhausted. It is astonishing that our orderlies continue to work with us; it can certainly be no pleasure to work for doctors with nerves as frayed as ours are. The Bendjabis naturally take advantage of our condition of overwork and worry to show us their worst side.

One day, in my despair at some of them who had once more been drawing polluted water, I threw myself into a chair in the consulting-room and groaned out: "What a blockhead I was to come out here to doctor savages like these!" Whereupon Joseph quietly remarked: "Yes, Doctor, here on earth you are a great blockhead, but not in heaven." He likes giving utterance to sententious remarks like that. I wish he would support us better in our efforts to hinder the spread of dysentery!

While we are thus overwhelmed with work in the hospital I have also to think about making good the whole of our leaf-tile roofing in view of the coming rainy season. Even roofs which are hardly a year old need some repairing. So with the idea of avoiding in future any loss of time on such work, I form the plan of gradually replacing all leaf-tile roofs with corrugated iron. The former have to be renewed every three years and need continual attention. In the course of a few years one spends as much on them as if corrugated iron had been used at first, and one has the trouble into the bargain of collecting the stitched leaves. What hours Dr. Nessmann spent in palavering about the leaf-tiles for the roof of our dwelling-house! What a number of crews we had to supply with food and presents in order to get the material here! So I proceed to order in Europe several hundred square yards of corrugated iron, although I am not sure that I have the means to pay for them.

In the middle of September we get the first rains, and the cry is to bring all building timber under cover. As we have in the hospital hardly a man capable of work, I begin, assisted by two loyal helpers, to haul beams and planks about myself. Suddenly I catch sight of a negro in a white suit sitting by a patient whom he has come to visit. "Hullo! friend," I call out, "won't you lend us a hand?" "I am an intellectual and don't drag wood about," came the answer. "You're lucky," I reply, "I too wanted to become an intellectual, but I didn't succeed."

17 *AUTUMN, 1925*

Now the famine has reached us too. It has, in fact, been here since the beginning of the summer, but its presence was concealed by the importation of rice from Europe. That has stopped for a time, and the famine is at once evident.

There are several circumstances to blame for this disastrous shortage of rice. First and foremost, the traders here estimated far too low the deficit in bananas and manioc root which inevitably resulted from the failure to plant what was needed last year. So from the very first they were ordering too little rice. Secondly, a ship bringing several thousand tons of rice for our West Coast was wrecked, the cargo getting soaked and ruined. Other ships, loaded with rice, lost, so it was announced, a great deal of time while discharging their cargoes, through unfavourable weather in our bad African roadsteads. So it will be some weeks before we get anything from them, and it will take months to make good the serious shortage. The panic that is setting in, and the accompanying storm of demands for the precious commodity only make the matter worse.

Worse off than any others are the small timber merchants, who have always relied on regular monthly deliveries, and who at their far-away outposts only learnt of the disaster when it was already upon us.

For the present, however, the feeding of the sick in our hospital is provided for. In June and July when the first signs of the shortage appeared and we also expected a rise in price, we laid in an emergency stock of over 5,000 lbs., so as to be prepared for all contingencies. In reliance on the loyalty of our friends in Europe we ventured on this huge purchase, though without the extra rooms provided by the new house I could not have dreamt of piling up such a supply. Nor without

the motor-boat could I have got it transported with the req-
uisite speed, for as soon as rice is brought it must be taken
away at once, or it runs the risk of being disposed of at other
places to our disadvantage. With our big reserve, for which
we are envied on all sides, we can, so long as it lasts, keep our
heads fairly well above water. Yet as soon as ever we hear
in the distance the siren of any steamer, big or little, off
I go with the motor-boat into the big channel where the factories are, so as not to be overlooked in the distribution of any
rice that may have arrived. Very often, however, the steamer
brings every conceivable thing except rice!

The number of sick who have to be housed and fed now
amounts to about 125. Then there is the hospital staff. From
130 to 175 lbs. of rice has to be dealt out every day, if not
more. Several times we have found ourselves with just enough
for a few days only, but on each occasion I have succeeded
at the last moment in unearthing a supply somewhere, and for
that my hearty thanks before all to the motor-boat!

How the hospital could be broken up and its inmates dispersed, if our supplies actually gave out, I cannot imagine.
Many patients are sixty or ninety miles from home, some even
further, and I see no means of getting them there. It is hard
enough in ordinary times to get the cured away as quickly as
we should like. Many of them have to stay on and be a burden
on our stores for eight or ten days, till a canoe or motor-boat
turns up which is going to their districts. Nor are they at all
anxious to leave us; elsewhere hunger is lying in wait for them.

Things look bad at the timber sites, work on most of them
being at a standstill. The Benjabis range the forest trying to support life with berries, fungi, roots, wild honey, palm-nuts, and
pineapples, which last grow wild here. Sometimes a gang of
them stumbles on an old manioc plantation in which they can
still dig up some tubers. At the end of November the mango
trees are in fruit, and can be found wherever there has been
a village. In December, maize sown in the first days of September is ready for cutting. Bananas cannot be reckoned on before
February.

It is refreshing to see how the timber merchants help each
other. Many a one of them who has managed to get some
sacks of rice gives some to his neighbour, although he is a
trade rival. I myself give a little help to the Mission at Samkita,
to two friendly merchants, and to an English factory.

Now that rice is the only available food, I get, unfortunately, ample confirmation of my experience that an exclusive diet of rice favours the appearance of dysentery among the natives of this country. There are at the present time dozens of walking skeletons among the population of our hospital.

In the middle of October Mlle. Emma Hausknecht joins us as a second nurse. She was a teacher in Alsace, and I have known her a long time; she promised years ago to come and help me some day. She now undertakes the housekeeping and the care of the white patients, setting Nurse Kottmann free for the hospital below.

What a relief it is for us that there is now someone who can have an eye on the patients and at the same time keep things straight everywhere! We ourselves are hardly able to stir all day from the consulting-room and the dispensary. Now it is possible to ensure that the dysentery patients get their soup and have their places cleaned. Now there is someone to see that the sick have what they need. All disputes which occur in the hospital are now brought to Nurse Kottmann and are decided by her. She superintends every day the distribution of the food rations, a business which hitherto has been left only too often to Dominic. She takes care that a fire is kept going under our store of dried fish, so that it may not go bad nor get infected with maggots. Every morning, too, she gives out spades, axes, and bush-knives for the work of the day, and counts them at night to make sure that they have all been returned. She also exercises supervision over the canoes. She has all the linen and the material for dressings under her care, and arranges who shall do the washing. When there are operations, she is the operation sister.

To find order and system thus gradually coming into the working of the hospital would give us all new courage for our work, if the situation brought about by our want of more space, by dysentery, and by famine were not so dispiriting. And it gets worse every day. The infection with dysentery germs gets worse and worse; almost every day someone is discovered who has caught the infection here, and fresh cases are continually being brought in. Not long ago a single morning brought us six at once.

This epidemic of dysentery makes me realise how detrimental it is to the work of the hospital that the site on which it stands is too small. If it were possible for us to erect isolation wards at a convenient distance from the rest of our buildings, and so keep the dysentery patients separated from the others, my hospital would not be so infected as it is with dysentery germs. The Mission, however willing, cannot afford to place any more ground at my disposal, because if they did, the hospital buildings would soon be too near the schools and the houses of the Mission families. To extend our buildings in any other direction than towards the Mission station is an impossibility, since in every other is either steeply rising ground, or a swamp, or the river.

How I regret that when I came back I had not the courage to rebuild the hospital on another larger site, instead of staying on the old one in order to make use of the old buildings, and not be compelled to start by clearing a new site for new ones. And yet, without workers, without canoes, without building materials, how could I have ventured on the task of building the hospital all over again on a site which would first have to be cleared and levelled?

Again, because I have not room enough, I cannot do what I ought for the poor mentally afflicted. The cell which I have for them, a dark den without a window, stands among the buildings which house the sick. I have no lock-up room which gets air and sunlight. Noisy mental patients I cannot take in for long periods, because the other patients cannot stand the noise so near. I therefore have to send them back in bonds to their village, where they will very likely be tormented to death, whereas under my care they might be cured. What I suffer at heart in such a case I have never let even my helpers know. If I only had a larger building site, I could house the mental patients at a distance from the others and carry out my duty to them as well.

But, anyhow, the area of my hospital is too small. It could hold the buildings needed for fifty patients, which was about the number during my first period of residence. But with the patients numbering permanently about 120, it is far too small. The activities of three doctors are carried on in two rooms, each about thirteen feet square, with two small side-rooms, one of which serves as the dispensary, while the other is at once laboratory and sterilisation room. In the room in which we examine the patients, Joseph makes the injections, two natives roll bandages, and two others wash bottles. There is a pushing and jostling as at a fair. We try in vain to get rid of the conviction that our work is seriously spoilt by these conditions with the fatigue and nervous strain that inevitably accompany them.

In the wards this want of space is distressing, even apart from the worry of the dysentery. We cannot put the dying by themselves; we have not even a separate place for the dead; they have to stay in the ward till they are carried out to the cemetery.

Nor can we house our staff properly; with the exception of Joseph and Aloys, the cook, they occupy odd corners and sheds. To keep them with us I promise that I will some day have them housed as befits human beings, but how that is to be done is a puzzle even to myself. If I could house all my workers properly, I should be able, in spite of the work being far from light, to get all the needed orderlies, the lack of whom hinders us so seriously in our work.

Then again, the danger of fire is so great that we dare not deceive ourselves by ignoring it. Our sick wards and all our buildings are so huddled together that if a fire did break out, they would all go up hopelessly in flames together.

Shall I, then, be angry with the dysentery, which so pitilessly drives me up against the insufficiency of my site and of my buildings?

The famine, for its part, does its share by warning me that it is an unsound and dangerous position when an undertaking like mine does not stand on its own ground, and is not surrounded by a piece of land on which it can produce some of its food supply. If at the beginning of summer I had been able to plant some maize, I should now have some to help with the feeding of my patients.

There are almost always in my hospital from twenty to thirty people who are capable of light work on the land. First of all come the attendants who accompany the patients, and whom I have to feed in any case. Why should they sit there all the day idle? That by such work they should to some extent pay for their own food and that of their sick companion is only fair and just. Then come a certain number of light and convalescent cases whom a little work will not hurt. Patients with ulcers on their feet whose skin is already granulating have often so little discomfort that they can quite reasonably be employed for a few hours. So I have a lot of labour power in my hospital, but it is unused because the hospital has no land.

It is only recently that this consideration has become weighty;

when there were only forty patients, the employable labour power meant much less than it does now with 120 or more. Nor had the idea of burdening oneself with farm work near the hospital anything attractive, so long as one could somehow manage to procure bananas and manioc. Now, however, when famine is raging, and it is becoming more and more evident that it is likely to prove a standing source of difficulty everywhere, I cannot but see that the hospital, if it is to continue its existence, must itself provide part at least of its own food.

On these and similar thoughts I ponder during these dismal weeks, and in the course of October my ponderings take shape in a resolution to remove the hospital to a bigger site, which will be its own property, and that as soon as possible. I already have the corrugated iron for the roofs. It was to have roofed the wards of the old hospital; now it will perform the same service in the new one. Nor shall I be short of labour, for he who has rice can always have labour. How subdued is the temper of our inmates to-day compared with what it was in the old days! They no longer try to evade the labour tasks, but even offer for them, because those who work get more to eat than the rest.

The decision thus arrived at I carry about with me without a word to anyone. I make solitary journeys to visit the piece of land which alone is worth considering for a site. It is three kilometres (one and three-quarter miles) upstream from here, on the same bank, and just at the point where the Ogowe divides into two branches. Once some big villages stood there, and N'Kombe, the "Sun-king"—for there were sun-kings in Africa too!—himself lived there. The spot was, therefore, once cultivated here and there, so that the forest which now covers it is comparatively young, and the labour of clearing the site will be correspondingly easy. Moreover, since there were once dwellings and plantations, there are oil-palms everywhere. A spacious valley not far from the river provides a good site for the hospital, and the gently rising hills just above it look as if formed to take our dwelling-houses.

I had been at the place many times, for Mons. Morel had drawn my attention to it during my first residence here. So the day after my return I revisited it, and regretted not being in a position to let the hospital rise again there in a new form, instead of my settling down amid the ruins of the old one. Now I come again, under the compulsion of dysentery and famine, to settle here after all.

My application for a grant of the land is met by the District Commissioner in the most friendly way. The formalities to be gone through will take months, but in consideration of the special circumstances and of the fact that no objections are likely to be raised, the site is put at my disposal provisionally, I am given about 70 hecatres (172 acres) as a "concession." This means that the land remains the property of the State, but is handed over to me to be built on or cultivated, whatever we build and whatever improvements we make remaining our own property. This is the only system of land-ownership in the colony.

On returning from my visit to the District Commissioner I call the doctors and nurses together and disclose to them what is under weigh. At first they are dumb with astonishment; then they break out into shouts of joy. There is no need to convince them of the necessity of the move; they have been for a long time even more convinced than I myself. Only we all wonder alike how we shall find the courage to face such an undertaking. The natives stare at us with astonishment; to such gesticulation and such a din of conversation among us they are quite unaccustomed!

I, however, think of the sacrifice it means for my wife and daughter. They expect to see me back again at the end of this winter (1925-26); as it is, I can scarcely hope to get to Europe before the beginning of the following one. The building cannot be done without my superintendence, and for the laying out of the hospital use must be made of my experience. Once the roofs are on the buildings, others can undertake the internal arrangements.

18 *AUTUMN AND WINTER, 1925*

THE first thing we have to do is to peg out the area provisionally granted us, so as to be able to make the ground plan which has to be handed in to the District Commissioner. Compass in hand, we work our way into the forest and cut tracks which make measurement possible. If we come upon a swamp, we have to content ourselves with driving long poles into the soft ground at intervals of twenty metres. If we stumble on a thicket inhabited by the formidable red ants, white men and black all try who can retreat the quickest. These ants establish themselves on the branches, and drop in clusters on invaders of their preserve.

While the pegging out is being done, the work of clearing the ground is also commenced, for we must as soon as possible have a piece of land ready for cultivation in order to sow some maize. Since it will be necessary for a longish time, so far as we can see, to feed our inmates with rice from Europe, it is a matter of giving them, in addition, some food containing vitamins.

For the deforesting everyone in the hospital who can move hand and foot is summoned each morning, provided with axe and bush-knife, and taken by canoe about two miles upstream to our new estate. This troop is composed of men and women who are staying with us as companions of the patients. There are in it also some patients who are now well again and stay to help us out of gratitude. All are willing, because those who work get a whole ration, while the ordinary hospital inmate, with the exception of those who are seriously ill, gets only two-thirds. There are periods, however, when even the workers have to be rationed sparingly, for the famine continues as bad as ever.

206

The workers get not only their food but a present as well. If I were to ask them what they would like for their present they would one and all ask for tobacco and some alcoholic drink. When the slave-trade flourished in these parts tobacco and alcohol, together with gunpowder and lead, represented the highest current values, and they have kept this position down to to-day. It is only with difficulty that these people are getting accustomed to receive their presents from me in a different form. I give only useful things: spoons—forks are hardly ever wanted—cups, plates, knives, cooking-pots, sleeping mats of raphia, blankets, material for clothes, and mosquito-nets.

It is no easy job to collect the people each morning for the journey. Dr. Nessmann and Dr. Lauterburg know something about that. Every day they have to shout themselves hoarse till at last the canoes are full. The native orderlies cannot help in this since they have not authority enough, nor can they decide who is fit for work and who is not.

If we have plenty of workers, the canoes are not sufficient, and the women have to travel in the motor-boat. There is then such a chattering that the noise of the motor stands out against it much as a harmonium would if played against a full orchestra.

We get, as a rule, about fifteen workers, which in view of the overwhelming amount that has to be done is far too few. And to ensure that some progress is made one of us must go with them as supervisor; left to themselves they would hardly do anything. Why should they, who happen to be here just now, exert themselves so that others, who will be in the hospital a few months hence, may have maize to eat, and even be housed in good wards!

A day with these people moves on like a symphony.

Lento: They take very grumpily the axes and bush-knives that I distribute to them on landing. In snail-tempo the procession goes to the spot where bush and tree are to be cut down. At last everyone is in his place. With great caution the first blows are struck.

Moderato: Axes and bush-knives move in extremely moderate time, which the conductor tries in vain to quicken. The midday break puts an end to the tedious movement.

Adagio: With much trouble I have brought the people back to the work-place in the stifling forest. Not a breath of wind is stirring. One hears from time to time the stroke of an axe.

Scherzo: A few jokes, to which in my despair I tune myself up, are successful. The mental atmosphere gets livelier, merry words fly here and there, and a few begin to sing. It is now getting a little cooler, too. A tiny gust of wind steals up from the river into the thick undergrowth.

Finale: All are jolly now. The wicked forest, on account of which they have to stand here instead of sitting comfortably in the hospital, shall have a bad time of it. Wild imprecations are hurled at it. Howling and yelling they attack it, axes and bush-knives vie with each other in battering it. But—no bird must fly up, no squirrel show itself, no question must be asked, no command given. With the very slightest distraction the spell would be broken. Then the axes and knives would come to rest, everybody would begin talking about what had happened or what they had heard, and there would be no getting them again into train for work.

Happily, no distraction comes. The music gets louder and faster. If this finale lasts even a good half-hour the day has not been wasted. And it continues till I shout "Amani! Amani!" (Enough! Enough!) and put an end to work for the day.

The sun is still well up in the sky. But the walk from the work-place to the river, the return in the canoes, the collecting of the tools and the paddles, and the distribution of the food ration takes nearly an hour and a half. And at the Equator darkness sets in just after six o'clock. To superintend the delivery of the axes and knives and the distribution of the rations by lantern-light is extraordinarily exhausting. Moreover, doctors and nurses are, as far as possible, to cease all outside work when darkness falls, that they may not get bitten by mosquitoes and so risk getting an attack of malaria.

Whoever is with the workers must, in the afternoon, continually watch the sky to see that no thunderstorm is threatening. As soon as he sees any suspicious-looking clouds, he must give the signal for return. The men must not be allowed to get wet, because that often brings on attacks of malaria. Nor must they be surprised by a storm on the river. Many of them come, of course, from the interior and cannot swim. If the canoe were to upset, they would be lost.

On December 4th the canoes are surprised on their return journey by a terrible thunderstorm. Dr. Nessmann, who was in charge that day, had not noticed the danger in time. We wait for an hour and a half in dreadful anxiety, but at last the storm abates. One after the other the canoes arrive in pitch darkness and under a deluge of rain. They had had just time to reach the bank somewhere or other, and no one was drowned. I mount to the doctor's house, almost dizzy with joy.

On that portion of the new site where the buildings are to stand, we leave some trees standing to provide shade. Where we want to plant, every tree must be sacrificed, oil-palms alone being spared. Big hardwood trees give us great trouble. Several men must work for several days before one of the giants comes down, and then it takes days longer to cut it up.

The simplest plan would be to leave where it falls everything that is felled, and then in the dry season to burn it, as the natives do when they lay out a new plantation. We act differently since we shall be glad later on to be spared the labour of hauling from a distance all the wood that the hospital needs for fuel. The logs are therefore built up into big piles on the spot, the trunks being left as they are. The tremendous roots, too, are left in the ground. What toil it would be to dig them out! But we shall sow between the trunks and the roots. To turn the forest into good arable land is a work of generations.

The piles of logs provide, unfortunately, a good home for snakes, but we acquiesce in the inconvenience as part of the bargain. There are so many in our grounds anyhow that a few hundred more make little difference. Every day as we clear further we despatch some, among them some of the most dangerous kinds.

Everywhere in the undergrowth we come across oil-palms, which can neither flower nor fruit, because the matted vines lie upon them like a thick carpet. We often have to cut a tunnel through this undergrowth to work our way to the foot of the palms. We cut the climbing plants through near the root, and then leave them to get dry and to rot; only then can we drag them down from the trees, and even then we have more than enough trouble with them. It takes on the average about a week to free a group of oil-palms from the carpet which covers them. How thankful the palms are when the sun can at last shine upon them!

There is always going on in the primeval forest, though without a sound to betray it, an uncanny struggle between creepers and trees. Anything which cannot work its way up above the creeper-growth into the sunlight, dies a slow and painful death.

The oil-palm is not a native of the primeval forest. It is only to be found on the outskirts of villages, or in places near which there once were villages. It has been spread by the action of birds and monkeys, who carry off into the forest the fruit of the trees growing near the huts, and after consuming the fibrous, oil-containing husk, let the nut, with its kernel, fall to the ground, where the latter takes root and grows.

So after getting rid of the other vegetation we find in many spots whole groves of oil-palms, which are valuable as a help in the feeding of our sick. In the course of years we shall be able to give the natives a good portion of their fat ration in the form of palm oil. We prepare it from the husk of the nut. It is well-known that the red nuts—in shape and size like walnuts—grow in several dozens together on a common receptacle, the whole forming a big cluster. Oil is got both from the fibrous husk which encloses the nut, the so-called fruit flesh, and from the hard kernel which is inside the very hard nut. To get the oil from the kernels strong presses are needed, so the oil is not prepared in Africa, but these "palm kernels" are shipped to Europe, where they are manufactured into oils and vegetable fats of the most varied sorts. When we have procured our oil from the fibrous husk, the nuts are shelled, and the kernels are exchanged for rice at a store. The nut-cracking is the job of patients suffering from ulcers on their feet and capable of no other work.

*　　*　　*

In the hospital we are still hard worked, for the dysentery epidemic continues, and we sometimes get half a dozen new cases in a single morning. Many of these poor creatures are mere skeletons, doomed irretrievably to death. Oftentimes there are not people enough in the hospital to dig the graves and carry out the bodies to the cemetery, and then we ourselves have to work as sextons and bearers.

And again and again it happens that patients who come with other diseases get infected. Menzoghe, a poor woman, who by her own wish had her arm with badly infected wounds taken off, catches it and dies. Similar is the fate of a poor sick man, deserted by his family, whom I brought to the hospital when I was on a journey upstream to save him from dying of hunger. And these are not the only victims whom we lose in this tragic fashion! At times I am so depressed that I can hardly summon up energy enough to work. I should like best to send away, till the epidemic is over, all the people who come for an operation. But they will not be turned away.

In November we operate on an elephantiasis tumour weighing more than 40 kilos (88 lbs.), the operation lasting from 10.30 to 4 p.m. For these cases there is no need, fortunately, to use a general anæsthetic. When Dr. Lauterburg, after the operation, proceeded to carry the patient to his berth, an old negro danced solemnly along in front of him. He knew of no better way in which to express his feelings. King David, no doubt, felt much the same when he danced before the Ark of the Covenant. Then all the hospital inmates crowded round the patient's berth, while he himself seized the doctor's hands and never wearied of stroking them and ejaculating, "Akewa! Akewa!" (Thank you! Thank you!)

About this time we operated on several smaller tumours, weighing only 10 to 20 kilos.

There are also a number of hernia cases. Everyone who gets relief from his sufferings sends to us hernia patients from his home district.

But of strangulated hernias we really get fewer cases now than when I was here before. That does not mean that there are fewer cases. But since nearly all the men are now at work getting timber and in the swamps far from their villages, there are often not enough people in the village to paddle at once to us the poor man whose hernia has got strangulated. So instead of finding deliverance with us, he dies a torturing death in his hut.

Accidents are continually giving us surgical work. Our worst case is that of a native, called Mefane, who had both his legs shattered below the knee by a gun-shot at very short range. He was sheltering for the night beneath the house, built on piles, of a European without the latter's knowledge, and he was hit by the charge from a gun which was accidentally fired through the floor. In this case again methyl-violet proved its value. We first removed the splinters of bone, and then by plugging and padding the wound with strips of gauze dipped in a solution of pyoktanin and kept moist, we succeeded in mastering the suppuration. But it will be a long time before the ends of the shattered bones re-unite again.

While the man is under treatment two of his relatives have to stay in the hospital to carry him to the operating-room for his dressings to be changed, and to help us in our various undertakings. Being in urgent need of workers, we always try to arrange that surgical patients who have relatives shall be accompanied by two attendants who are capable of manual work and who, from the day of the operation till the patient is discharged, shall help in the clearing of the new site in return for food and presents. We often do manage this, but cannot insist on it too decidedly. The result might be that, to escape having to work for us, relatives would abstain from bringing sufferers who ought to be operated upon. With the natives one cannot adhere rigidly to principles; one must always act with due consideration for all circumstances which ought to be taken into account.

Towards Christmas our little rooms for white patients get filled up. The case which causes us most anxiety is that of Herr Stähli, a Swiss, who came to us with a row of deep-seated abscesses and a severe sunstroke. We do everything we can for him, but without much hope; he lies in a state of almost unbroken coma. On Christmas Eve we bring him a little tree decked with candles and sing carols at his bedside. He has a clear moment or two, and understands what it means, a happy smile lighting up his thin, yellow face.

That very evening there is great excitement among the patients. A maniac is secretly deposited here, and causes universal confusion.

In the afternoon of Christmas Day our Swiss patient dies. As the burial must take place next morning—a body cannot be kept above ground in the tropics—the coffin has to be taken in hand at once.

19 *1926*

FROM the beginning of 1926 I have to be on the new site almost every day. While Mlle. Kottmann leads the clearing party, I undertake with another team the work on the actual building-site.

How are we to build? We are unanimous on one point— that we will not have in the new hospital any bamboo huts or any leaf-roofs. These huts require constant repairs, and after every storm holes have to be mended in the roofs. The storm, that is, lifts the light leaf-tiles and pushes them together, so that uncovered spaces are left. And every three years the roof has to be replaced by a new one.

It often happened that the doctors could devote only the morning to the sick, and had to employ the afternoon on building repairs. So now that we are reconstructing the hospital we intend to have permanent buildings which will not require constant maintenance.

Buildings of stone or brick are unthinkable; they would cost us too much time, and far too much money. So we decide for wards of corrugated iron on a framework of hardwood. Hardwood it must be, since ordinary timbers would, in a few months, be the prey of termites.

These corrugated-iron wards we shall build on piles. Why? The hospital will spread out along the river, having to be built near it because the natives are accustomed to live near water. They like, too, to have their canoes within sight. The hospital will, indeed, stand on the slope of a hill a few metres above the normal high-water level, but we have to allow for exceptionally high floods. These might carry my buildings away if they stood on the ground itself; if they are on piles, the water flows away between the piles. Piles, therefore, on account of the river.

But also on account of the hill. For if two or three thunderstorms descend on us during the night, torrents of water rush
down the hillside above us, and these would endanger my
buildings if they stood on the ground itself; if they are on
piles the water flows away between the piles.

So I shall be a modern prehistoric man, and build my
hospital like a lake-dwellers' village, but of corrugated iron.

Learned men dispute whether the lake-dwellings of our
ancestors were built actually in the water or on the edge of it.
On the whole the latter are doubtless right. When primitive
man intends to make a permanent settlement near water or
on a hillside, he is obliged to help himself out with piles. Piles
safeguard him from danger caused by the water, and relieve
him, a very important matter, of the toil of levelling a site.
The road from the hut to the stone building leads over
the pile-dwelling.

Next there comes for us the question of getting the piles.
The most suitable material is a special kind of hardwood
which is somewhat rare. One of my black friends is kind
enough to tell me of a spot higher up the river where there
are groups of such trees not too far from the water. It must be
upstream, because in canoes with a heavy load of timber
we can only travel downstream. And only trees standing near
water can be considered, because we cannot haul the heavy
timber any but short distances over land or through swamps.

Dr. Nessmann is given the duty of fetching the piles. If we
were to send the natives by themselves, they would come
home with only a few poles in the boat.

The place indicated is about sixteen miles away on a
mountain stream, which has rapids in it and is only navigable
when the water is high. So Dr. Nessmann will be getting piles
till spring comes. He made his first journey on January 4th,
1926, and returned a few days later with thirty piles. To secure the needed number the expedition will have to be repeated several times.

Meanwhile, to provide fuel, I get palm branches cut and
piled in layers to dry. For it is necessary to char the piles in
order to make them last longer, and this work I must superintend. Left to themselves the natives would either burn them
altogether, or not char them sufficiently, and they would
never have more than three or four piles in the fire. My plan
is to throw up a broad bank of earth on which twenty already

barked piles are so laid that one end projects as far as possible beyond the bank into the fire, which is kept burning the whole length of the bank. When this free end is sufficiently charred, the fire is allowed to go out and the pile is reversed, so that what rested before on the bank becomes the free end and rests on the fire. Thus the pile gets charred from end to end. The charring is made especially effective if water is poured over the glowing end before it is taken from the fire. If everything goes well, I can char from twenty to thirty piles a day.

By February 15th the store hut is erected and roofed with corrugated iron, with a room inside it which can be locked, for the tools used by those who work at the felling and the digging. Now we need no longer waste time at the start from the hospital over giving out axes, bush-knives, pickaxes, billhooks, and spades, nor in the evening go through the wearisome task of calling in, counting, and storing away all the tools in the darkness.

The store hut erected, we proceed at once to the driving of the piles for the first sick ward. The important thing is that the hole for the pile shall have a strong and well-stamped-in layer of stones at the bottom for a foundation which will not give way. If a pile sinks with the weight of the house, the building, of course, comes out of the perpendicular.

Moreover, in fixing the piles care must be taken that they stand exactly in line, and that their top surfaces are exactly level. If they are not, the fixing of the beams upon them is very troublesome, for some have to be wedged up, others to have a piece cut away, according as a pile is too low or too high.

I set the piles fairly close to one another. Measured from centre to centre the distance is about 1½ metres (4 feet 9 inches), so that four, five, or six rows are needed, according to the width of the building. With the piles so close together the beams that are to rest upon them need be of 10 to 15 centimetres only (4 to 6 inches) instead of 8.

The ward we begin with is 25 metres (about 80 feet) long and 5 wide. It is to contain two rooms for surgical patients, and a few small ones for the native orderlies. How it weighs on me that in the old hospital they have to live in holes and corners. They are now to have rooms with wooden floors and mosquito-proof netting. The pleasantness of their quarters will induce them to stay with me, even if the work is hard and the pay not high.

I am in a hurry to get this first building roofed. It will let me house Monenzalie, the black carpenter, and his helpers, and also some of those who work on the new site. That will mean two more hours a day secured for work, hours spent hitherto in journeys out and back.

At the end of February Dr. Nessman is to return home in order to perform his military service, and on the 22nd Dr. Trensz, who is to take his place, arrives; he also is the son of a pastor in Alsace. He has scarcely unpacked, when he is taken by Dr. Nessmann on the last journey the latter will make for pile-getting. He has to learn the business, for it will now fall to his share.

I try sometimes leaving the building workers to themselves for an afternoon, or even for a whole day, because I so urgently need time for letters, for making out orders for goods, and for getting into touch again with the working of the hospital. But each time I have to repent it. If I am not here, either nothing is done or the work is done in such a way that it has to be done over again. On one such afternoon a carpenter sawed twenty valuable beams by wrong measurements.

I have written to Europe asking them to find me in either Alsace or Switzerland a young carpenter, to be sent out as quickly as possible for the beginning of the dry season.

And now there is some building work needed in the old hospital. For in March an insane patient who had been brought to me fastened in some stocks, tears down the cell made for the mental patients and breaks out of it, spreading terror everywhere in the hospital. With a heavy heart I have to give him back to the people who brought him.

Amid all the work and anxiety caused me by the new hospital there is one thing that comforts me, viz., that I shall have there safe rooms for several mental patients, and shall not have to turn any away because I have not enough cells, or only cells which are not strong enough. But in order to be able in the meanwhile to take in at least one or two such sufferers, I rebuild the cell that has been ruined. It now has two doors —a solid inner one and an outer one with openings in it. If the patient is comparatively quiet, he need not sit in darkness; the inner door is left open, and through the openings he gets light and air with a view over the landing-place and the river.

The cell is only just ready when there comes an inmate for it. How glad I am that I did not shirk this temporary work, but did, in defiance of the parable, put a piece of new cloth on the old garment.

While the carpenters are working on the first building, I set the piles for those which are to follow, this difficult work taking weeks. Often I have to push or to turn the heavy pile just a centimetre or two so as to get it into the right position, and while this is being done I cannot let a native touch it. They cannot judge any movement, and would push it or turn it right out of place. There is nothing for it but to get into the pit myself, put my arms around it, and move it as required. If all goes well, I can get a dozen piles into position in a day.

The new hospital is becoming a regular village. It is to provide accommodation for two hundred patients and their attendants. In the part which stands furthest downstream it will consist of three parallel lines of buildings. At the upper end of these lines there will be only two, so that the big building in which the doctors carry on their work shall have an empty space in front of it and get some breeze from the river.

Every building has its central line running east and west, so that the sun rises and sets opposite the gable ends, and never strikes the side walls. For we are close to the Equator, and the sun travels very little towards north or south. Hence the side-walls of a building so oriented and provided with a projecting roof only catch the sun about Christmas and midsummer. The building is therefore considerably cooler than one built north and south, on the walls of which the sun's rays would rest every morning and evening. These building rules should be much more observed and followed in the tropics than they usually are.

I also purposely make these buildings long and narrow, the form which the sun can injuriously affect least. The problem also of light and air, a problem which is so important with tropical buildings when there is a projecting roof, is easier to solve with narrow buildings than with wide ones. And so in my buildings the rooms are not side by side, but end to end.

In the course of the spring I have fixed the piles for the entire hospital village. Besides the building measuring 27 yards by 5½, which is now approaching completion, there will be four others with dimensions of 14½ yards by 7½, 28 yards by 7½, 39 yards by 5, and 24 yards by 9.

Simultaneously with the buildings for the black patients, I begin a house for the white ones. It will be higher up the river than the main block of buildings, and will be 24 yards by 9, supported by forty-eight piles.

On April 26th Hans Muggensturm arrives, a young Swiss from St. Gallen, and now I can breathe, though not quite freely. The great question is whether he can get on with the natives. If he has not that gift, his work will be much less valuable than it might be. But in a few days it is clear that he has it.

And what is the gift? It consists in being able to combine in right measure firmness and kindness, to avoid unnecessary talk, and to find a jocular remark at the right moment.

So now the new European helper takes over the superintendence of the three carpenters and their labourers, and I can devote myself to the fixing of the piles, the preparation of the sites, and the collecting of the materials. My first duty now is to see that the various kinds of work fit into one another, and that timber and iron, screws and nails, are always at hand when wanted.

Now I can undertake the necessary journeys to get timber without the building work coming to a stop. For time is precious. In the dry season—from the end of May to the middle of September—the most important buildings must be roofed. In the autumn, when the rainy season begins, we shall work at the partitions and the fittings.

During the dry season, too, we shall begin digging a well down by the hospital, and in the autumn I shall fix the piles for our dwelling-house on the hill above; 105 piles for a house 33 yards by 9.

The garden, upstream from the hospital, which we laid out and sowed in the spring, now gives us beans and cabbages. Unfortunately, its lower part was reached by the exceptionally early autumn flood, and we lost part of the crop.

* * *

In the early months of the year the work for the patients is so heavy that the two doctors can hardly get through it, for we always have from 120 to 160 black patients on our hands. Speaking generally, we can say they suffer from malaria, frambœsia, dysentery, leprosy, and sleeping-sickness, but nearly a third of them are, as usual, with us on account of the phagedenic ulcers. From fifteen to twenty berths are occupied by patients who have had, or who are waiting for, an operation.

Accidents bring us just now a lot of surgical work. One man falls from a high tree on which he was getting honey, and is brought here with a serious fracture. Another is cutting down a tree on which he believes there is honey, so as to secure the tasty spoil in comfort, and the tree falls upon a hut and kills an unfortunate woman. From a timber site we receive a man who had got caught under a rolling tree-trunk. In spite of his severe injuries we cure him.

A longish time is spent with us by a native hunter, whose hand had been torn by a gorilla with its terrible teeth. He shot at the creature, which encountered him unexpectedly on the forest path, and thought himself lucky that it retired instead of rushing at him. But it lay in wait behind a tree to catch him when he came back, and there was a struggle in which the hunter had a hair's-breadth escape from death.

Another native's encounter with an elephant had a less happy ending. The elephant came to a spot near Samkita, where mahogany was being felled, but on seeing the men there made a leisurely retreat. The men determined to bring him down by their traditional method of sneaking after him and cutting the Achilles tendons of his hind legs, the crafty way in which in earlier times thousands of elephants in the forests of Central Africa had been rendered helpless and then cruelly done to death. But the Samkita negroes have not the skill of their forefathers; the elephant noticed the coming onslaught and charged. The nearest native he threw into the air, and then, having bored him through with his tusks, he quietly trotted off. The man's injuries were so severe that we could not save his life.

The primeval forest also witnesses accidents caused by careless shooting. One morning we received a native whom, while he was digging for roots in the bush, another had taken for a wild boar and had shot him in the back. The unhappy shooter, N'Zigge by name, accompanies his victim, whose wound proves a fatal one. Immediately after his death N'Zigge sends for his wife and child to come as soon as possible, and I keep them all in the hospital because their lives are now unsafe. I accompany N'Zigge also to the District Commissioner's where the case is dealt with, lest he should be murdered on the way. As it is only a case of homicide through negligence, his sentence is only to pay a considerable sum of money to the family of the dead man, and give them a goat as well, the latter in obedience to the rule that when a life has been lost something living must be given as part of the compensation. In order to be safe and to earn the money, N'Zigge, who is a pleasant, quiet fellow, remains with his family here, and helps in the tree-felling. He becomes in time our best and most loyal worker.

Once we have brought to us all at once half a dozen injured men, victims of a fight which took place on a timber site between the workers.

On another occasion we receive two natives in a terrible condition, because on a road-making job about ninety miles to the south they had been blasting stone with dynamite and had not taken shelter quickly enough. One dies a few days after his arrival, the other is saved.

At the beginning of the year we receive several mental cases, many of them, however, with merely temporary derangements, due to sleeping-sickness or to poisons which cause nervous excitement. One of the former, N'Tsama by name, was reduced to a skeleton. We treat him with tryparsamid, the new sleeping-sickness drug from the Rockefeller Institute, which we have just received for experimental purposes. N'Tsama's excitement slowly disappears, but his mental disturbance remains in the form of an uncanny kleptomania which exposes the poor fellow to unpleasantly rough treatment from the hospital inmates who suffer thereby. Having also, like many sleeping-sickness patients, an abnormal appetite, he coaxes to him my poultry, so as to make them a contribution to his cooking-pot, and many a one falls a victim to his wiles. Then, like so many other patients, N'Tsama catches dysentery and hovers for two months between life and death, so weak that he has to be fed by others. At last, as spring approaches, he gets over the dysentery, and the treament with tryparsamid can be resumed. Then the kleptomania slowly disappears, and, having become strong enough to walk about, he stands nearly all day on the river bank and fishes, though without catching much. One day, when there were planks to be unloaded and taken up to the hospital, I laughingly called to N'Tsama to leave his fishing and help us, whereupon he lifted up a plank and carried it away on his head. There is much jubilation over this in the hospital, because it is thus evident to all that even sleeping-sickness sufferers in the last stage of the disease, who have hitherto been doomed to death, can now be restored to healthy life. At the beginning of the summer N'Tsama asks to be allowed to help with the forest clearing, and he stays with us as a labourer. "The Doctor is my father (he says) and the hospital is my village." The only relic of the sleeping-sickness is a proneness to fatigue and irritation. On account of this he is only allowed to work when one of us is present, so that too much exertion may not be expected from him, and that the others may not excite him by making fun of him. Since then we have had many excellent results from the use of this drug.

"Bayer 205" (called also Germanin), the drug produced by the Bavarian Dye Company, constitutes, with the American tryparsamid, a great advance in the fight with sleeping-sickness. Each of them has its own advantages and disadvantages. Tryparsamid is more effective in advanced cases than Bayer 205, but has the disadvantage that, like the atoxyl we used to employ, it often damages the optic nerve and may result in blindness. In spite of all our caution we, too, have one case of blindness to register.

With how much more confidence than hitherto we now hold our position in the fight against sleeping-sickness. We have had this month to diagnose three Europeans as in the early stage of the disease, but they were all saved. And they had no need to go to Europe to recruit; as soon as the cure was over, they could go straight back to work.

And what a number of natives get cured now, whom in past days we should have had to give up as hopeless cases because they had come to us in the last stage of the disease!

One day I have some business at the factories and see a native lying asleep at the side of the path. No one can tell me anything about him. "He has been lying there for a day, and is probably drunk," said the natives whom I questioned, and off they went their several ways. I put him into my boat and brought him to the hospital, where the microscope revealed that there in the hot sun his sleep was not that of the drunkard, but that of the victim of sleeping-sickness. When, some weeks later, he recovered his power of speech, we learnt that he was coming up from the coast, and wanted to go to his home in the interior.

We also got several poison cases one after the other. The na-

tive timber merchant who told me where to find the piles for
my new building notices that his quite intelligent son is beginning to stumble, and to sit staring stupidly in front of him.
I at once suspect poison, so the boy is isolated, has to take
powdered charcoal, and gets no food but what has been prepared under careful supervision. He slowly recovers. Probably
someone was poisoning him to wreak his revenge on the father.

Another native timber merchant whom I know is brought
here in a strange condition. He seems to be fully conscious, but
can neither speak nor swallow. His muscles show a remarkable
rigidity, and his arms and legs tremble persistently, though only
gently. He shows cataleptic symptoms, keeping his arms, for
instance, in the position in which another person has placed
them. He asks by signs for a pen, but is unable to write. As he
spits all food out of his mouth, he is fed for weeks through the
nose with a tube, and his cure depends on whether we can
effectively overcome the tension of the muscles. He is treated
with chloral hydrate, and intravenous injections of various
drugs.

What trouble Dr. Trensz has with this man, the first case
of poison that he has to deal with! He is well enough to be
sent home at the end of three months, but has no recollection
of what was done to him in the hospital.

This timber merchant had shortly before had a dispute over
money with some family connections who had a share in the
business. These, then, will have been the persons who gave
the poison, someone suggests. But one must not make such obvious inferences in Africa! To anyone familiar with native
mentality it will seem probable that an enemy who had been
planning against him for some time, or someone who wanted
him out of the way, was using the quarrel as an opportunity
for poisoning him, because he reckoned that suspicion would
fall on the relatives who were engaged in the dispute.

What an uncanny place Equatorial Africa is with its many
tragedies in which poison plays a part!

Frequently, however, the poisoning is unintentional. The sick
man who seeks help from a medicine-man is given too much
of the dangerous stuff in which the latter deals. Such a patient
was brought to us this spring in a terrible condition. He could
neither stand, nor speak, nor swallow, and it cost us endless
toil and trouble to snatch him from death.

Simultaneously with him we had with us a medicine-man

with a severe ulcer on his tongue. We found the causative organisms to be fusiform bacilli and spirochætes, such as are found also in the tropical phagedenic ulcers. We treated the medicine-man as we should a colleague, because our policy is to keep on good terms with all of them, so that they may send to us of their own accord the sufferers for whom their art can do nothing.

* * *

For the treatment of the phagedenic ulcers we have now, to guide us, our own tried method, which is much simpler than the usual one, and gives much better results.

The latter consists in putting the patient under an anæsthetic, and then scraping his sore with the sharp-edged spoon, in order to remove all diseased tissue, after which it is covered with disinfecting compresses which are renewed daily. This is a very troublesome method. What a way of commencing treatment when five or six savages are to be put on the table one after the other, and anæsthetised! The method is also expensive, for ether and ethyl chloride, being inflammable commodities, have to travel on the ship's deck and pay even a higher freight.

So our efforts have for some time been directed towards managing without an anæsthetic and scraping, especially since many of the natives, upset by the shriek that others made when the anæsthetising began, were afraid of being put to sleep, and preferred to have themselves taken home uncured, rather than face the scraping. One evening we heard a patient, who had just gone through the anæsthetising and the scraping, say to his neighbour: "Yes, the doctor wanted to kill me. He put some poison into my nose, and I was actually dead. But he hadn't enough poison, and I came to life again!"

We began by substituting for the scraping of the sore a dabbing of its surface with a sublimate pastille, and this is repeated on several consecutive days. This made possible a very satisfactory removal of the diseased tissue, only this was very painful. We, therefore, tried whether we could not do as well with a daily syringing. And it was successful! This new method allows us to avoid any touching of the sore at all—even the gentlest is very painful, as I know by experience—and yet at the same time to get the antiseptic down through the thick layer of nectroic tissue to the very base of the ulcer much better than before. The pus is wiped off with a gauze swab, and all loose sloughs are removed; but all rubbing or pressure is avoided, for both are extremely painful. After this the ulcer is washed out with sterile water, and irrigation treatment is instituted. The fluid we use is a 1-6000 solution of mercury cyanide. The ulcer is treated every morning from five to twenty minutes according to its size, with drops which fall, about sixty to the minute, from a height of 50 to 75 cm. (20-30 inches). Drops from such a height cause at first acute pain, so for the first few days the height is kept to a few centimetres only; but the drops gradually make their way through the thick superficial layer of necrotic tissue. The splash breaks it up, and enables the antiseptic to make its way down to the base of the ulcer. Probably, also, the continual "hammering" of the drops of liquid has a stimulating effect. At any rate, the ulcer gets cleansed in the course of a few days; it assumes a good, red colour, and shows a tendency to heal which we never could show to follow with any other method.

If it is a very large and rapidly extending ulcer, it is exposed to the drops both morning and evening; we also make the solution stronger, taking a gram of oxycyanide of mercury to three, or even to two, litres of water (3⅜ or 2¼ quarts).

What is put upon the ulcer for the bandaging between the washings is comparatively unimportant. We generally mix for it equal quantities of iodoform, dermatol, and salol.

Even when the ulcer is beginning to granulate, the dropping is continued steadily, but with weaker and weaker solution, so as to avoid any injury to the newly formed tissue; we end with 1 gram to 10 or 12 litres of water.

When the ulcer is perfectly clean we try, if it is a very large one, to hasten the growth of the new skin by skin-grafting, and if this is successful the time wanted for the healing is shortened by at least a third.

But this treatment by falling drops gives good results with other kinds of ulcers too, many of them responding well to a solution of half a gram of sulphate of copper in a litre of water. And it makes possible the use with any kind of ulcer of any desired disinfectant in a solution of any desired strength.

Extraordinarily useful in combating the many varieties of ulcer is a new disinfectant, a Swiss speciality called Breosan, which we usually apply in the form of a salve. Its success with the most varied kinds of ulcer is especially surprising when it is used on quite recent ones. We use hardly any other remedy than this for the so-called craw-craws from which Europeans suffer, and the origin of which is still obscure, although bacteriologically we frequently find staphylococci in pure culture.

I have tested Breosan on myself. Previously, every scratch I got on one of my feet turned into an ulcer, which gave me trouble for weeks. If on the new site I knocked my foot against a beam, or if it got chafed by my shoe, I knew that it meant an ulcer. But since beginning to treat every such abrasion with Breosan I have not had an ulcer on either foot. We have now made it a rule to give every European a tube of Breosan for his travelling drug-box, and have been thanked for it again and again. I believe that Breosan ointment is going to play a big part in tropical medicine.

We are caused great anxiety by the cases, happily not numerous, in which the phagedenic ulcer infects deeply the surrounding tissues. As a rule the infection is confined to the ulcer itself, the difference between healthy and infected tissue being clearly marked. But if, as occasionally happens, the infection spreads along the subcutaneous fascial planes, or along the intermuscular septa, or along the tendon sheaths, or if it reaches the bone, the case becomes very serious. If this complication is noticed at once, an extensive incision into the tissues may be effective. Otherwise hardly anything can be done; the infection spreads further and further, and death results. Anyone, therefore, who is treating such an ulcer, must be on the watch for any possible undermining of its edge. If that begins, an immediate intervention with the knife is called for.

There is at present no explanation of the facts that phagedenic ulcers form only on the lower leg, and that—in the Ogowe district at any rate—women are hardly ever attacked by them.

*　*　*

While treating the unhappily still numerous dysentery patients, Dr. Trensz makes a valuable discovery. It is well known that there are two sorts of dysentery, that caused by the unicellular amœbæ, and that which is traced back to dysentery bacteria. In the bacteriological laboratory which he has fitted up with the most primitive apparatus, Dr. Trensz undertakes the making of cultures from fæces of patients in which no

226 The Primeval Forest

amœbæ had been found. In these he proved the presence not of the dysentery bacilli but of vibrions closely akin to the cholera vibrions, and distinguished from them only by a different form of combination. It follows that what passed for bacillus dysentery is, in most cases, if his investigations prove correct, severe cholerine, produced by a paracholera vibrion.

Examination of the local water shows that this vibrion is endemic in the Ogowe district. Hence it is called the Vibrio Gabunensis, and Dr. Trensz has embodied his study of it in a good-sized scientific pamphlet.[1] So, perhaps, the dysentery which in Equatorial Africa always breaks out among the labourers engaged on road or railway building is in a large number of the cases in which the presence of amœbæ cannot be proved, not bacillus dysentery but this cholerine. I long ago dealt with unexplained cases of dysentery by taking a hint from cholera-therapy and treating them with white argillaceous earth (*bolus alba*) dissolved in water. The results were favorable, and now Dr. Trensz's researches explain why this treatment was effective. We have to deal with a complaint which is akin to cholera.

Cultivation of the vibrions in the laboratory enables Dr. Trensz to prepare a vaccine with which such cases of cholerine can be cured in two or three days.

In ordinary circumstances these water-borne cholerine bacteria are not dangerous to the natives. It is only when a diet of rice has destroyed the resisting power of the intestine that the infection is able to establish itself.

The fact that we doctors in Lambaréné are now three in number allows us to work scientifically and make researches of great value for the treatment of our sick.

The doctor who works in the primeval forest single-handed is so fully occupied with the daily routine that he has neither time nor energy left for the investigation of puzzling cases. In every tropical hospital there should, therefore, be at least two doctors. Too small medical establishments are as unprofitable here as are too small mission stations.

Again, since there are several doctors, necessary journeys can be undertaken without the hospital work being affected. Almost every month we each spend some days travelling. At the beginning of June Dr. Lauterburg undertakes a jour-

---

[1] This has since been published with the title: "Etude sur une diarrhée épidémique à vibrions observée au Gabon" (Strasbourg, 1928).

ney which is to last several weeks, made partly by water, partly by land, in the districts south of Lambaréné. He is away an unexpectedly long time, and no news of him reaches us, so that we are beginning to get anxious, when one fine day we see him step out of a canoe, thin, indeed, but healthy and happy. He was the first doctor who had ever been seen in those parts, and he at once won the confidence of the natives, who knew of the Lambaréné hospital by hearsay.

His report confirms us in our design of undertaking regularly long journeys like his, for there are numbers of sick far away from here who cannot travel to the hospital. The journey is too long, or the current of the river makes it too difficult, which is, indeed, the case for the districts lying to the south. Often, too, there is nobody to bring the sick to us. If, then, so many who need us cannot come to us, we must go to them.

If the hospital is to make available its full power for good, one of the doctors ought really to be continually going about with a well-supplied travelling dispensary, and the most necessary instruments, so that the necessary care may be given to those who can be treated where they live, and those who need hospital treatment can be brought back with him to Lambaréné.

But for this plan there must always be three doctors, one for the ordinary work, one for surgery, and one for travelling. It is to be hoped that I shall be able to find the necessary men and means.

*   *   *

We are not compelled, fortunately, by the bacteriology to cut down the surgical work. Many and many a victim of hernia or elephantiasis gets relief from his suffering through the knife wielded by Dr. N'Tschinda-N'Tschinda. And the patients are as a rule, very grateful. It may happen, indeed, that some man who has been operated upon is not prevented by gratitude from making off secretly in the night and taking with him as a souvenir the mosquite net lent him by the hospital. Such was the experience of Dr. N'Tschinda-N'Tshcinda with a patient who had an enormous hernia, and gave the surgeon a great deal of trouble. However, the joy the surgeon felt at having given the needed relief prevented him from worrying over the ingratitude.

By way of precaution we require that the present made in return for the operation—usually bananas or other fruit, seedlings of bread-fruit trees, or of banana plants, or smoked fish—shall be brought by the relatives while the patient is still in the hospital. If he himself expresses an intention of bringing it after his discharge, there is reason to fear that he will be hindered from doing so through a change in his feelings or through circumstances. One of them, who really means his promise, wants to leave his second wife with me as a pledge, until he returns with the present. I decline his offer on the ground that the pledge will be difficult to look after.

With operations on elderly people, i.e., over fifty years of age, one must in Equatorial Africa be extraordinarily careful. The cannot endure being for so long on their backs. They often lose their appetite after an operation, and fall into a condition of weakness which may be very dangerous. Our experience has made us refuse to operate on elderly people, unless such drastic treatment is absolutely necessary to save their life.

Since April we have had with us Mlle. Martha Lauterburg, the doctor's sister, as a nurse. She arrived at the same time as Hans Muggensturm. Our new, very experienced nurse takes over the service of the hospital, so that Mlle. Kottmann can now devote herself entirely to the work of the plantation, the garden, and the new building site. A European, too, Mons. Ganne, has been helping us for months with the supervision of those who are felling the trees.

Mlle. Emma Hausknecht manages the housekeeping, which is in truth the heaviest department of all our activities. She has a world of trouble with the cook to make him prepare the food with care and absolute cleanliness, not endangering our health by the use of unboiled water. Almost every day there are from twelve to fifteen Europeans to cook for. And the housekeeping is especially complicated because almost every day is washing-day, and there is always linen to be mended. The tidying of the rooms of the European patients also falls to Mlle. Hausknecht. She has at her disposal, indeed, for helpers the "boys" who have come with their sick masters, but what a job it is to keep these half-dozen boys in order!

Then there is still the care of the poultry and the goats. To avoid having to pay hard cash in Switzerland for all our milk, we are trying to rear a herd of goats. It is, indeed, only half a glass of milk a day that we get from each of these half-wild creatures, but we hope with time to improve the breed.

Mlle. Hausknecht, the ever busy, seldom appears on the scene alone; Fifi, the baby chimpanzee, is always holding on to her apron; Fifi was brought to us a year ago when only a few days old, by the native hunter who had shot her mother. Mlle. Hausknecht was at first terrified by the frightfully ugly creature, and would not touch it, but pity triumphed finally over all æsthetic inhibitions. Fifi has now got over her teething and can feed herself with a spoon without help. She has had for some time a playmate in a somewhat older baby chimpanzee, which a European left with us when he returned to Europe, in order that he might know it to be in good hands.

* * *

Europeans who are going home on leave often bring their dogs to us for the time, since they know that the animals will be well looked after. They never venture to entrust them to the natives, because the latter are quite capable of letting them die of hunger or thirst, or of treating them with thoughtless cruelty.

But while I am setting the piles I am allowed to discover that sympathy for the lower creatures can be aroused in even the most savage of the natives. Before the pile is lowered into the pit I look whether any ants, or toads, or other creatures have fallen into it, and if so, I take them out with my hands so that they may not be maimed by the pile, or crushed to death later by the earth and stones, and I explain why I do this to those who are standing by. Some smile in embarrassment; others pay no attention at all to what they have heard so often. But one day a real savage, who was working with me, was fetched to work in the plantation at cutting down the undergrowth. A toad being espied in it, his neighbour wanted to kill it with his bush-knife, but the first one seized his arm and unfolded to him and to a listening group the theory that the animals were, like ourselves, created by God, and that he will some day hold a great palaver with the men who torment or kill them. This savage was the very last on whom I should have expected my deeds and words to make any impression.

Our natives hear, with a lively interest, of a European magician who is touring the West Coast and giving performances in Cape Lopez. He also gives personal interviews in which, in return for a fee, he reveals the future, and gives information about things which have been lost. Till now it has been only those natives who could read the newspapers who got to know about the luxuriant crop of superstition that flourishes among the whites, and many a time have I been questioned by native "intellectuals" about the advertisements of clairvoyant men and women who are at work in the big towns of Europe.

What is *our* position, i.e., the position of those who try to combat the superstition of the natives?

"So the white people too have magicians!" a native said to me. "Why have the missionaries and you, too, concealed that from us?"

The victorious advance into the colonies of European superstition is an event of far-reaching significance. It gives another tremendous blow to our spiritual authority, which has already been cruelly shaken by the war. The intelligent, reflecting natives are shocked by the discovery that there is superstition prevalent among us also, and at present heathen superstition is triumphing, thanks to the unexpected ally who has come to its support from across the sea.

And the professional European superstition is now beginning to exploit the negro. Natives in this neighbourhood, some of our orderlies among them, have had sent to them a prospectus from Roxroy Studios, 42, Emmastraat, Haag (Holland). They must send fifty francs, a lock of their hair, and the date of their birth, so that their horoscope can be cast, and they may receive the "Ki-Magi" talisman which corresponds to those signs of the zodiac which bear on their life. They must also say in their letter whether their talisman is to ensure success in business, good fortune in love, good health, or luck at cards. A talisman is offered which will bring success in all the four, but it costs considerably more than the others.

Full of joy that they can obtain some of the advantages of this mysterious wisdom, two of my orderlies come to me about it, and ask me to advance them part of their wages, so that the money demanded and the other requisites may go off by return of post. One of them regretfully admits that he does not know when he was born, but he hopes that the hair he sends will enable the astrologer to cast his horoscope. I am afraid that in spite of my explanation and my refusal of any advance, the prospectus was answered.

*   *   *

In the course of the summer Joseph leaves us, since the wages he gets from me are no longer sufficient. He has got married, and wants to spoil his wife—an energetic and prudent woman—with clothes from Europe, just as two or three native timber merchants who have made something out of their business, spoil their wives. But he cannot manage this on an orderly's wage, so he is going to devote himself to the timber trade exclusively.

The departure of the man who was my only helper in the early days grieves me, but we remain good friends. If either of us can do a service for the other, he does it, and Joseph continues to style himself, "Dr. Albert Schweitzer's first medical assistant." Fortunately, we have managed to attract several new black orderlies. The best of them is Bolinghi, and he is entrusted with the care of the surgical cases.

We find the painting of the completed buildings a heavy task. They must be colour-washed in some way to make them last longer, and we prepare the wash by adding size dissolved in warm water to a solution of well-sifted lime. Properly prepared and laid on, this colour-wash is in the tropics very nearly as serviceable as the much more expensive oil paint. We use the latter only for those parts on which the rain beats during a thunderstorm.

We believe at first that we can train natives to do the colour-washing, but their chief contribution to the work is to ruin most skilfully the few brushes that we possess. If a primitive gets a brush into his hand the brush has in two days not a hair left. I do not know how they manage this, but so it is, and, as the colour-wash must also be laid on very carefully, there is nothing for it but to do the work ourselves. Doctors and nurses vie with each other in the practice of this unfamiliar art.

Mlle. Kottmann is at work for many days on eighty sacks of rice which had got wetted during transport. First, space had to be made for the sacks to stand side by side instead of being piled one upon another. Then each one had to be cut where it was wet, the damp grains taken out, and then the sack sewn up again, after which the whole lot had to be carefully watched, to see that the contents of the sacks were not spoiling. A couple of handfuls of damp rice is enough in this hot climate to make the whole sackful mouldy.

We still have to keep something like two tons of rice permanently in store. The famine is diminishing, but only because sufficient rice is now coming from Europe. Had we to depend on locally produced food only, we should be in an uncomfortable position. Bananas and manioc are scarcely procurable. What we do manage to secure is only enough to feed a few patients who are absolutely unable to take the rice. Not till the New Year comes, when the newly-planted banana trees begin to bear, will the country be able once more to feed its inhabitants.

We burden ourselves with some extra work out of compassion for the palm-trees, with which the site of our future home is crowded. The simplest plan would be to cut them all down. An oil-palm is valueless, there are so many of them. But we cannot find it in our heart to deliver them over to the axe just when, delivered from the creepers, they are beginning a new life. So we devote some of our leisure hours to digging up carefully those which are transplantable and setting them elsewhere, though it is heavy work. Oil-palms can be transplanted even when they are fifteen years old and are quite big.

That one should feel compassion for the animals my natives can understand. But that I should expect them to carry heavy palm-trees about, so that they may live instead of being cut down, seems to them a perverted philosophy.

The hospital is never without Europeans as inmates. At the beginning of the year two European babies first saw the light under our roofs, one of the mothers having come a very long journey from the south along the sea coast in order to go through her confinement at Lambaréné. For fourteen days she was carried by natives through forest and swamp, till she reached Cape Lopez, and was able to finish her journey in the river steamer. For her return journey I discovered a motor-boat which was going as far as the Fernando Vaz Lagoon, which lies due south from Cape Lopez. In the Catholic Mission station there she found hospitality till her husband could be summoned by messenger and could fetch her away with native carriers.

A few days later a European lady, seriously ill, arrives from the interior with her husband, an official, during the night and amid pouring rain. White patients are turned out, so that there may be a room free for them. And when she has been examined and provided for, there are the fifty natives to take in who were paddling the whole day in pouring rain without anything to eat. For they have come from the famine district. How we have to talk and scold to get the inmates to make room for them in the already overcrowded wards, and to give them some wood for their fires. Then by the light of lanterns the whole of the baggage has to be unloaded from the canoes, got under cover, and put in charge of watchmen. Finally, there is a liberal distribution of food, and it is past midnight when, tired and wet, we mount up to the doctor's house.

Since the lady is fit to travel and wants to get home, we take her the following evening to a small river steamer which is going down to the coast. Dr. Nessmann leaves us by the same boat. The inmates escort their departing doctor by torchlight to the canoe which is to take him to the steamer's stopping-place, but the farewells there are hurried. We have scarcely put our dear helper and his baggage on board, when we have to be off at once, so as to get home before the burst of a thunderstorm that we see gathering.

Not long after this there arrives from the Mission station at Ovan, which is situated in the interior, three hundred kilometres from Lambaréné and in the famine district, Madame Rusillon, a missionary and missionary's widow, to recruit for a time in our hospital. She can hardly realise that she is living once more under normal conditions. As soon as ever we heard of the severity of the famine at the Ovan mission station, the missionaries here and we ourselves determined to send some foodstuffs to it, and did so by the most varied methods of transport. I now learn that a small sack of eighty pounds of rice, which I entrusted to one of my European patients, was the first gift to arrive and just at the right time. What had been sent before that either arrived later or was lost *en route*.

In the dry season the bosun of the crew of a canoe in which Dr. Trensz and Mlle. Lauterburg were coming home just as night was falling, noticed with his sharp eyesight an unusual object on a sandbank near the hospital, and stopped the canoe. The object was a European who had got injured and was lying unconscious on the sand with his bundle. It turned out that he was coming from the interior, where he had been engaging negroes, and that his crew—newly engaged men from the interior—had found it simpler to put him out on the sandbank than to bring him to the hospital. The poor fellow recovered in the hospital so far that he could be sent to Europe some weeks later.

On the whole, Europeans decide much too late to come to the hospital; they often come when it is too late to help them. The responsibilities which they have to bear at the timber sites, or in the distant factories, are so heavy that they decide to leave their post only under the pressure of the extremest necessity. To whom can they entrust the foodstuffs and the wares for which they are responsible? Who will see that the trunks are rolled at the right time into the swamps and lakes and streams to catch the expected high water which will allow them to be piloted into the River Ogowe? To go into hospital, if there is no substitute to take their place, means often nothing less than risk of ruin. It is touching to see how in such cases Europeans in the forest mutually help each other, and undertake the duty of a neighbour, even if they live far apart and can only visit each other at the cost of a laborious journey.

Again, Europeans often leave the hospital too soon. A young man whom malaria and heart disease had left in a very bad way, insisted on returning to his post upstream because there was just then a good opportunity for travel. All entreaties and warnings were in vain. Three weeks later came the news that he was dead.

20 *1927. IN THE NEW HOSPITAL*

THIS year I can give to writing even less time than I could last year. The continual to and fro between the old and the new, and the work on the latter, fatigue me so much that I am incapable of work with the pen. I have no energy for anything beyond practising regularly on my piano with pedal attachment.

At the beginning of the year there are so many buildings finished that patients can be lodged in them, though there is still much to be done inside. But we must use the short, dry season for the removal, and further, we must empty the old buildings, so as to be able to use the materials in them for completing the new ones. In the primeval forest every old plank and every old beam is very valuable.

On January 21st the removal begins. Dr. Lauterburg, his sister, and Mlle. Hausknecht look after the loading in the old hospital; Mlle. Kottmann and Hans Muggensturm receive the patients and their belongings at the new. I myself am on the river the whole day towing the full canoes upstream, and bringing them back empty. Some white patients also come to our help with their motor-boats.

In the middle of it all a European arrives with his wife, who is expecting her confinement. Fortunately I have made allowance for such tricks of fate, and have had three rooms, with two beds in each, made ready in the house for the white patients. A quarter of an hour after their arrival the lady is settled in, and the removal can proceed.

In the evening I make the final journey and bring up the last patients, the mental ones among them, and the latter behave excellently. They have been told that in the new hospital they will live in cells with wooden floors, so they imagine that they are moving into a palace. In their old cells the floor was the damp earth.

I shall never forget the first evening in the new hospital. From every fireside and from every mosquito net they call to me: "This is a good hut, doctor, a good hut!"

For the first time since I came to Africa my patients are housed as human beings should be. How I have suffered during these years from having to pen them together in stifling, dark rooms! Full of gratitude I look up to God who has allowed me to experience such a joy. With deep emotion, too, I thank the friends in Europe, in reliance upon whose help I could venture to move the hospital, and replace the bamboo huts with corrugated iron wards.

On the day following the removal Dr. Trensz returns from a journey. He has no idea of what has been accomplished, and is intending to go further downstream. It is only with hesitation that he acts on the news that is shouted to him from the bank, and lets his canoe be put in here.

From this time onward, Dr. Lauterburg, Dr. Trensz and Mlle. Lauterburg live in the house for the European patients in the new hospital. Hans Muggensturm had already taken up his quarters there in the autumn. The rest of us remain for a time in the old Doctor's house at the Mission station, and the cooking is done at the old place. A canoe—which we call the "Restaurant Car"—conveys their food to those who now live in the new hospital.

Three days after the removal there sets in such a stream of European patients that we hardly know where to house them. As soon as the dispensary has been emptied I start demolishing the buildings which are our property. Some of the buildings belong to the Mission, and were only lent for our use. How carefully I have to watch to see that the natives do not injure the beams and the planks! And what a labour it is to draw all the nails out of the wood, and to hammer them straight so that they can be used again!

The planks we thus obtain are used mostly for constructing the sleeping-berths, which, in the new wards, as in the old, are in two storeys, one above the other. This work Dr. Trensz superintends in his spare time, and he, practical man that he is, devises a method of construction which allows the bed frames to be lifted down, so that they can be washed outside and left in the sun.

But before the last berth is finished he has to lay down his hammer and start for Europe, having been unable to keep himself free to stay for more than a year. On February 18th he leaves us, but we join him in hoping that at some future time he will be able to devote himself once more to the Lambaréné hospital.

To replace him there arrives on March 23rd Dr. Ernst Mündler, from Switzerland, and accompanying him is an English lady, Mrs. C. E. B. Russell, who wants to help us in our labours. And she at once finds her proper sphere. She takes over the command of the people who are felling the forest and are working in the plantation, whereby Mlle. Kottmann is set free for other activities.

The natives soon make friends with their new feminine superintendent and obey her willingly. It is remarkable that the white woman has the greatest authority over primitive men.

An inseparable companion of Mrs. Russell is a little tame monkey, which I gave her as a present on her arrival. It goes with her every morning into the forest, and even if it does take a walk up in the trees, it always comes back loyally to its mistress.

As we have more work than we can manage to get through, we thankfully accept an offer of help for an indefinite time from a Mons. Karl Sutter, a Swiss, who has till now been in the timber trade. He works with Mrs. Russell because we want to get a big piece of forest cleared during the dry season.

Meanwhile we have fortunately got ready for use some of the rooms in our house on the hill; otherwise we should not know where to put the newcomers. And early in the summer the kitchen near it gets its roof on, so that cooking can be done up there. Before long, too, the fowl-house and the goat-kraal are ready, so that our livestock can be transferred.

While the doctors complete the internal arrangements of the hospital, and Hans Muggensturm finishes off the dwelling-house on the hill, I set the piles for a house to contain five rooms, on the slope of the hill facing the hospital. It is for the doctors to live in some day. The other house on the hill is meant first of all for the nurses, but it contains also a room for sick European women, the common room in which we dine, and store rooms in addition. For in African houses there is neither loft nor cellar. Everything has to be stored in rooms.

I am also still at work building a big shed for the canoes and the boats.

* * *

Early in July the chief buildings are finished, though there is still much to do in the matter of internal arrangements.

The big pile-built village has quite a dignified look! And how much easier the work is now, for at last we have space enough, air enough, and light enough! How delightful we feel it, doctors and nurses all, to have our new rooms distinctly cooler than our old quarters were!

For the isolation of the dysentery cases wise precautions have been taken. Their rooms have no opening towards the hospital, and are approached on the side next the river. But from the river they are separated by a fence, so that they cannot pollute the water.

For the mental patients eight cells and a general sitting-room are in prospect. That I can provide for them so well I owe to an endowment which the congregation of the Guild House in Eccleston Square, London, has created for the sake of these poorest of the poor in my hospital in memory of a former member, Mr. Ambrose Pomeroy Cragg.

If the people concerned are patient sheep, and a number of them will go into one fold, the hospital can house some 250 patients with their attendants. And it is generally occupied by between 120 and 160.

While the two doctors are organising the routine of the new hospital, I get ready for my return home. It is three and a half years since I left Europe. Everything is now so well in order that I can leave the hospital to the care of my helpers.

The report that I am going to Europe has reached a mental patient, N'Tschambi by name, who is now allowed to go about in freedom. With tears in his eyes he comes to me and says: "Doctor, have you given orders that no one can send me away while you are in Europe?" "Certainly, N'Tschambi. No one can send you away without first having a great palaver with me." Deeply relieved, he presses my hands, and the tears stream down his cheeks. He had been brought to us some months before in chains, having in his mental darkness killed a woman. In the cell he gradually became quiet, and now he is so far restored that under a certain amount of supervision he can walk about, and even busy himself with a little work. He sharpens the axes, and goes with Mrs. Russell into the forest, where he helps with the tree-felling. As soon as it is noticed that he is getting restless, he is kept in his cell under observation. His continual fear is that he may be compelled to leave the hospital where he has been so well cared for, knowing well as he does, what sort of fate awaits him in his village. He is afraid, too, that while he is out of his mind he will be guilty of fresh misdeeds. How glad I am that I can offer to him and to others in the same misery a refuge for a long period!

On July 21st the hour strikes for my departure. Mlle. Kottmann and Mlle. Lauterburg are travelling with me. The former goes to recruit in Europe after three years' work here; the latter goes home to get married.

We have to wait several days at Cape Lopez for the steamer, which struck a sandbank in the Congo, and was got off it with difficulty. But on the 29th we go on board. The boat pushes slowly out of the bay in bright sunshine, and with my two loyal helpers I gaze at the disappearing coast, hardly able to realise that I am no longer in the hospital. All the needs and all the work of the past three years sweep through my memory, and with deep emotion I think of the helpers of both sexes who have shared them with me, as well as of the friends and associations as whose deputy I was allowed to start this work of mercy. Joy at the success of it is not what I feel; rather I feel myself humbled, and ask myself how I earned the privilege of carrying on such a work, and in such a work attaining to success. And there breaks through, time and again, a feeling of pain that I must leave it for a time, and tear myself loose from Africa, which has become for me a second home.

It seems to me incomprehensible that I am leaving the natives for months. How fond of them one becomes, in spite of all the trouble they give one! How many beautiful traits of character we can discover in them, if we refuse to let the many and varied follies of the child of nature prevent us from looking for the man in him! How they disclose to us their real selves, if we have love and patience enough to understand them!

But the far-away green strip, behind which our thoughts would fain see Lambaréné, is getting less and less distinct. Is it still there on the horizon? Or has it at last disappeared below the waves?

Ah, now there is no room for doubt. . . . There is nothing to be seen but water. So without a word we three press each other's hands and go down to stow away our belongings in our cabins, and so deaden a little the pain of parting.